D1709952

No Tomorrow

Winner of the Walker Cowen Memorial Prize

for an outstanding work of scholarship in eighteenth-century studies

No Tomorrow

~: The Ethics of Pleasure in
the French Enlightenment

Catherine Cusset

University Press of Virginia   *Charlottesville and London*

Acknowledgments for previously published materials appear on page xi.
The University Press of Virginia
© 1999 by the Rector and Visitors of the University of Virginia
All rights reserved
Printed in the United States of America

First published 1999

∞ The paper used in this publication meets the minimum requirements of the
American National Standard for Information Sciences—Permanence of Paper for
Printed Library Materials, ANSI Z39.48-1984.

Library of Congress Cataloging-in-Publication Data

Cusset, Catherine, 1963–
    No tomorrow : the ethics of pleasure in the French Enlightenment /
Catherine Cusset.
      p.   cm.
    Includes bibliographical references and index.
    ISBN 0-8139-1860-x (cloth : alk. paper)
     1. French fiction—18th century—History and criticism.
    2. Pleasure in literature.   I. Title.
PQ618.C87   1999
843'.509353—dc21   98-55780
                                          CIP

One of the specific diagnoses of any French passion, science or art, is to elude the excessive, the absolute and the deep.

Baudelaire, *On the Essence of Laughter*

The text is (should be) this uninhibited person who shows his behind to the *Political Father.*

Barthes, *The Pleasure of the Text*

Contents

Illustrations

PREFACE

THIS BOOK is an extended version of my study *Les Romanciers du plaisir* (Paris: Champion, 1998). Shorter versions of chapter 3 and 5 were also recently published as prefaces to Crébillon's *Les Égarements du coeur et de l'esprit* and Vivant Denon's *Point de lendemain* in *The Libertine Reader* (New York: Zone, 1998) edited by Michel Feher, whom I thank for allowing me to reproduce these texts.

I feel immensely honored by the Walker Cowen Award I received for this book, knowing that I address issues that go against the main current of ideas: not only do I speak of pleasure, which is less than ever a *politically correct* idea, and even of an *ethics of pleasure*, thus implying that libertine works may teach us a lesson, but I defend a notion that it is fashionable to criticize today: reason.

Reason, this gift of the Enlightenment, is held responsible for the excesses of both technocratic societies and totalitarian regimes. This book is concerned neither with political philosophy nor with cultural history but with literature and art. It is useful to return to the texts of the period to understand what reason meant. I found in these works a nuanced and sophisticated mechanism that is not about fashioning the world but about enabling a rapport with it.

ACKNOWLEDGMENTS

I AM immensely grateful to the two professors who guided and inspired me throughout my studies: Georges Benrekassa, in Paris, who directed my dissertation on Sade; and Peter Brooks, at Yale, who gave me such strong intellectual support, as the chair of the French Department when I first came to Yale in 1986, as my dissertation adviser between 1988 and 1991, and as the director of the Whitney Humanities Center, where I spent two wonderful years as a fellow. I am also indebted to Denis Hollier for giving me precious advice and, as the chair of the French Department at Yale between 1991 and 1997, for making it such a stimulating place. I thank all my colleagues, with whom it has always been a pleasure to work, and professor David Marshall, who, as acting chair for the Whitney Humanities Center in 1995, gave me a chance to expose my ideas to academics in other disciplines. A Morse Fellowship from Yale University provided me with the time necessary to complete the research on this book.

A warm thank to my students Jeremy Billetdeaux, Susie Brubaker, Jeremy Sabol, and Allison Tait and to my friend Hilari Allred, who assumed the delicate task of transforming my English, and sometimes my French, into English and made some helpful comments on the text they edited. A special thanks to Susie, who mentioned the Walker Cowen Award competition, and to my parents-in-law, Ann and John Jenkins, on whom I could count in difficult times.

I also wish to express my gratitude to Mrs. Cowen, Cathie Brett-schneider, Deborah Oliver, and everyone at the University Press of Virginia, who have been so encouraging and enthusiastic about my book. Finally I wish to thank Joanne Allen for her careful work in copyediting my manuscript.

What I owe my husband, Vlad Jenkins, is beyond thanks.

INTRODUCTION

AT THE museum, we recognize the French eighteenth century by those little paintings, with bright tones or pastels that show women at their bath, in their bedrooms, or in a garden, being seduced or caressing themselves, where even the stone statues and the mythical goddesses seem to become flesh and solicit the viewer with winks of complicity: Watteau, Pater, Lancret, Boucher, Fragonard.[1] We open up a libertine novel: Crébillon, Diderot, Dorat, Duclos, Laclos, Marivaux, Prévost, Sade.[2] We read about nothing but pleasure, desire, and manipulation of others with seduction in mind.[3] "When I entered society the idea of pleasure was the only one I had in my head," the hero of Crébillon's *Les Égarements du coeur et de l'esprit* says at the beginning of a novel that ends with a scene of sensual pleasure.[4] In this frivolous world of marquises, vicomtes, *roués*, and *petit-maîtres* who seem to be oblivious to any other reality than pleasure,[5] is anything relevant for us today?

These novels and paintings have provoked a great deal of interest recently because their titillating subjects seem ideal for arousing the reader's curiosity and securing commercial success. Hence the uninitiated reader is deceived, who discovers these texts to be much more prolix and less stimulating than what the words *libertine* and *erotic* would imply.[6] We are left with the consolation of giving a historical value to these old-fashioned erotic texts: they tell us, at least, about a world brought to an end by the French Revolution, a world of privileged classes without political concerns who, to escape the boredom that threatened their unlimited leisure time, developed "the art of pleasing" and cultivated pleasures like the art of conversation—

an art some would like to revive today in order to make our own society more civilized.[7]

The Ethics of Pleasure

This book is concerned primarily with the moral meaning of pleasure, not with its social or erotic value. What interests me is an ethical issue. I would like to understand what conception of human beings stems from the focus libertine works placed on pleasure. Pleasure never had good press, as Roland Barthes reminds us in his 1973 essay *The Pleasure of the Text*: "Futility and—or guilt, pleasure is either idle or vain, a class notion or an illusion. An old, a very old tradition: hedonism has been repressed by nearly every philosophy; we find it defended only by marginal figures, Sade, Fourier. . . . Pleasure is continually disappointed, reduced, emptied, in favor of strong, noble values: Truth, Death, Progress, Struggle, Joy, etc. Its victorious rival is Desire: we are always being told about Desire, never about Pleasure."[8]

Libertinage is the sole literary and artistic movement that speaks of nothing but pleasure. Libertine novels were written in a philosophical context of resistance to metaphysics. The materialist philosophers d'Holbach, Helvétius, La Mettrie, and Condillac made use of Locke's empiricism to fight Descartes's transcendental philosophy: they argued that the aim of human life was to seek pleasure and to avoid displeasure.[9] Libertine novels likewise focus mainly on pleasure and on the body. This is the reason why even today *libertinage* is not considered a great literary movement. Of course, it is no longer ignored as it was in the time of Gustave Lanson, whose *Histoire de la littérature française* (1896), for reasons of both moral and social censure, does not even mention the libertine writers. But an esthetic censure still exerts itself. Several of Lanson's judgments have persisted, especially the one concerning Rousseau, whose work represents the inauguration of a sensitive literature that "touches" our soul more deeply, says Lanson, than that of the materialists.[10]

For modernity, literature and art are indissociable from lack and suffering, which did not interest the libertines. *Les Liaisons dangereuses* may be the only libertine novel to be considered a masterpiece. Is this not precisely because this novel ends with a catastrophe that strikes all the libertine heroes and thus seems to prove the failure of *libertinage?* Modernity begins with Rousseau, with Goethe. With *Julie, ou la nouvelle Héloïse*, published in

1761, love is henceforth placed under the sign of sacrifice, of the surpassing of the self, of sublimation. What ennobles literature from the end of the eighteenth century is a feeling of infinitude that transcends the limits of the body, of sensations, and of reason. "What is man, this much-vaunted demi-god?" Werther asks. "Always brought back to the desolate and cold conscience of his insignificance, while wishing to lose himself in infinity?" The phenomenon enacted by Werther in Goethe's *The Sorrows of Young Werther* (1774) and by Julie in Rousseau's *Julie, ou la nouvelle Héloïse* is the sublime as it is described by Kant in the "Analytic of the Sublime," in his *Critique of Judgement*. In the experience of the sublime, which presents a formless object to reason and does violence to the imagination, the latter's incapacity to produce forms adequate to the greatness of the ideas of reason becomes the proof of the supersensible vocation of reason. "The sublime," writes Kant, "is that, the mere ability to think which, shows a faculty of the mind surpassing every standard of Sense."[11] The sensation of the sublime, then, becomes the very sign of the infinitude of human beings.[12] Kant's analyses in the *Critique of Judgement* reduce French materialism to an incapacity to surpass sensuous pleasure and to experience the infinite.

Libertinage is incredulous of infinity. The claim of the libertine novel is precisely the impossibility of ignoring what Casanova calls "the present enjoyment of the senses," which is the opposite of transcendence. *Libertinage* is one of the only literary movements to resist the metaphysical dimension of man. This book intends to show that resistance to metaphysics is also a metaphysical gesture and that *libertinage*, which believes in neither infinite phenomena nor the supersensible vocation of reason, has an ethical dimension. Libertine writers and artists teach their readers a useful lesson: they transform their metaphysical skepticism into a positive argument for the limit. Indeed, in order to be able to accept one's own, or the other's, inclination for pleasure without uttering immediately a moral judgment condemning human weakness, frivolity, and sensuality, one needs to be able to rid oneself of prejudices and to become a tolerant "philosopher." Casanova, the expert in pleasure, writes in *Histoire de ma vie*:

> "What is pleasure? and what do you mean by prejudices?" "Pleasure is the present enjoyment of the senses [*jouissance actuelle des sens*]. It is their complete satisfaction in everything they covet. . . . Now, the philosopher is the person who does not stint himself of any pleasure. . . ."

> "And you say that we can do this by ridding ourselves of prejudices?
> Tell me, then, what are prejudices, and how it is possible to get rid of
> them." "You are asking me a question, my dear, which is not easy to
> answer. For moral philosophy does not know any larger question, any
> that is more difficult to resolve. That is why this lesson lasts all one's
> life. I will tell you in brief that we call prejudice any so-called duty
> having no ground in nature."[13]

Casanova speaks of a lifelong lesson. Pleasure, indeed, is both an immediate feeling and the result of a constant struggle against every prejudice that impedes the satisfaction of pleasure. One understands, therefore, why most libertine works have a polemical tone: They fight "prejudices." They fight the resistance to pleasure—to the light, weak side of oneself.

The most important word in Casanova's definition of pleasure, "jouissance actuelle des sens," is probably *actuelle* (meaning both "present" and "in act"): pleasure takes place only in the present moment and therefore implies a relation to time different from that of any other feeling.[14] This is how pleasure is defined in Diderot and d'Alembert's *Encyclopédie* in 1765: "Pleasure, (Moral) Pleasure is a feeling of the soul that makes us happy at least during the time when we feel it; we could not too greatly admire how nature is careful to fulfill our desires. If nature drives matter only through movement, it is also only through pleasure that it drives human beings." It is impossible to define or justify pleasure by anything other than itself. There can be no value judgments of pleasure, no hierarchy of pleasures. Pleasure cannot be controlled; it imposes itself through sensation. Pleasure is a driving force, since it is analogous to "movement," which drives matter. It is a principle of life and energy.[15]

Let us compare this materialist definition of pleasure with the earlier definition in Furetière's *Dictionnaire universel* (1690): "Pleasure: Joy that the soul or the body feels, when excited by some agreeable object. The contemplation of God, or of Truth, gives solid pleasures to spiritual people: by comparison, worldly pleasures are nothing. There are honest and innocent pleasures. This man experiences the pleasures of life. Pleasure, is also called voluptuousness and dissolute passion. Pleasures of the flesh are dirty and brutal. Debauched people seek pleasures of the bed and table, they are addicted to every pleasure." Furetière's definition contains a distinction between good and bad pleasures, true and dirty pleasures, those of the soul and those of the flesh. Such a moral judgment is missing in the *Encyclopédie*, which neither condemns nor extols pleasure but rather observes that pleasure is a reality.

I am interested in this absence of moral judgment, in the libertines' descriptive, rather than normative, morals.[16] As Saturnin, the hero of the pornographic novel *Histoire de Dom Bougre, portier des Chartreux*, says, "Yes, here is pleasure: it shows itself and escapes. Have you seen it? no: the sensations it has excited in your soul have been so fleeting, so quick, that annihilated by the strength of its impulse, your soul has been unable to grasp it."[17] Pleasure is a feeling experienced by the soul, but so ephemerally that the soul cannot know it. This impossibility of knowing, of rationally mastering, is characteristic of pleasure. Pleasure is accompanied by a certain ignorance of oneself. This ignorance can lead to blindness to oneself and to self-delusion—which is why libertine novelists are interested in pleasure.

They are, indeed, moralists: they unmask the hypocrisy of the social being who claims high moral principles while his or her body obeys another law, that of the senses. They reveal how acts often contradict principles and how the denial of pleasure leads to intolerance. Libertine writers teach us a lesson—a paradoxical lesson, yet a lesson. Against the "doxa," libertine writers work on revealing the hidden face of things. If *ethics* can be defined both as a science of morals and the art of leading one's life, it is appropriate to speak of an *ethics of pleasure* since libertine writers use their critical observation of human reality to teach us to be more true to ourselves and, consequently, to the other as well. They also teach us tolerance by warning us that our harsh criticism of others may soon apply to ourselves. "Monsieur has good eyesight," the libertine Jacob says, in Marivaux's *Le Paysan parvenu*, to the young chambermaid Toinette, who has just criticized Geneviève for yielding to their master's advances: "It's Geneviève's turn to be loved today, tomorrow it may well be yours, and then what about all the nasty things you're saying about her? Believe me, show a little charity for your own sake if not for hers."[18]

Paradoxical Morals and the Novel

The new value bestowed upon pleasure provides for the beginning of the modern novel. The form of the novel changes considerably at the beginning of the eighteenth century.[19] This change arises from the desire expressed by such novelists as Marivaux, Prévost, Crébillon, Diderot, and Sade to paint only what is true.[20] What they call "the true" or "the truth of the heart" is often evaluated by the effect it produces on its readers, or more accurately, on its female readers; in terms of the pleasure felt by a category of readers, the true is evaluated by its effect on women, whose instincts are not clouded over by the knowledge of scholarly rules. As Marivaux says in 1712, and Diderot in 1770, one should write a novel as one would speak to a woman: with the goal of pleasing her and holding her attention; the style must be spontaneous and retain the breath of life.[21]

Narrators may be male (des Grieux, Meilcour, Jacob) or female (Marianne, Susanne, Thérèse); they all recount something that happened when they were young. Eighteenth-century literature before Rousseau is not yet interested in childhood, but in the age of crisis, which today we call adolescence, and which, in the Enlightenment, corresponds to the discovery of pleasure, to the age when the body of the other is both unknown and desirable. There is probably no other period in the history of literature in which we find so many very young protagonists. Seventeen is the preferred age: it is the age of des Grieux at the beginning of *Manon Lescaut*, which covers a period of two years, of Suzanne Simonin in Diderot's *La Religieuse*, of Meilcour in Crébillon's novel, of Faublas in Louvet's *Les Amours du chevalier de Faublas*, at the end of the century. The heroine of Marivaux's *La Vie de Marianne* is fifteen when a vicar takes an interest in her fate—when her story truly starts; Théophé, the heroine of Prévost's *Histoire d'une Grecque moderne*, is sixteen; and Sade's famous sisters, Justine and Juliette, are twelve and fifteen at the beginning of their adventures. In *Les Liaisons dangereuses* the thirty-six-year-old Comte de Gercourt seems an old man to Cécile de Volanges. Seventeen—the age when one enters the *world*, meaning the social circles of the adult world; above all, the age of first sexual experiences, the age at which bodily relations with the other begin.

The first-person narrative allows the reader to follow closely an experience that is recounted in detail with thrilling naiveté.[22] In retrospective narratives the sensual pleasure of the adventure is augmented by the pleasure of a distant, ironic narrative that mocks the illusions, the ignorance, and the stupidity of youth, as well as society's hypocrisy. Libertine novelists unmask the hypocrisy of emotional, social, and religious codes. They reveal the disparity between social appearances and the reality of the body. Hence the abundance of scenes staged to transform reader into voyeur. Everyone can experience pleasure: men and women, young and old, aristocrats and peasants. "The prolific essence distilled in a vigorous street-porter's dance is no less sublime than that which is produced in a monarch's ball," Nerciat writes in *Le Diable au corps*.[23] The libertine novel takes an interest not only in the microsocieties of the privileged class, which survive outside of history, but also in the transgressions authorized by the instinct of pleasure. It is this pleasure that draws the fifty-year-old bourgeois women to the young Jacob in Marivaux's *Le Paysan parvenu*, des Grieux to Manon, Meilcour to Mme de Lursay, Danceny to Mme de Merteuil.[24]

From physical principle, pleasure becomes a psychological dimension. With the notion of pleasure the libertine novelists clear a space for the unconscious, for the idea of a blindness to the self.[25] I choose to speak of pleasure, not of desire, for two reasons: first, *pleasure* is the term encountered most often in libertine texts; second, *desire* connotes lack, and lack does not interest the libertine novelists. The psychological model they valorize is based on "moment": they are struck by the contradiction between our moral being, which defines itself in terms of duration, consequence, and continuity, and this other being, at once physical, moral, and imaginary, which compels us, in the "moment," to commit acts incompatible with all our moral values.

In the "Preface by the Author of *The Memoirs of a Man of Quality*," at the beginning of *Manon Lescaut*, Prévost starts by recognizing that the "most agreeable moments" of our lives are those that we spend "examining with a candid mind the charms of virtue, the joys of friendship, the ways of attaining happiness, and frailties of human nature." Then he asks, "How then does it come about that we so easily fall from these lofty speculations and find ourselves so soon brought down to the level of the most commonplace of men?"[26] "Lofty speculations" are helpless to resolve the moral conflicts and contradictions of the subject. Morality is powerless when it does not address the human dimension par excellence, that of sensation. Prévost justifies the novelistic genre as "a moral treatise entertainingly put into practice" [*un traité de morale agréablement réduit en exercice*]. "Moral treatise"—

we recognize the most familiar principle of Aristotle's poetics, associating the agreeable and the useful. Throughout the century, novelists, and in particular Diderot in his *Eloge de Richardson*, defend the moral value of the novelistic genre.[27] The words "put into practice" [*réduit en exercice*] are more interesting. "Reduced into an exercise," Prévost says literally. We encounter this word *reduced* (*réduit*) throughout the current study; if the eighteenth century favors an operation, it is reduction—from great to small, from ideal to real, from emotional to sexual, from metaphysical to physical. This reduction has also been referred to as "analysis," quite literally a reduction to the simple, a decomposition of elements (from *luo, is, ere,* "to dissolve," and *ana,* a prefix indicating a return to the source). The word *exercise* is also important, for it emphasizes practice, the present "moment," over which abstract discourse has no power.

Prévost's preface to *Manon Lescaut* contains two essential ideas. The first is that it is not enough to defend the novel by saying that it has a moral import; morals must necessarily be transmitted by the novel because pleasure is the only means for affecting the reader. What is at stake here is the place of the reader. The novelist, unlike the moralist, does not seek to draw readers above the melee in order to wisely contemplate the "most commonplace of men." On the contrary, he immerses readers in practice, he seduces them, he betrays them, lays traps for them, mocks them, plays with them. The foremost victims of the novels must be readers, seduced despite themselves by the techniques of illusion and subjected to the power of pleasure, which makes them turn page after page.

The second idea is the necessity, in the plot, of dealing with human reality—the "fall." "How then does it come about that we so easily *fall* from these lofty speculations?" The libertine novel analyzes man after the fall, man always in the act of falling, but without giving the word *fall* a theological and eschatological value. The "fall" is simply understood as a first principle. The notion of the fall is reflected in a libertine word often used by Crébillon and his followers, such as La Morlière: *occasion,* from the Latin *cado, is, ere,* "to fall." The occasion is the moment of seduction. The libertine novel is interested in the perturbations of order that are tied to the body; hence the importance given to these moments cut off from past and future, these *égarements,* momentary lapses, wandering, swerving. The libertine novel accepts the fall.

My claim, like Prévost's, is that novels contain more powerful moral lessons than do philosophical and moral treatises precisely because they put morals into practice and convey morals through pleasure: morals in novels are more subtle, more ambiguous, and therefore closer to human reality, which is full of contradictions.[28] Which is why this book on the ethics of pleasure examines novels rather than essays by Locke, Helvétius, d'Holbach, La Mettrie, or Condillac: I am interested in the ethics that is "entertainingly put into practice." Each chapter in this book treats a question of morals, to which the novel analyzed brings a specific, subtle, and original answer.

The pleasure I talk about in this book is not only sensual satisfaction; it also includes mental pleasure, all the feelings that lead to a happiness of the moment. What matters is the opposition between the solid, lasting values favored by traditional morals and the superficial and ephemeral, yet powerful feelings described by libertine novelists. The aristocratic Cartesian ethics of generosity, analyzed by Paul Bénichou in *Morales du grand siècle*, is countered in the eighteenth century by what one could call an ethics of superficiality (*frivolity* in the eighteenth century):[29] all that concerns surfaces, whether of the body (the skin) or of the soul (vanity), for, as Nietzsche writes in *Human, All Too Human*, "Vanity is the skin of the soul."[30]

Which is why libertine novelists also stress the role played by vanity. If Valmont dies at the end of *Les Liaisons dangereuses*, it is not from love; it is, as Mme de Merteuil makes clear with murderous irony, from vanity: "Yes, Vicomte, you loved Mme de Tourvel very much, and you love her still; you love her like a madman: but because it amused me to make you ashamed of your love, you have brashly sacrificed her. . . . Oh, what vanity brings us to! The Sage is truly right, when he says that vanity is the nemesis of happiness" (letter 145, my translation). *Les Liaisons dangereuses* reveals that vanity is a psychological motor as powerful as love. Long before Laclos, Crébillon wrote in *Les Égarements du coeur et de l'esprit*: "I have come to the conclusion . . . that it is far more important for a woman to flatter a man's vanity than to touch his heart" (55). And Marivaux, around the same time: "In love affairs, however committed you are already, your *vanity* at pleasing somebody else makes your heart so unfaithful!"[31] Libertine novelists give a fundamental role to the moral and psychological dimension they call vanity.

What is vanity? *Webster's* defines vanity as "emptiness, worthlessness, from vanus, vain," and "the quality or fact of being vain or excessively proud of oneself." The eighteenth-century definition is not very different, even if one detects in it a theological reference that is gone today: "It seems that man became vain since he lost the sources of his true glory, by losing this state of sanctity and felicity in which God had placed him," De Jaucourt writes in the article "Vanité" of the *Encyclopédie* (1765). The word *vanity* comes from the Latin term *vanitas, vanitatis*, itself formed from the adjective *vanus*, which means "empty." The seventeenth-century moralists La Rochefoucauld, La Bruyère, and Pascal emphasized the "vanity" of man precisely in order to underline man's nullity compared with the grandeurs of the divine. Any use of the notion of vanity, from the seventeenth century to the twentieth, implies a moral condemnation of the vain subject and of the interior void implied by a concern for worldly appearances. Seventeenth-century paintings depicting vanity contain all sorts of objects contributing to the worldly pleasures one can enjoy juxtaposed with a symbolic object, such as a skull, indicating the limited duration of human life and consequently the absence of pleasure in the face of the truth and the eternity of the soul. The use of the word *vanity* implies a condemnation of the frivolous and the superficial.

Eighteenth-century libertine artists and novelists, in contrast, did not reprove the superficial and worldly dimension of man; they stated it as a fact. They then went further: they revealed that this dimension could be more powerful, hence truer, than what one would call the truth, that is, the love of God or the exclusive love of one woman. One certainly should not assume that an ethics of pleasure implies a propaganda of pleasure; this is really not the point. Libertine novelists are actually the first to elaborate the negative consequences of pleasure: numerous libertine novels, such as those of Dorat, Duclos, Laclos, and Louvet, end with their heroes' madness, death, or repentance. But this does not diminish the value of pleasure. Even though the heroes later acknowledge that they were wrong in their youth, they nonetheless yielded to the pleasure of the senses or of vanity, and the past cannot be rewritten. The libertine novel shows the irresistible power of the "moment." The insight of the eighteenth-century libertine novel is its analysis, both ironic and amoral, of the functioning of human psychology—of man as a being that exists nowhere else but "hic and nunc," "in the moment," and "in the world."

Content and Method

The works analyzed in this book are Watteau's *Pèlerinage à l'île de Cythère*, Prévost's *Manon Lescaut*, Crébillon's *Les Égarements du coeur et de l'esprit*, the anonymous pornographic novel *Thérèse philosophe*, Diderot's *La Religieuse*, and Vivant Denon's short story *Point de lendemain*. I chose these works because they trace an evolution throughout the century, from 1717 to 1777, that refines what I call the ethics of pleasure. It starts with Watteau as an esthetic position, an ironical view on the metaphysical nature of man and on his quest for meaning. It continues with Prévost as a very ambivalent relation to pleasure, both repressed by moral discourse and yet triumphant in its effect on the characters. With Crébillon the representation of pleasure and of the decisive role it plays in life allows for a cynical, "realistic" conception of man as a social being. In *Thérèse philosophe* pleasure is on the side of reason, but the mechanical aspect of pleasure shows at the same time the limits to the power of reason. Diderot's *La Religieuse* becomes an apology of pleasure as the wisest of God's laws since only monsters could live without physical desire. *Point de lendemain*, finally, is probably the most paradoxical of these works, and this is why it gives its title to my book: this short story affirms what has always been negated, namely, that there exists an art of enjoying the moment while avoiding any bad consequences. From being criticized but accepted as a fact of life, pleasure becomes, little by little, a major quality and a proof of humanity.

One would probably expect to see the names Marivaux, Laclos, and Sade. Sade is omitted because his work poses problems that are not simply accounted for by an ethics of pleasure and because his work occupies an exceptional place not only in the libertine eighteenth century but also in the history of literature. I do not devote a chapter to *Les Liaisons dangereuses* because it is the most well known of the libertine novels, and I preferred working on authors less frequently read, such as Crébillon and Vivant Denon; nevertheless, throughout the book, *Les Liaisons dangereuses* is a constant reference.[32] An analysis of Marivaux's *La Vie de Marianne* or *Le Paysan parvenu* would have easily found a place here, but it would have treated similar issues to those covered in the chapters on Watteau, Prévost, and Crébillon. As for Restif de la Bretonne, his work emphasizes pleasure with such a heavy moral tone that it does not enter into the much lighter, subtle, and ambiguous framework of an ethics of pleasure.[33]

Nor are Mme de Graffigny, Mme du Tencin, Mme Riccoboni, Mme de Genlis, and Mme de Charrière present here. Even if some of these novelists portrayed libertine characters, *libertinage* was neither their chosen esthetic form nor the goal of their work. Women write from the point of view of the victims. The play, the irony, and the ambiguity of *libertinage* do not interest these women writers, no doubt because they had more pressing preoccupations: first they had to obtain social and economic liberty. I would agree with Nancy K. Miller that the irony of *libertinage*, this polemical assertion of pleasure, is a luxury permitted by certain social and political conditions that in the eighteenth century probably was not available to women, not even to the elite circle of aristocratic women.[34] If writing by women in the eighteenth century has an object, it is marriage: the suffering and misunderstanding caused by marriage, and the unfaithfulness whose victims they become because of the ideology of pleasure. Yet I believe that it is possible to read libertine works from a perspective other than that of gender. The female characters in the novels analyzed in this book are not so much representations of real eighteenth-century women as allegories through which libertine novelists address moral issues that concern both men and women. In each of the novels studied here the main female character embodies the moral issue at the heart of the novel. The author's vision of the world contained in libertine novels is frequently allegorized by a female character and by her adventures.

Chapter 1, "1717: Cythère, or Ambiguity," takes its title not from a woman but from a place, Cythera, in Greek mythology the island near which Venus was born. This chapter examines the resistance to interpretation of Watteau's *Le Pélerinage a l'île de Cythère* and explores the esthetic and moral value of ambiguity. I compare Watteau's Cythera and Rousseau's Elysium in *La Nouvelle Héloïse* in order to highlight the contrast between two conceptions of pleasure that frame the eighteenth century, the first immanent, the second transcendent. The comparison also shows how Watteau's work paves the way to the ironical ambiguity that characterizes the ethics of pleasure in libertine works throughout the century.

Chapter 2, "1731: Manon, or Pleasure," questions the place of the heroine in *Manon Lescaut* as the object of desire and mourning. This chapter explores the conflict, not so much between two social classes, but, rather, between two radically different sentiments, Manon's inclination for pleasure and des Grieux's passionate love for her. Does the masculine, noble framing of the narrative represent, as most critics have argued, a repression of Manon and therefore of pleasure?

Chapter 3, "1736-1738: Mme de Lursay, or Vanity," studies the contrast between two feminine characters and the ontological values they come to embody, vanity and truth, in Crébillon's *Les Égarements du coeur et de l'esprit*. Why does this novel lead the reader to expect a moral or sentimental ending and then not deliver? This chapter shows how the missing end of the novel, with its promise of endless *égarements*, displays Crébillon's irony toward the reader and suggests a new conception of the self.

Chapter 4, "1748: Thérèse, or Reason," analyzes one of the most famous eighteenth-century pornographic novels, *Thérèse philosophe*, so as to explore an issue addressed in recent studies, namely, whether there is such a thing as enlightened pornography? What kind of *philosophe* is Thérèse, and why do pornographic novels claim to be philosophical, when the mechanical effect of voyeurism on the reader's body seems to contradict the power of reason?

Chapter 5, "1760: Suzanne, or Liberty," examines the definition of liberty proposed by Diderot in *La Religieuse* through the story of Suzanne Simonin, a character who fights for her freedom at the same time that she is used textually as erotic enticement. This chapter explores the issue of legal and sexual innocence and the relation between the body, the law, and imagination in order to show how the novel gradually reveals that liberty consists in accepting the limits of the body.

Finally, chapter 6, "1777: Mme de T———, or Decency," examines the relation between physical pleasure and social reality in Vivant Denon's short story *Point de lendemain*, which was published anonymously in 1777 and 1778 and under Denon's name in 1812. This final chapter shows that *Point de lendemain,* in which many critics have seen a utopian dream of pleasure, is rather a discourse on the method of pleasure: this story redefines the moral and social notion of decency as an art of negotiation and a science of nuance that allow us to enjoy the "moment" without paying its consequences.

This book proposes a successive reading of texts rather than a thematic division of chapters in the conviction that a literary work perishes when it is cut up in the interest of thematics. As Peter Brooks writes in *Reading for the Plot,* a text is an organism brought to life by reading, by the desire to read that it inspires and by the propulsion toward the meaning and toward the end of the text that are already contained in its very first lines. The meaning of a text lies in its words, which contain a vision of the world and a conception of human beings. The analytic method applied in this essay is the product of a bias toward hermeneutic coherence. Only by taking into account all the elements of a narrative, its development from beginning to end and its apparent digressions, can the deep coherence of a work of art, beyond all its contradictions, be discerned. Only the desire provoked by the text and its own response to this desire give the text its meaning. Ethics is not to be found in the connection between the text and the society in which it was produced; ethics is inscribed within the text, in the coherent vision of the world it proposes, and in the connection it establishes with its reader. The absence of an end is a characteristic of several of the texts analyzed here, such as Crébillon's *Les Égarements du coeur et de l'esprit* and Diderot's *La Religieuse,* and other eighteenth-century novels, such as Marivaux's *La Vie de Marianne* and *Le Paysan parvenu.* The lack of an ending in these novels is as meaningful as a denouement containing a "moral" conclusion would be in the face of the reader's unchanging desire, which is a desire for meaning. A conclusion would bring a resolution. Libertine writers show that resolving the contradictions in the human mind is not so simple since humanity is contradiction. They are interested, not in the conclusion, but in the moment in which all contradictions are revealed.

One

1717∾ Cythère, or Ambiguity

LE PÉLERINAGE à l'île de Cythère, Watteau's best-known painting, is one of the most commented upon paintings in art history. In 1712 Watteau presented the project at the Royal Academy of Painting and Sculpture, and it was approved as a project for a history painting; Watteau only needed to show the completed work to be officially received at the Academy. Being accepted as a *peintre d'histoire* at the Royal Academy of Painting and Sculpture was certainly a great social promotion for Watteau, born the son of a roofer in Valenciennes in 1694, who had come to Paris with no money and no connections around 1700 and had started his career painting copies for a merchant on the Pont-Neuf.[1]

It is strange, then, that it took Watteau more than four years and four reminders by the Academy to finish the painting. *Le Pélerinage à l'île de Cythère*, which can be seen in the Louvre today, is a painting of rather small dimensions. Furthermore, we know that Watteau did not spend much time working on it, since a recent restoration at the Musée du Louvre revealed that Watteau painted the foliage and the landscape quickly and carelessly, as if all he wanted was to finish the task.[2] Why did Watteau take so much time? Reading Caylus's biography of Watteau, in which the former criticizes his friend and master's "unfortunate inconstancy of character," "instability," "listlessness," "laziness," and desire to paint or draw very quickly, we are free to imagine that the idea of a "planned" and official painting contradicted the spontaneous pleasure that always guided Watteau's practice.[3] This hypothesis seems to be confirmed by the fact that three years later Watteau painted another version of *Le Pélerinage à l'île de Cythère*, as if he had gained interest in his subject once he was rid of official formalities. The second version, in the Charlottenburg Castle in Berlin, is known under the title *Embarquement pour Cythère*.[4]

The length of time Watteau took to finish the work is not the only surprising thing about *Le Pèlerinage à l'île de Cythère*. The project had been accepted as a history painting because this category included paintings with historical, religious, and mythological topics, and the word *Cythère*, which is the name of the island near where Venus was born, implied that the painting would represent a scene from mythology. The category "history painting" was the highest in the Academy's hierarchy, above *scènes de genre*, portraits, and landscapes. Whether its subject was historical, religious, or mythological, a history painting was a painting for which there existed a written narrative that could justify all the details in the painting: thanks to the written text (a book of antique or modern history, the Bible, Cesare Ripa's *Iconologia*, or Ovid's *Metamorphoses*), every element in the painting could be explained. In a history painting the image is subjected to the text, as Norman Bryson argues.[5] When confronted with the completed *Pèlerinage à l'île de Cythère*, the secretary of the Academy crossed out the original title—the only one, among the titles of his paintings, that Watteau had chosen himself—and replaced it with the simple notation "fête galante," thus taking it out of the category of history painting. As suggested by many art historians, the rejection of the title reflects the impossibility of defining the subject of Watteau's painting and of producing a narrative that would explain the action of the characters in it. What does the painting represent? Are the characters on an island or on the mainland? Are they embarking for Cythera or leaving it? Why are aristocrats mixed in with peasants? Are the peasants aristocrats in costumes? Or are they real peasants mixed in with real aristocrats, as was the case in these fairs with which Watteau was probably familiar and in which improvised plays were performed, some indeed representing pilgrimages to Cythera?[6] What kind of boat do we see in the background? Is it Charon's boat, the boat that carries dead souls to the other side of the Lethe in Greek mythology? Why does Watteau paint characters with modern costumes in a scene that is supposed to be mythological? None of these questions can be answered definitely. The only thing one can assert without a doubt is that there is an air of festivity and rejoicing in the whole painting, in its characters' modern costumes and in its soft landscape, hence the new title "fête galante," defined by Furetière's 1690 *Dictionnaire universel* as a "rejoicing of courteous people."

Nothing in Watteau's painting recalled a history painting since it did not refer to any mythological story. Nor was it a scene of private life, a portrait, or a landscape. The title chosen by the secretary of the Academy led to the creation of a new genre, that of *fête galante*, intermediate between history painting and landscape. With this painting, Watteau unknowingly opened a new space for painters, one that he and his followers—Pater, Lancret, Boucher, and, later, Fragonard—fully explored. In a sense the *fête galante* was a frivolous space, to the extent that it was not submitted to academic rules. In *Word and Image*, Norman Bryson coins the term *semantic vacuum* to designate the discrepancy between figural and discursive elements in Watteau's paintings: there are elements that contain the beginning of a narrative, but these never suffice to make the narrative consistent and explain every detail in the painting. This discrepancy, Bryson argues, emancipates the image from its submission to meaning and also justifies the melancholy myth surrounding Watteau's paintings. Bryson equates melancholy with a feeling of frustration experienced by the viewers because their desire for meaning is not satisfied. For Bryson, this is the very sign of Watteau's modernity: he is one of the first painters in the Occident to affirm the independence of image from words.

Le Pèlerinage à l'île de Cythère was an esthetic event since it modified the beholder's sensibility and opened a way to modern painting. However, the first chapter in this book is devoted to this painting because *Le Pèlerinage* represents pleasure. Cythera, the island near where Venus, goddess of carnal love, was born from the sea, stands as an allegory of sensual pleasure. There exists a link between the theme of the painting—pleasure—and the modernity of its form: by freeing his painting from the subjection to language Watteau redefines the relation between pleasure and meaning.

For the purpose of this analysis, I will introduce a paradoxical point of comparison: Rousseau's *Julie, ou la nouvelle Héloïse*. Rousseau's novel was published in 1761, almost half a century after Watteau's painting was accepted by the Academy. Only a fragment will interest us here, letter 11 in the fourth part of the novel, which Saint Preux writes to Milord Edouard to describe Elysium, Julie's garden. Saint Preux's eighteen-page description of Elysium, a small part of the seven-hundred-fifteen-page novel, could be considered a mere digression, but it has a very important place in *La Nouvelle Héloïse*, first, because this is the only nonproductive site in the Clarens economy (after Julie's wedding to M. de Wolmar), the only place devoted to amusement and pleasure; and second, because it is also the site of an internal experience that transforms Saint Preux's feelings for Julie.

This chapter brings together Watteau's Cythera and Rousseau's Elysium in order to explore the contrast between two concepts of pleasure that frame the eighteenth-century imagination. Both Cythera and Elysium are at the same time gardens and magic islands, places devoted to leisure, amusement, contemplation, and conversation.[7] Both Watteau and Rousseau represent an allegorical garden in order to define the function of pleasure in a human economy.[8] Both names, Cythera and Elysium, come from Greek mythology and anchor the representation of pleasure in a myth: Cythera is an allegory of sensual pleasure, and Elysium, the paradise for virtuous souls after they passed the Lethe, river of death and forgetfulness, an allegory of virtue. Finally, both representations stand out as events in their time— Cythera in the first half, Elysium in the second half of the eighteenth century—and marked generations of artists and writers.[9] Rousseau's influence on the formation of a modern sensibility has been abundantly asserted and thoroughly analyzed: Rousseau, whose work revealed a new subjectivity, is considered the father of modernity.[10] Watteau seems to belong to a much earlier time, when aristocrats spent their time dressed as shepherds and cared about nothing but seducing and pleasing one another. Thomas Crow, for instance, writes that Watteau's art is a "belated phenomenon" because it depicts an aristocracy that is closer to the late seventeenth century than to the Enlightenment.[11] I argue, however, that Watteau is modern in his representation of pleasure, that is, as we shall see, in the painting's address to the beholder.

One could say that it does not make sense to compare a painting and a text because they do not have the same relation to time and, therefore, to meaning. Watteau's painting can be seen entirely in one gaze, whereas Elysium, as a text, is slowly discovered, page after page and line after line.

Yet it would be wrong to conclude that text and painting are perceived in radically different ways. Painting, like text, must be deciphered. The gaze does not seize all the details at once: it reads the painting, and generally in the Occident this reading progresses from left to right. There is also a temporality of painting.[12] Painters have various means to represent time, either through juxtaposition of scenes (Watteau uses this technique in *Le Pèlerinage à l'île de Cythère*) or through the choice of the represented moment. Even though a painting uses visual and not linguistic signs, the moment represented can contain a whole narrative; hence the many discussions, from Diderot to Barthes, on the importance of the choice of the moment.[13] Finally, that Watteau painted two versions of *Le Pèlerinage à l'île de Cythère* is important: these two versions constitute a series, which is the equivalent of a narrative sequence. From the first to the second version Watteau made changes that can be considered corrections or refinements. It is therefore possible to go beyond the traditional distinction between word and image and argue that Watteau's paintings, like Rousseau's text, contain a statement.[14] It is this statement, underlined by the changes Watteau introduced in the second version, that this chapter intends to decipher.

The Direction of the Walk

Both Cythera and Elysium represent an enchanting vision of pleasure. In the two versions of Watteau's *Le Pèlerinage à l'île de Cythère*, the soft and warm colors of the landscape, the curved lines, the golden or blue background, the characters, who are all in couples, the statues of Venus, and the little putti, who fly everywhere, underline the delightful aspect of the island of pleasure. If the sixteen characters walking on the soft slopes of the hill were not dressed in costumes of modern pilgrims, which give an indication of early-eighteenth-century reality, one could believe that the painting represents a mythic and utopian vision of pleasure, an *enchantment* in the strong sense of the word, that is, a magic operation transporting the viewer into a dream world. This is exactly Saint Preux's initial impression, in Rousseau's *La Nouvelle Héloïse*, when he first enters Julie's garden. Elysium appears to him like an island, a magic place remote from the real world. As soon as he is inside and turns backwards, he discovers that the gate has disappeared, as in a fairy tale: "Seeing no door, it seemed as if I had dropped from the clouds."[15] Saint Preux's enthusiastic exclamations reflect his enchantment: "O Tinian! O Juan Fernandez! Julie, the world's end is at your threshold!" (133). Saint Preux calls Julie's garden by the names of recently discovered desert islands, and he insists on his surprise and ecstasy: "Being seized with astonishment, and transported at so unexpected a sight, I remained motionless for some time" (133).

At first glance Cythera and Elysium produce the same effect: surprise, the impression of being on an enchanted island at the end of the world. But the difference between the two gardens lies precisely in the progression from a first to a second glance. In Rousseau's text the impression of magic is soon dispelled, to be replaced by a rational explanation. "On my entrance into this disguised orchard," Saint Preux writes to describe his initial impression, "I was seized with an agreeable sensation; the freshness of the thick foliage, the beautiful and lovely verdure, the flowers scattered on each side, the murmuring of the purling stream, and the warbling of a thousand birds, struck my imagination as powerfully as my senses" (132). During the walk, all the elements of this confused and wonderful sensation are methodically explained. One page describes where "the freshness of the thick foliage" and "the beautiful and lovely verdure" (473) come from; another accounts for "the murmuring of the purling stream" (474); two pages explain how one can hear "the warbling of a thousand birds" (475–76). In extremely precise detail Saint Preux elucidates the technical causes of the feeling of enchantment. The charms of magic give way to another pleasure: the satisfaction of analysis and understanding. The purpose of the walk is, as Julie states, to bid farewell to enchantment: "Go, and you will understand it. Farewell, Tinian! farewell, Juan Fernandez! farewell enchantment! In a few minutes you will find your way back from the end of the world" (135).

The first, "Watteauesque" vision of enchanting nature is articulated by Rousseau only to be left behind and replaced by the pleasure of understanding causes, all of which are human, not magical. During the narration and the walk the verb *to see* (*voir*) changes meaning. First used as a transitive verb, it signifies "to perceive through the eyes": "I thought I was seeing the most wild place," "I saw here and there bushes of roses" (135), "You might see the springs rise and bubble out of the earth" (137), "I saw several of them alight and come towards us" (140). In its literal and sensory meaning, the verb *to see* simply designates the visual perception of the walker, who notices plants, water, and birds. But it also has another meaning: "I saw then that all the contrivance consisted in managing these streams so as to make them flow in meanders" (138), "I see that you want guests instead of prisoners" (141). In these sentences the verb *to see* is followed by a subordinate clause and means "to understand," to perceive through reason, not through the eyes. This double use of the verb, at every step of the walk, indicates the passage from a sensory to a rational perception. The Rousseauist vision goes beyond sensation. Seeing the garden does not mean simply having one's eyes charmed by its beauty and giving oneself to the reverie inspired by this spectacle; it also means understanding which elements make up the garden and being able to reduce the garden to its elements, that is, to analyze it, as a botanist and gardener. Analysis, understanding, and naming produce pleasure. Rousseau was a botanist in his leisure time; his interest in nature is not romantic and sentimental but precise and technical. Hence the scientific precision of Saint Preux's description when he names the plants that produced such a wonderful sensation of enchantment: "Little plantations of lilac, hazle-trees, alders, seringa, broom, and trefoil . . . embellished the ground, at the same time that it gave it the appearance of being overgrown with weeds" (135–36).[16]

The Rousseauist walk has a direction: it consists in passing from the magic charm of sensation to the satisfaction of analytical explanation. Walking further into the garden, one comes closer to the scientific reality of nature: one moves away from sensual reverie into the realm of understanding.

The direction of the characters' walk in Watteau's *Le Pélerinage à l'île de Cythère* is much less clear. The ambiguity of the painting has become a commonplace among critics today. What does Watteau paint? It is difficult to answer this question because the painting represents two contradictory and simultaneous temporal sequences. The movement from right to left—toward the boat in the background—seems to depict a departure. But if we follow the "natural" movement of the eye and read the painting the other way, from left to right, the progressive enlargement of the figures invites us to understand the painting as an allegorical representation of the stages of love or courtly seduction, which would be the opposite of a departure. The seated couple on the right, absorbed in seduction, are closest to the viewer and the most visible; they are completely indifferent to, and their posture contradicts, the movement of departure that is taking place from right to left. The statue of Venus above them confirms an allegorical interpretation and justifies the couple's indifference to anything unlike love or intimate conversation. We can read the painting equally well from either direction. This absence of a compulsory direction allows two contradictory interpretations of the painting.

This ambivalence is accentuated by the fact that *Le Pélerinage à l'île de Cythère* lacks a focal point. If we look at the painting from some distance, we see three focal points. The first is the sky, in the upper left corner, which absorbs our gaze like a dreamland. Even before the recent restoration of the Paris version, in which the removal of thick layers of varnish revealed that the colors used by Watteau had been much brighter and lighter, there was a strong contrast between the sky, almost white in the first version and yellow in the second, and the rest of the painting. A bright spot on the other side of the painting also attracts the eye; it is the white dress of a seated woman. Listening to a man on his knees, this woman with downcast eyes seems cut off from the general movement of departure and from the hazy sky to which she turns her back. The third focal point is the standing couple in the center of the painting. Dominating the other characters, they stand atop the hill that divides the painting into two distinct halves, the sky and remote background, painted in cold colors, and the earth, painted in warm colors.

These three focal points are connected by a sinuous line, a rococo arabesque that structures the painting.[17] The arabesque is a decorative form that follows a purely ornamental logic. There are economical, social, and cultural explanations for Watteau's use of ornamental forms, since Watteau painted in a time when nouveau riche financiers commissioned small-scale paintings to decorate their new Parisian mansions. But the arabesque also has a semiotic value. As Jacques Derrida argues in *La Vérité en peinture*, the ornament—the parergon, that which is beside the work itself, which is added and unnecessary—determines the meaning of a work by revealing the lack of a central meaning.[18]

1. *Le Pèlerinage à l'île de Cythère* (Pilgrimage to the Island of Cythera) by Jean Antoine Watteau. Louvre, Paris. (Courtesy Giraudon/Art Resource, New York)

The man atop the hill stands with his back to us and, with his arm around the waist of his companion, tries to coax her along in the direction of the hazy background, where other couples are already embarking. The woman's body is moving forward in the direction of the boat, but her face is turned backwards, toward the foreground and the seated woman in the white dress. The small dog at the feet of the central couple mirrors the dynamic manifest in the woman's posture: ready to advance but with head turned back. This couple indicates the dispersion of the gaze and consequently the impossibility of reading the painting in a single way. Because this couple advance toward the background by the movement of their bodies and at the same time retreat toward the foreground by the movement of their gaze, they are the figure of the painting's ambiguity, or of what Donald Posner calls Watteau's "narrative inconsistency."[19] Far from dispelled, this inconsistency is only strengthened in the second version.

In *L'Embarquement pour Cythère* Watteau replaced the rowboat on the extreme left with a rigged vessel bearing a large red sail, and the bust of Venus on the extreme right with a statue that looks almost alive, whose stone body seems to become flesh as it—she—plays with a putto. Between the ship and the statue of love Watteau added four couples, two in the left half, two in the right half. The two couples on the left, embarking on the ship, reinforce the idea of departure. The two couples on the right, at the foot of the statue, absorbed in various acts of love, confirm an indifference to the movement of departure. The couple seated on the grass is in an embrace that seems proper to kissing; the other couple stands behind the woman in the white dress. The man is placing roses on the woman's outstretched apron, and a large red rose adorns her low-necked corsage. These roses make the meaning of the crown of roses deposited on the bust of Venus in the first version much more explicit.

What is striking in the second version is not that Watteau gave the painting warmer and more sensual tones, as all critics have acknowledged, but, rather, that he reinforced the painting's ambiguity by simultaneously stressing the movement of departure in the left half and the indifference to departure in the right half. While the general movement of the painting represents a departure, that is, a temporal dimension, the absorbed couples on the right represent the "moment" in the sense that Crébillon later gave to this important concept, that is, the physical instant of seduction, or the complete oblivion of a temporal dimension that would limit the moment.

Pleasure and Meaning

Watteau's painting, as we shall see, resists interpretation because of its simultaneous representation of two contradictory temporal processes. Rousseau's text, in contrast, aims to establish the meaning of Julie's garden. Saint Preux's dialogues with Julie and Wolmar frame the walk and keep both the walker and the reader from wandering into reverie or ambiguity.

From the beginning of the walk, Julie introduces herself as the garden's "superintendant": "Nature has done everything, but under my direction" (134). From the moment they enter the garden she plays a pedagogical role. When Saint Preux expresses his initial enthusiasm, she merely smiles and proceeds to ask him questions, which abruptly replace the poetic expression of his enchantment with a prosaic vocabulary of economics: "What do you imagine it may have cost me to put it into the condition you see?" (133). Julie gives Saint Preux two lessons: one in economics and one in natural sciences. She is very proud to reveal her tricks and to see Saint Preux astonished at learning how she accomplished a miracle through human means.

The description of the garden is followed by a long conversation in which M. de Wolmar is the principal speaker. He addresses Saint Preux, who responds with his approval; Julie is almost entirely excluded from this male dialogue. Whereas Julie simply describes the transformation of her garden in technical terms, Wolmar uses more abstract terms and refers to one central theme: nature. He compares Julie's garden with the gardens of the rich, which are unnatural sites of vanity and boredom (480–81); he criticizes gardens that follow the French fashion, arguing that nature does not use "the square or rule" (482); and eventually he justifies the organization of Julie's garden by virtue of a natural principle: "He will introduce water, and will make the walk verdant, cool, and shady; for nature herself unites these properties" (153).

Nature is the final reference. What is nature? Does nature mean instinct and impulse? When Saint Preux first walks into the garden, he believes that it is the "most wild and solitary place in nature" (133). To Julie's first question concerning the garden's cost, he answers: "It is indeed a delightful spot, but wild and rustic; and I can discover no marks of human industry" (133). But the walk and the conversation that goes along with it reveal this apparently natural garden to be in fact the result of great industry. The garden cannot be nature because nature cannot be found among men; it exists only "in the tops of mountains, in the midst of forests, in desert islands" (147), places far from a social and civilized world. Nature, like Rousseau's utopian model of "le bon sauvage" in his philosophical writings, is therefore a hypothesis, an idea that guides human industry and helps mold human beings. Nature has been recreated, or rather fabricated, by Julie's and Wolmar's art. Nature, then, is the result of a process so perfectly completed that all its marks have been erased. Nature is a hypothetical ideal that allows human work to go beyond natural disorder, that is, to transcend immediate instincts. The first garden, in which Saint Preux, as Julie reminds him, played with Claire by throwing peaches, a rather sensual and childish game, was arid, with "thinly planted trees, offering very little shade, and . . . no water" (133). Recreated by Julie, it has become a beautiful garden: "You find that now it is fresh, verdant, cultivated, embellished with flowers, and well watered" (133). This garden is, paradoxically, both the most beautiful state of wild nature and the most cultivated product of human work. Only labor and industry offer a truly beautiful vision of nature. Julie's garden thus becomes a metaphor for a moral and psychological process that we can call sublimation.

Wolmar theorizes the process of sublimation. It is in the bird grove, where birds remain in spite of their freedom to fly away, that M. de Wolmar interferes for the first time. In words more abstract than Julie's he reveals the real causes of the garden's transformation: "Time and patience . . . have worked this miracle" (141). Time and duration make progressive transformation possible; patience is a specifically human quality that implies the acceptance of time thanks to an anticipated future. The miracle Wolmar mentions here is the gathering of numerous birds that remain in the groves as "voluntary inhabitants." In the context, however, we are invited to give a double meaning to the sentence: it suggests Julie's transformation, her acceptance of the role of wife and mother and her voluntary renunciation of more sensual pleasures. When Julie comments on this miracle, she immediately evokes the scenes of reproduction and the nesting of eggs that took place two months earlier, thus revealing "the birds' paternal and maternal fondness": "Had you been here two months ago, you might have feasted your eyes with the most lovely sight, and have gratified your feelings with the most tender sensations in nature" (143). It is clearly because the birds remind Saint Preux of Julie's metamorphosis that he suddenly expresses a nostalgic sadness: "'Madam,' said I, somewhat gravely, 'you are a wife and a mother; these are pleasures of which it becomes you to be susceptible'" (143).

Although Saint Preux addresses Julie, M. de Wolmar, not Julie, answers him: "You have friends, and those friends have children; how could you be a stranger to paternal affection?" (143). Wolmar's question produces an effect that is critical to the whole novel; it is sufficient to transform the soul of Saint Preux, who testifies to the power of the word: "I do not know by what strange effect a single word can make such an alteration in our minds, but since that moment M. Wolmar appears to me quite another man" (143–44).

Elysium is the site and the vision of an evolutionary process. It is the place where a "natural" and instinctive self is transformed through time, patience, effort, and word into an ideal nature that represents the highest human accomplishment. This is why conversation plays this role in a letter devoted to the description of a garden. Only words can indicate the meaning of the garden and reveal the quality of the human work that realized a perfect nature. Which is why Wolmar's discourse, questions, and answers frame Saint Preux and Julie's walk—not because he must keep an eye on them, being the husband, but rather because he theoretically frames Julie's transformation.

It is therefore not by chance that M. de Wolmar himself answers Saint Preux when the latter suddenly casts a doubt regarding Elysium's utility. On the other side of the house, says Saint Preux, there are "such charming and neglected groves" offering as pleasant a walk. Whereas Julie, "somewhat disconcerted" by the question, tries to elude it, Wolmar answers Saint Preux quite directly: "My wife has never set her foot in those groves since she has been married. I know the reason, though she has always kept it a secret from me. You, who are no stranger to it, learn to respect the spot where you are: it has been planted by the hands of virtue" (157). The grove, site of the first kiss between Julie and Saint Preux, is a place of immediate memory, desire, silence, and dreams; the garden, "planted by the hands of virtue," is a place framed by an ideal and inhabited by words. The discourse of Wolmar, who answers Saint Preux's indiscreet question for his wife, ultimately takes hold even of this forbidden place, the grove where he will soon lead the former lovers. He leaves room for neither escape into memory nor any reverie that words could not penetrate, analyze, and transcend.

The Rousseauist garden, therefore, is not a place of vague and sensual reverie, as one might believe. M. de Wolmar strongly criticizes the taste for "beautiful perspectives," which allow one's eyes to escape into an indistinct horizon. A person who takes pleasure in oneself, Wolmar says, "will not be anxious about opening distant and beautiful perspectives. The taste for perspectives and distant views proceeds from the disposition of men in general, who are satisfied only in places where they are not. They are always desirous of what is distant from them" (153). The words "perspectives" and "distant views" refer to French gardens in the style of Le Nôtre, which were regular and symmetrical and aimed to create beautiful perspectives easily embraced from one central point, generally the castle. Rousseau criticizes seventeenth-century French gardens for being "non-natural." But his garden is no more natural: it simply fits a different idea—or hypothesis—of nature. Elysium is the metaphor of a self that does not try to dominate the outside world but rather works on, and transforms, oneself. In Rousseau's text the beautiful perspective is replaced by a discourse that rationally defines the only "view" (aim) of the garden: to prove to the visitor that he will find pleasure in himself once his corrupted nature has been transformed by the sublimation of instinct and the acceptance of temporal limits. The Rousseauist garden is not a place of dreams and sensual reverie but one of moral satisfaction, the satisfaction given by a practice that makes sublimation possible and recreates an ideal nature.

Wolmar's strong rejection of perspective contrasts with the yawning chasm in the sky of Watteau's landscape. This sky seems to represent an invitation to a journey, an escape into a remote dream. It is a specific feature that differentiates Watteau's *fête galante* from earlier representations of a similar theme from which he likely borrowed some elements, such as Rubens's

Conversation, also entitled *The Garden of Love*, or Claude Duflos's engraving *The Island of Cythera*.[20] An iconographic or cultural interpretation, which would explain all the painting's elements through allegorical, aristocratic, or theatrical codes, would not account for the white and bright opening of the sky in the upper left part of the painting.[21]

This white opening is problematic. It is probably the basis for the melancholy myth surrounding Watteau's painting. It seems to justify metaphysical interpretations and to allow for a dialectic reversal that endows a representation of pleasure with sadness—exactly the kind of reversal the Goncourts effected in their attempt to rehabilitate a painter generally disliked in the first half of the nineteenth century for the frivolity of his topics and the theatricality of his representations.[22] The Goncourts' article was published in 1856 in the review *L'Artiste* under the revealing title "La Philosophie de Watteau," already suggesting a philosophical meaning behind the apparently empty representation of pleasure. "Enchanted isles separated by a crystal ribbon from the land, as carefree as they are unpastored . . . The Elysian Fields of a master painter! . . . In some fortuitous and uncharted spot, there exists, beneath the trees, an eternal indolence. Sight and thought languish into a vague, vanishing distance. . . . A Lethean stream spreads silence through this land of forgetfulness" (6). For the Goncourts, Cythera has no reality on earth and is only a dream of pleasure. Cythera has become the Elysian Fields. The Goncourts can make sense of the painting insofar as they transform the representation of pleasure into a dream and the viewer of the painting into a melancholic dreamer, nostalgic of a lost paradise. The white opening of the sky saves Watteau from being a superficial painter and makes him an artist with a pre-Rousseauist sensibility. The island of pure pleasure does not exist in the world: there is only one real pleasure, that of dreaming, and only one space of pleasure, Elysium. We are not far from the Rousseauist garden—from a common but improper concept of it—since, as we have seen, the aim of Rousseau's garden is not nostalgia but a rigorous transformation of the self.

The Goncourts' interpretation of Watteau denotes a nineteenth-century sensibility, which has been transformed by the wide impact of Rousseau's influence. For the Goncourts, the image of pleasure painted by Watteau must hide a recess in order to make sense, a "behind" that only discourse can reveal: "It is indeed true that in the recesses of Watteau's art, *behind* the laughter of its utterance, there murmurs an indefinable harmony, slow and ambiguous; throughout his *fêtes galantes* there penetrates an indefinable sadness" (8, my emphasis). The Goncourts are looking for what is behind the apparent immanence of pleasure. Without this "behind" a metaphysical meaning could not graft itself onto Watteau's painting, which would remain superficial and frivolous. Only a metaphysical meaning allows us to understand the painting. Eventually, only the death of Watteau, of pneumonia in 1721 at the age of thirty-seven, gives sense to his work: "It is an art that we are made to look upon as the pastime and the distraction of a mind that suffers, as we might look, after its death, upon the playthings of an ailing child" (8). Cythera, which the Goncourts mistake for Elysium, exists only in relation to the background of death.[23]

Not only does the feeling of melancholy come from the frustration of the viewer, who cannot understand the meaning of the painting, as Bryson argues in *Word and Image*, but melancholy means more than pleasure because it reopens the temporal perspective that pleasure eliminates. And this temporal perspective indeed has a place in Watteau's painting since the open sky seems to represent it. Michael Levey's famous 1961 article "The Real Theme of *The Embarkation for Cythera*" is the most striking modern attempt to reconstruct the meaning of the painting and to replace the image of immanent pleasure with sadness and melancholic regret of the past. By focusing his analysis on the movement of departure from right to left Michael Levey declares that the second version of the painting, like the first, represents not an embarkation but a departure, that is, the end of the party, the end of pleasure. Levey writes: "The demand of time is inexorable. . . . Watteau was not painting two bits of stage nonsense, ravishingly beautiful but resistant to any real interpretation."[24] Levey's argument, which has been vigorously refuted,[25] reveals the challenge facing critical interpretations of Watteau: they attempt to overcome Watteau's *resistance* to interpretation and to prove that Watteau did not paint "nonsense." Only the idea of departure, of ending, of the inexorable demand of time, gives meaning to the painting.

The sky in Watteau's painting is somewhat troubling. It is very tempting to interpret it as a divine warning, like the statue of the Commander in

Don Juan. If this sky does not represent an eschatological threat or reopen a metaphysical perspective negating immanent and sensual pleasures, what, then, does it mean? If the painting simply represents an allegory of seduction, as argued by Le Coat, or the pleasure of aristocratic conversation, as shown by Mary Vidal, if we do not need to look for a meaning beyond the image of pleasure, if, in other words, pleasure is so simple, why, then, this large and white opening offered to our gaze?

Immanence versus Transcendence

It is important to note that we, the viewers of the painting, are the only ones to look at the sky. Not a single character in the painting is turned toward the sky. All the characters are in couples, and their eyes are all absorbed by those of their partners or turned toward another couple. It is surprising that they all turn their back to the sky, when the sky opening is so attractive. There is a striking contrast between the characters' indifference to the sky and the melancholic effect the same sky produces on us.

If we look more closely, we notice that the sky is not empty: in both versions of the painting a few putti are ascending in the sky. These little cupids can be found in all representations of love from the sixteenth to the eighteenth century; here their presence is all the more justified since they add a mythological element to a painting that represents a pilgrimage to a mythological island of pleasure. It is clear that Watteau considered their role important, for he multiplied them fourfold from the first to the second version. In the first version there are only twelve, and all save one are near the sky. In the second version they number forty eight and can be found everywhere, in the sky and on the earth.

Putti add an element of playfulness to erotic paintings, as Philip Stewart argues in *Engraven Desire*: in a humorous way they reveal the reality of carnal desire, which decency prevents painters from representing openly.[26] This is true in the second version of Watteau's painting: putti fly everywhere on the earth side, above couples and the statue of Venus. Their naked, plump, pink bodies stress the idea of carnal pleasures, which is only discretely suggested by the couples absorbed in the "moment." Since all the putti are in couples and in physical contact with each other, they offer a playful and bold version of the adults' action, reflected in a kind of ironic mirror.

2. *Embarquement pour l'île de Cythère* (The Embarkation for Cythera), by Jean Antoine Watteau. Charlottenburg Castle, Staatliche Schloesser und Gaerten, Berlin. (Courtesy Bildarchiv Foto Marburg / Art Resource, New York)

In the second version of the painting the postures of the putti in the sky are even more explicit than those of the putti on the earth side. One putto on the slope of the hill catches another from behind and prevents him from rising toward the sky; another leans over his companion, who is lying on his back, legs spread apart, and threatens to attack him; and yet another rises in the sky while firmly holding his companion between his legs as a third eagerly attempts to catch them. Two more, in the back of the ship, abandon themselves to more solitary activities: one clasps a cable on the mast, while the other embraces the sculpted stern of the ship.[27] All these postures reinforce the playful and sensual aspect of the painting, which is also highlighted by colors. In the second version Watteau used warmer, brighter, and more dawnlike colors and replaced the hazy and foggy mountains in the background of the first version with the bright light of the sun piercing through the cloudy sky. The first painting is blue-green, the color of dusk and haze, whereas the second is golden, the color of sun and wheat, evoking the presence of flesh more than the irreality of the dream.

In both versions, but more often in the second, the putti exhibit to the viewer mainly their naked bottoms. If there truly is a behind in Watteau's paintings, then it is very visible, being that of the putti, indecently and humorously exposed to the viewer. This behind with dimples, as plump as the bottoms of Rubens's fleshy Flemish women, seems to comment ironically on any attempt to look for the "behind" of the scene, to use the Goncourts' word. The putti's behind serves to deride the viewer's gaze, which is absorbed in the view of the remote background, whereas a sensual and playful show is offered to him or her. There is a contradiction in the sky itself between the metaphysical perspective absorbing the gaze of the viewer, who is looking for a meaning "behind" the scene, and the immanence of pleasure represented by the playful putti's plump behinds.

The putti, however, do not simply mirror the adults' implicit activities. Their role in the painting's second version is even more subtle and more ironic. In the first version four putti ascending toward the sky form a small circle. In the second version a much larger circle, now formed by about twenty-seven putti, adds itself to the small circle, which becomes only one element of the big one. This circle, to the left of the pole, which clearly

3. Detail of ship, *Embarquement pour l'île de Cythère* (The Embarkation for Cythera), by Jean Antoine Watteau. Charlottenburg Castle, Staatliche Schloesser und Gaerten, Berlin. (Courtesy Bildarchiv Foto Marburg/Art Resource, New York)

suggests departure and may also refer to the "inexorable demand of time" in a metaphysical interpretation of the painting, is a form that the viewers of religious paintings can easily decode: it is, indeed, reminiscent of glories, paintings of luminous skies in which whirling angels and saints delimit a central point where the divine figure is revealed. In Watteau's painting there is nothing inside the circle formed by the flying putti. It is not enough, however, to say that there is nothing, for the putti, by forming a circle around nothing, encircle and highlight the nothingness.

As in the first version, none of the couples in the second version is turned toward the sky. However, the addition of the circle of putti stresses the attraction exerted by the sky as a source of reverie and a ground for meaning and interpretations. Not only is the sky empty but it is shown as empty by the circle of putti. There is not only nothingness but an ironic representation of nothingness. This irony contains the painting's statement about pleasure.

Irony functions as a reflection on the notion of pleasure. It turns derisively on interpretations that attempt to resolve the painting's contradictions and make up for narrative inconsistency. It is because of this ironic statement that Watteau's painting resists interpretation. It does not simply represent pleasure thematically through elements such as the statue of love, allegorical cupids, the joyful pilgrimage, the physical contact between characters and cupids, the declarations of love, the couples absorbed in seduction. It also makes a statement about pleasure, by showing that pleasure is not a utopian dream that ignores deep meaning and metaphysical thought but, rather, a deliberate rejection of metaphysics and an ironic address to the viewer that aims to deride the latter's desire for meaning. This ironic gesture consists in simultaneously representing the sky, which contains the threat of an end, while showing its emptiness, and couples who are absorbed in the moment and who turn their back to the sky. It is this gesture that allows the moment of pleasure to exist outside time and outside a narrative that tries to circumscribe it.

It is important to understand that pleasure is not the "meaning" of the painting. Rather, pleasure is a rejection of meaning since it consists in choosing ambiguity and rejecting a moral lesson, thus producing an unbearable lightness of meaning for the viewer, who longs for a coherent interpretation. Pleasure has an ironic meaning: it mocks all metaphysical interpretations, which attempt to endow superficial pleasure with a deep meaning. Pleasure does not ignore metaphysics but contains a comment on metaphysics; in that sense pleasure too is metaphysical. The metaphysical perspective of the sky only serves to highlight the immanence of pleasure, but the assertion of immanence is a metaphysical statement in itself: it proves that pleasure is not such a simple and superficial feeling since it implies the negation of that which negates pleasure.

Rousseau's Elysium, in contrast, is totally deprived of the irony that characterizes Watteau's Cythera. Julie, Wolmar, and Saint Preux seriously and thoroughly explain the garden's every element and function and replace sensual playfulness with a clearly articulated meaning. The aim of the garden is not pleasure but a process of meaning which replaces the spontaneous sensation of pleasure with a moral lesson.

Yet Saint Preux starts his letter to Milord Edouard by saying that pleasure is the only aim of work: "We only work for pleasure [*pour jouir*]; this alternation of labor and recreation [*jouissance*] is our natural state" (130). This sentence led Louis Marin to suggest, in a beautiful analysis of Julie's garden, that the whole Clarens economy could be reversed and that in the end the reality principle was subjected to the pleasure principle in Rousseau's work.[28] Louis Marin's paradoxical interpretation, seductive though it may be, overemphasizes the role of pleasure (*jouissance*) in Rousseau's ethics, unless pleasure is redefined to exclude sensual connotations: Rousseauist characters, indeed, enjoy a pleasure whose value is primarily symbolic and nonsensual.[29]

The symbolic value of pleasure is confirmed by Saint Preux's solitary return to Julie's garden the day following the walk. Although Saint Preux uses the pretext of feeding birds, his real intention is to contemplate, inhale, and even kiss Julie's work, that is, the traces of her body; he therefore intends to have a sensual experience: "I shall see nothing which her hand has not touched; I shall kiss the flowers which have been her carpet; I shall inhale, with the morning dew, the air which she has breathed" (159).[30] No sooner is he in the garden, however, than his sensual reverie stops and is replaced by the memory of a word, not a sensation: "As I entered Elysium with this temper of mind, I suddenly recollected the last word which M.

Wolmar said to me yesterday very near the same spot. The recollection of that single word instantly changed my whole frame of mind. I thought that I beheld the image of virtue, where I expected to find that of pleasure" (159).

This last word was M. de Wolmar's answer to Saint Preux's question about the usefulness of the garden, when he told Saint Preux that Elysium had been "planted by the hands of virtue." Wolmar's words have the power to change radically Saint Preux's state of mind and that of his body. Although Rousseau does not use the word *revolution*, Saint Preux's phrase— "a changé sur le champ tout l'état de mon âme"—is the very definition of a spiritual revolution. This revolution reminds us of a scene Julie recounts to Saint Preux in letter 18 of the third part, in which she justifies her wedding to M. de Wolmar, betrayal of the past, and renunciation of sensual love. In the church where her wedding to M. de Wolmar takes place Julie has the feeling that she hears God's voice in the voice of the priest. "All this made such an impression on me that I thought I felt a sudden revolution inside me." Julie's experience in the church is very close to the feeling of the sublime described by Burke and Kant: what she feels, indeed, is a "kind of emotion" she had never felt, a "terror" that seizes her soul in a place full of the majesty of God, and a "sudden fear" that makes her shiver and almost faint. She has the sensation of something "absolutely great," to use Kant's words, which transcends her personal feeling of sadness and regret for the past. In the church Julie hears God's voice in that of the priest; in the silence of the garden, where he came to enjoy a sensual memory of Julie, Saint Preux suddenly hears M. de Wolmar's words. In both cases an internal revolution takes place that allows for the transcendence of individual and sensual desire. Both Julie and Saint Preux suddenly understand the "supersensible purposiveness of Reason," to use Kant's words again.[31] They have very similar experiences, experiences that can be called sublime. Julie's garden is a human and worldly echo of a sacred space that makes possible the process of sublimation; this sacred space has no reality in itself: it is nothing but a striving toward infinite progress and the feeling of a supersensible faculty. If the garden is allegorical, it is an allegory neither of virtue nor of Julie's beautiful soul but of a spiritual sense of the self that makes possible the transcendence of an immediate and sensual pleasure.[32]

The spiritual revolution experienced by both Julie and Saint Preux consists in linking the moment—the pleasure of the individual—to the duration of mankind and the common cause of human beings, that is, in renouncing the selfish pleasure of the individual. On the day following the walk Saint Preux completes the first step of the process symbolized by Julie's garden. Instead of dreaming of Julie and desiring her while breathing and touching her work—instead of fetishizing the experience—he sublimates his initial sensation. He discovers another pleasure, a specifically Rousseauist one "which the wicked never know and which consists in being pleased with one's self," a pleasure "no other pleasure can equal" (161). This pleasure is the result of the effort Saint Preux expends on himself and of the process he is pursuing, which only "time and patience" can make successful.

The walk in Elysium therefore represents a crucial moment in *La Nouvelle Héloïse*, a moment whose importance can be understood only by placing the letter in the narrative continuity of the novel. It comes immediately before the letter in which Julie tells her cousin Claire how M. de Wolmar led her and Saint Preux to the grove where their former love blossomed. Saint Preux's next long letter is letter 17, in which he describes the ultimate test of his strength to Milord Edouard: a return to the past with Julie, that is, their excursion to La Meillerie without M. de Wolmar. Wolmar has deliberately left on a trip so that the lovers, by themselves, might undergo the experience of, or rather the miracle produced by, time. In the grove, as at La Meillerie, the lovers remain within M. de Wolmar's gaze, under a spiritual and moral power that pulls them out of nostalgic reverie and forces them to discover that the past is nothing but the past, a moment transcended by time. In the grove Wolmar asks Julie and Saint Preux to give each other a kiss, thus profaning the place, that is, taking away its sacred value as a prohibited place of memory, as a repressed memory. "This kiss was nothing like that which rendered the grove terrible to me. I sadly congratulated myself, and I found that my heart was more changed than I had hitherto ventured to imagine" (177), Julie writes. The walk in Elysium can be read as the first step in a therapeutic process that leads not to repression but rather to a transference that makes possible the sublimation of desire. The garden is emblematic of the therapeutic miracle because it is a place where time, patience, and words produce effects that seem at first purely magical. The garden is not "natural": it produces a nature that is the closest possible approximation of a truly desirable but hypothetical nature. The garden is a site of transference, a transference through art, from disorder to nature; through time, from past to present; and, through patience, from melancholy to self-satisfaction.

This is not to say that Rousseau's novel is not ambiguous at all. Many critics have been struck by the ambiguity of its ending.[33] Indeed, Julie's death raises many questions: does not her death, which resembles a suicide, indicate a failure of the sublimation process allegorized by her garden? In her posthumous letter to Saint Preux, Julie reveals that she never stopped loving him and that she wished to die. Does this ambiguous ending represent a sudden negation of the entire novel? In *Jean-Jacques Rousseau: La Transparence et l'obstacle* Jean Starobinski argues that even Julie's death belongs to the same dialectic process of transcendence. I agree with this interpretation. The ambiguity of the novel's ending does not transform ambiguity into an ethical ideal but, rather, makes the morals of the novel more subtle, more complex, and more spiritual. Reading carefully Julie's final and posthumous letter, one sees that she does not simply reveal her love for Saint Preux; she also asks him to care for her husband. This letter allows us to interpret her death not as an ultimate rebellion against the violence done to her nature but as a last sacrifice, completing the process of transference by giving Wolmar's role, that of the therapist, to Saint Preux and thus endowing Saint Preux's life with a spiritual meaning. "You know him to have been your deliverer, as well as the husband of your friend. . . . As he restored your taste for virtue, so show him the object and the value of it. . . . He has done his duty; I will do mine; and you must hereafter do yours" (279–80). Julie's "first feeling," like the first state of her garden, exists only to be sacrificed, or sublimated through work, time, patience, and death. Rousseau's genius consists in giving the strongest affective value to this sacrifice: "You will lose no more of Julie than you have long been deprived of. Her better part remains with you" (278), Julie writes to Saint Preux in her final letter. Her "better part" is not her sensual passion for Saint Preux but the "miracle" she teaches him when she gives him her own key to the garden, a symbolic key that gives him no access to her body since it represents the apprenticeship of sublimation.

It is the very process allegorized by Julie's garden that constitutes Rousseau's modernity. Rousseau replaces the dualist Cartesian model, in which reason is sovereign and triumphs over mastered passions, with an "ethics of singularity," as Francine Markovits argues. Wolmar embodies the human articulation of Rousseau's ethics, in Markovits's words, "the theory of an intelligent sensibility, the definition of affection as passage, the determination of the subject as history, and therefore, what was so scandalous, the idea of a transference of affections."[34] It is precisely because Rousseau defines affection as a "passage" that time plays such an important role in *La Nouvelle Héloïse*, whose story covers a long period of time. In *Jean-Jacques Rousseau* Jean Starobinski stresses the importance of evolution in Rousseau's novel and describes the dialectic movement Rousseau invents in order to reconcile opposites and to allow for the transcendence of oneself.[35] Beyond a discussion of Julie's death and the ending of *La Nouvelle Héloïse*, it is important to understand that time is a crucial element in Rousseau's writing: only time makes passage, history, and transference possible; only time allows characters to be transformed through the mediation of the word. This is why *La Nouvelle Héloïse* "in so many ways announces the nineteenth-century tradition," as Peter Brooks suggests.[36]

Rousseau's and Watteau's gardens represent two contradictory relations to time and meaning. Whereas the Rousseauist garden is inscribed in a temporality that allows for dialectics and transcendence, the pleasure represented by Watteau ironically rejects the temporal and discursive limits of pleasure. Watteau paints not simply pleasure but rather resistance to a temporality that puts an end to pleasure and to interpretations that attempt to define and therefore to limit pleasure: he paints an ironic resistance to analysis and to sublimation. In that sense his work is as metaphysical as Rousseau's and also contains an ethical claim.

Yet Watteau's Cythera suffers from the posterity of Rousseau's Elysium. Watteau's painting is caught in a dichotomy that destroys its specific claim: either it is considered a ravishingly pretty but frivolous representation of aristocratic pleasures, and therefore condemned as a superficial painting having no meaning and no consistency, while preserved as a document of the aristocratic art of pleasure; or it is considered a melancholic painting highlighting the vanity of worldly pleasures before the threat of death and revealing that pure pleasures exist only in utopia and is then saved thanks to this metaphysical meaning, which gives it some depth. We have inherited the dichotomy of frivolity and depth from Rousseau's influence and from the late-eighteenth-century political and moral use of his thought. Watteau's Cythera, however, is neither frivolous and superficial nor melancholic and deep but both frivolous and deep, as Vivant Denon, the author of the libertine, Watteauesque tale *Point de lendemain*, the founder of the Louvre Museum, and the owner of the second version of Watteau's painting, was the first to claim in 1829.[37]

A dichotomous system of values would establish a division between Elysium, meaning, depth, transcendence, metaphysics, bourgeois morality, nature, and sensibility, on the one hand, and Cythera, nonsense, superficiality, immanence, physical pleasure, aristocratic decadence, artificiality, and theatricality, on the other. The aim of this chapter is to show that Watteau's representation of immanence contains an ironic reflection on transcendence and that the rejection of meaning has a specific meaning. Watteau's Cythera is not simply the antithesis of Rousseau's Elysium. The elements crucial to Rousseau's garden, mainly time and the process of transcendence, are also represented in Watteau's paintings, but they are derided at the same time.

The ethical value of this derision is less easy to understand than that of Rousseau's lesson of transcendence through time. Whereas everyone, regardless of his or her opinion of Rousseau, is aware of his immense contribution to the formation of modern sensibility, the importance of Watteau's ethical gesture has not yet been recognized, even though his esthetic modernity is widely acknowledged. His ethical claim lies, not in a thematics that could be considered somewhat archaic, but in an ironic address to the viewer. This irony is the awareness that metaphysics represents an irresistible temptation for human beings: pleasure is a resistance to this temptation, and the putti's plump behind a resistance to the viewer's desire for a "behind" of the scene. This irony contains an inversion of traditional metaphysics and, to that extent, an ethical claim: that man must learn to accept the lightness of meaning.

The unresolved contradictions in Watteau's paintings open a space of playful ambiguity and irony that is the basis for an ethics of pleasure. This irony consists in mocking the metaphysical tendencies of the viewers, who cannot help looking for a deep meaning. It is because of its ironic dimension that Watteau's representation of Cythera transcends its cultural and social context. This irony, which is both an awareness and a playful mockery of a tendency that pushes us to always look for definite meaning and for morality, addresses twentieth-century as well as eighteenth-century viewers and allows us to speak of Watteau's modernity.

Watteau defines a specific mode of address to the viewer that we will find in all the novels and stories we are about to examine. These novels, unlike *La Nouvelle Héloïse*, cover only a short period of time. Libertine novelists are not interested in a duration that finally resolves the contradictions of the self through a dialectical movement but, rather, in the contradictions of the self in one single instant and in what happens in that "moment."

Two

1731 ∾ Manon, or Pleasure[1]

IN HIS preface to the seventh volume of his *Memoirs* the Man of Quality warns his readers that he will tell them the story of a young man of good birth "who obstinately refuses to be happy and deliberately plunges into the most dire misfortunes" and who "chooses an obscure and vagabond life in preference to all the advantages bestowed by nature and fortune."[1] In this preface Manon is not mentioned even once, as if des Grieux's crime consisted in choosing not Manon but a "vagabond life." The stakes are clear: Manon represents this vagabond life.[2]

Des Grieux starts his narrative by describing his "good and regular life" before meeting Manon: "My conduct at college had been so good and regular that the masters quoted me as an example to others" (12). At the end of his narrative he describes his intention to resume a "good and regular life": "I had made up my mind to return to my country and to atone for the scandal of my conduct by a good and regular life" (154). We find exactly the same words, "good and regular" [*sage et réglée*], used at both the beginning and the end of the narrative to describe des Grieux's life before and after the perturbation brought on by his encounter with Manon. What Manon stands for, that is a "vagabond life," seems to be condemned in the end and to leave no trace in the narrative except guilt. This moral framing is confirmed by the fact that des Grieux addresses his narrative to an older man, the Man of Quality, whom he met twice by chance, first with Manon on his way to America and then alone when disembarking from America: "'Sir,' he said, 'you have been so good to me that I should reproach myself with ingratitude if I kept anything back from you. I am prepared to acquaint you not only with my misfortunes and sufferings but also with my follies and shameful weakness'" (11). By using the words "ingratitude," "acquaint," and "follies," which belong to an aristocratic and moral set of values, des Grieux seems to acknowledge his guilt and repudiate his wandering (*égarement*).

The Man of Quality, both the outside narrator and des Grieux's addressee, is the first character to describe Manon to us: not knowing who she is, he depicts her exactly as he sees her—chained to a dozen harlots.[3] Even though she looks beautiful and distinguished, her condition does not allow him to take her for a noble person. Through the eye of an impartial witness, the first image we, the readers, have of Manon is that of a woman of pleasure. But as soon as he sees des Grieux, the Man of Quality feels naturally attracted to him in spite of his misery, since "a mere glance is all you need to gauge a man's birth and upbringing" (8). It is clear that there is a solidarity of social class between des Grieux and the Man of Quality, which later becomes a solidarity of values and souls. When addressing his narrative to the Man of Quality, the first image des Grieux gives us of Manon is also that of a woman of pleasure: "I gathered that she was being sent to the convent against her will, and I see now that it was certainly to check the pleasure-loving tendencies that had already shown themselves in her, and that were to cause subsequently all her misfortunes and mine" (13). This is a mere hypothesis, which des Grieux reconstructed a posteriori, and yet he states it as a certainty. This allows him to designate Manon as the only source of all his misfortunes. The two men's solidarity against the "woman of pleasure" makes the moral order win out and erases the threat brought by the female element.

This is the general interpretation of *Manon Lescaut*. Most critics read *Manon Lescaut* as the story of a social conflict between two antithetical worlds and as a love story in which the woman's voice is repressed and negated. Nancy K. Miller writes in *French Dressing*: "Thus, although the novel appears to belong to the eighteenth-century tradition of constructing fictional texts around a heroine's name and fate, in its narrative and in its ideology it is structured by the apprenticeship of masculine identity."[4] In *Enlightenment and the Shadows of Chance* Thomas Kavanagh argues: "His [des Grieux's] telling his story to Renoncourt thus represents in a very real sense an aggressive taking control of all that remains of Manon's life."[5] We find a consensus among critics about the moral framing and the repression of Manon's voice.[6]

I would like to call this interpretation into question because of an element in the narrative that I see as an inconsistency and that has not been highlighted to this day. At the beginning of his story des Grieux blames Manon's "pleasure-loving tendencies" for all their misfortunes; by the end he says that his only real misfortune is Manon's death, "a tragedy without parallel" that he is "destined to bewail . . . for the rest of my days" (152). But Manon's "pleasure-loving tendencies" are not responsible for her death. What causes the tragedy, on the contrary, is her newly found virtue and the lovers' desire to be reconciled with heaven through marriage. In America Manon becomes a saint and makes des Grieux as happy as a man can be. And yet, as he starts his narrative after Manon's death, he remembers and describes Manon only as a woman of pleasure, as if she had never redeemed herself.

It may seem strange to accuse a novel of narrative inconsistency. Yet one must ask why des Grieux's narrative mourns the woman of pleasure, not the redeemed sinner. Why is it that the men's gaze constructs the image of a frivolous and unfaithful woman, when in fact Manon died faithful and repentant? Should we read this as one more sign that the novel tries to save the moral order and to repress Manon's voice? This narrative inconsistency and des Grieux's "bad faith" warrant further examination, for they indicate that pleasure is the object, the heart, the central stake of the novel: as an object of mourning it is also an object of desire. As an object of desire its relation to higher, aristocratic feelings is more complex than merely one of repression.

Manon: The Embodiment of Pleasure

It has often been said that Manon embodies contradiction.[7] She is both tender and cruel, fickle and faithful, constant and treacherous. She loves des Grieux and betrays him with men she does not love. When des Grieux finds her at M. de G.M.'s home, she seems "overjoyed" to see him again and reproaches him for being "so gloomy and pained." When she betrays des Grieux with the young G.M., she is extremely surprised by des Grieux's anger at her perfidy.

When des Grieux tries to understand Manon, he finds only one explanation: Manon's inclination for pleasure. The word *pleasure* becomes des
Grieux's only key to resolving Manon's enigma, in an analogy with his own
passion for Manon: "Manon was pleasure mad and I was mad on her" (36).
Strange, admirable, and *extraordinary* are the adjectives des Grieux uses to qualify Manon's character and to express his own wonder: "Manon had a most
extraordinary character. . . . She had to have pleasure and amusements. . . .
So long as the day could be spent in pleasure she never troubled her head
where the money came from. . . . But this ceaseless round of pleasures was
so essential to her being, that without it there was no relying on what she
might feel or do" (44). Des Grieux calls Manon "strange" and "extraordinary" because she stands outside the system of values he received from his
birth and education. He can hardly conceive of a being whose actions and
feelings are determined not by social rules but by the temporary and individual sensation of pleasure.

This is not to say that pleasure in the eighteenth century is incompatible with social rules. We know that the "art of pleasing" first developed in
the sixteenth and, even more, the seventeenth century as an art practiced by
courtiers. But there is an important difference between the aristocratic art
of pleasing, which consists both in pleasing and in being pleased, and
Manon's pleasure, which consists only in being pleased. The art of pleasing
is an art of ruling and polishing the relation to the other, a codified practice that aims to make life in society agreeable within the limits of social
and moral decency.[8] Taste is taught through sociability: only the world, that
is, aristocratic society, can teach the art of pleasing by refining what is too
rough or crude in an individual. Manon does not belong to the world;
Prévost purposely emphasized her common birth in the 1753 edition.
Manon has no origins and no family other than the parents mentioned
briefly twice at the beginning of the novel and a brother, Lescaut, a soldier
and pimp, who encourages her to prostitute herself. Manon's difference is
also a moral, since ancien régime literature always establishes an equivalence
between nobility of birth and nobility of the soul.

Manon's impulsive character gives way to the almost simultaneous
expression of two feelings that are absolutely incompatible not only for
des Grieux but for any reader who has some sense of moral values. One

moment she expresses her love for des Grieux in almost Racinian terms: "She repeated, amid floods of tears, that she was not trying to justify her abominable behavior. 'What do you want, then?' I cried. 'I want to die,' she answered, 'unless you give me back your love, for without that I cannot live'" (32). A moment later she justifies her betrayal with venal reasons: "He had held out in front of her such dazzling promises that she had given in little by little" (33). For Manon, there is no contradiction between sublime feeling and venal pleasure, between tragedy and comedy. The contradiction exists only in the code of values that frames the narrative through des Grieux's voice. *Inconstant, fickle, unfaithful, disloyal, perfidious,* and *perjured* are all adjectives des Grieux uses to qualify Manon throughout his tale; they all signify change, movement, rupture of oath, lack of stability. In spite of his attraction to Manon, des Grieux's rhetoric is still moral and aristocratic: he expresses a desire for order and stability. "I am quite sure that with my loyal and affectionate nature I should have been happy for life with Manon if only she had been faithful to me" (17). Faithfulness, or fidelity, is one of the main aristocratic values, not a bourgeois, sentimental fidelity to one's lover but rather as a sense of honor that makes people keep their word. When des Grieux calls Manon "my unfaithful" [*mon infidèle*], he remains within an aristocratic system of values that his fascination for Manon violates. "My unfaithful" is an oxymoron: the possessive "my" contrasts with the unreliability and the impossibility of possession expressed by "unfaithful." The novel itself is based on this oxymoron.

Almost all the rare passages in which des Grieux recounts Manon's words in direct style before the exile in America concern money and calculation. The numbers are very precise: "I should take the jewelry and close on sixty thousand francs I have got out of him in these two years" (34), Manon says before leaving M. de B. for des Grieux. "Of course, he has kissed my hands more than a million times, and it is only right that he should pay for the pleasure. I don't think the price of five or six thousand francs is too high when you take into account his money—and his age" (54), she declares when she gives up the old M. de G.M. for des Grieux. "It seemed to me that it would be a pity to spoil our chances of so much money in the long run, by merely being content to disappear there and then with the ten thousand francs and the jewels. Here was a fortune ready to drop into our hands, and you and I might live very comfortably at G.M.'s expense" (110), she tells des Grieux in order to justify her decision to betray him for the young G.M.

The sealed letter she leaves for des Grieux in her bedroom after betraying him for the second time expresses what des Grieux calls her "coarse, materialistic outlook" (50): "I swear that you are the idol of my heart, my dear Chevalier, and there is nobody in the world I love as I love you. But don't you see, my poor darling, that loyalty is a silly virtue in the pass we are in? Do you really think we can love each other with nothing to eat? . . . I love you, do believe me, but try to leave our affairs in my hands for a little while. Woe betide whoever falls into my clutches!" (49). Such style does not require a comment: it should be enough to shock the reader's sensibility. Manon, who puts side by side love declarations and vulgar images of swindling and gives feelings a material limit, does not seem to have any moral conscience.

Des Grieux's father laughs about his son's love for a woman who is really not worth it: "'You left Amiens on the 28 of last month. It is now the 29th of this month. It is eleven days since M. de B. wrote to me. Let us suppose it took him eight days to get to know your lady friend properly. So if we take eleven and eight from the thirty-one between the 28th of last month and the 29th of this, we get twelve, or thereabouts.' More roars of laughter" (24). The father's calculation aims to reveal Manon's villainy and the venality of her soul. It also anticipates Manon's own calculations in later episodes. The idea of calculation, which still has negative connotations today, as is shown by the French expression *comptes d'épicier*, is supposed to decrease the value of des Grieux's passion by taking away its romantic and spiritual dimension.

For Manon, however, material pleasure is perfectly compatible with true love, as is faithfulness of the heart with unfaithfulness of the body: "The fidelity I expect of you is that of the heart" (111). Is she passionate or fickle, tender or perfidious, faithful or traitorous? The contradiction of terms exists only in des Grieux's system of values, which is also that of the Man of Quality, of the father, and of the whole novel. This is why it is so difficult to define a character who escapes the binary terms and the dichotomous values that underlie the entire plot structure.

Manon's "extraordinary" character also distinguishes this novel from other romances, from the medieval courtly novel to the seventeenth-century heroic and picaresque novel. A comparison with another heroine who is said to have served as a model for Manon reveals Manon's strangeness. The heroine of "Histoire de Monsieur Des Frans et de Silvie," in Robert Chasles's *Les Illustres Françaises* (1713), betrays the man she loves and continues to love him even after the betrayal, which her lover witnessed with his own eyes. Des Frans, who, like des Grieux, is the narrator of the story, presents himself as the victim of his passion for Silvie. Silvie's persistent love for des Frans leads the narrator to comment on the "incomprehensible" nature of women: "The more I think about and remember her proceeding, the more I tell myself that women are incomprehensible."[9] The Man of Quality expresses the same wonder at the beginning of *Manon Lescaut*: "She sounded so charming and modest that I found myself making many a reflection on the incomprehensible nature of woman" (10).

There is, however, a fundamental difference between Silvie and Manon: Silvie is extremely surprised by her own betrayal and approves the physical torture des Frans inflicts upon her as a punishment. Silvie has a noble soul; her own betrayal remains incomprehensible and horrible to her. "It seems to me that the delusion in which I hurled myself is a dream. The more I examine myself, the more I examine also the feelings I always had for you, the less I can understand my fall. I don't accuse my destiny; I don't accuse the charm of my senses, I was forced to do it by some supranatural power."[10] The story does not threaten the system of moral values that condemns Silvie's infidelity since Silvie, unlike Manon, is the first to accept that system and must find a supranatural cause to explain her infidelity.

Manon is also different from all the female characters in Prévost's *Mémoires d'un homme de qualité, Cleveland, Le Doyen de Killerine,* and *Histoire d'une Grecque moderne.* Sélima, the Man of Quality's wife, Diana and Nadine, the Marquis de Rosemont's lovers, and Théophé, the Greek woman, are foreigners, but their social rank is not inferior to that of their lovers and manifests itself through their noble souls—through their constancy and their capacity to love and sacrifice themselves, transforming a carnal passion into a spiritual energy. Since all of Prévost's novels are written from the point of view of a male narrator, the stake of the narrative is usually the hero's Corneillian conflict between his passion for a woman deserving his love and the social, religious, or moral duty contradicting this love. Prévost's heroes endlessly question themselves on the madness of love, but this madness has a moral limit, as the object always deserves their love. If Sélima were not worthy of the Man of Quality's passion, the *Mémoires d'un homme de qualité qui s'est retiré du monde* would be inconceivable: the title refers to the hero's passionate desire to withdraw from the world after the death of his beloved.

The last story in *Mémoires d'un homme de qualité*, at the end of volume 6, just before *Manon Lescaut*, starts exactly like the story of Manon and des Grieux: a young man, called "le Chevalier," falls madly in love with Rosette, but his father forbids him from marrying her because she is poor. The Chevalier, unlike des Grieux, obeys his father's orders and marries another woman. Rosette, unlike Manon, remains faithful to him; the Chevalier's first wife dies, and he can finally marry the woman he never stopped loving. Neither respect for authority nor honor has been violated. Volume 6 ends with a tale of love within the frame of social, moral, and sentimental order.

Is Manon closer to the most monstrous and most original female character in *Mémoires d'un homme de qualité*, a serial killer? The Man of Quality meets this woman while traveling through a forest. She is well dressed and looks like a decent bourgeois woman. Seeing her alone and without a carriage, he proposes his help, which the woman gratefully accepts. Soon after, they are stopped by a guard who warns them about an extremely dangerous and clever serial killer, a well-dressed woman who lures her victims into the woods and kills them with a sharp knife. The Man of Quality thanks the guard and pretends that he has not seen this woman. He then makes a deal with the serial killer after taking her weapon: he will not turn her in to the police if she will tell him her story and surrender of her own free will when they arrive at the next town.

The woman's surrender submits her to the moral and social order. Since this ending is comparable to Manon's repentance in America, this is not where the difference between Manon and the serial killer lies. This violent woman, like Manon, disrupts the social order. But she becomes a murderer only because she was seduced, deceived, and abandoned by a first lover who had promised to marry her. After several bad experiences with men she decides to take revenge: "Then I wished that all men together had only one life, and that I could take it with my teeth and nails" (245). The serial killer fights exactly what Manon stands for: deception and betrayal. The constancy and the legitimacy of her hatred almost make it a noble feeling in spite of its excessive violence.

Manon is therefore the first of Prévost's heroines not to be integrated into a heroic or courteous code of values. When the novel was first published, its title was not *Manon Lescaut* but *Histoire du Chevalier des Grieux*, and it was only the seventh volume of *Mémoires d'un homme de qualité*, published at the same time as volumes 5 and 6. This last volume, probably added because Prévost was in need of money, is now published under the name of the heroine, whom Prévost does not even mention in the preface, and it is the only volume of the *Mémoires* to be read today as a classic; clearly, this story goes well beyond the author's intentions. *Manon Lescaut* is both integrated into and external to the structure of the *Mémoires*, integrated since the Man of Quality himself introduces des Grieux's narrative as a part of his *Mémoires* and external since the main narrator is no longer the Man of Quality, who remains silent after ten pages of introduction and reappears only once in the middle of the narrative, but the Chevalier des Grieux, whose voice ends the *Mémoires* and breaks their perfect closure. The Man of Quality listens to des Grieux silently and transcribes his narrative without a single reflective comment: "This is his tale, and I shall add nothing to his own words, from beginning to end" (11). There is no moralizing conclusion, and the Chevalier des Grieux, not the Man of Quality, has the last word. The Man of Quality does not simply withdraw from the world: in the last volume he also withdraws from his own narrative.

Manon takes us away from courteous and heroic literature. But she is not a nineteenth-century heroine either: she is not Zola's Nana or Huysman's Marthe, a courtesan or *cocotte* whose body represents the corrupting power of flesh and evil. The pleasure Manon claims does not have an immoral dimension, through which it would be integrated into the system of moral values as the very corruption of this system. Manon's pleasure is of a different sort. It is simply the desire to have fun, not to get bored.

She does not attach any value to material goods in themselves: "No woman was ever less attached to money for its own sake, and yet she could not for a moment endure the risk of being without it. She had to have pleasure and amusements, but she would never have wanted a sou if enjoyment could have been free of charge. So long as the day could be spent in pleasure she never troubled her head where the money came from; and so as she was not particularly addicted to gambling, nor dazzled by the mere display of wealth, it was the easiest thing in the world to satisfy her by supplying from day to day the sort of amusements she liked" (44). Manon's pleasure cannot simply be bought; it is not a material good but a feeling. This feeling is the only thing that male characters in the novel can neither take away from her nor restrain. Manon is looking for opportunities to laugh. What she wants is play in all the senses of the word—games, jokes, acting, and comedy. Manon's taste for theatricality mocks the moral system of values that is based on social and moral identity and stability.

Three important scenes reveal her strong inclination for theatrical pleasure. The first is the scene in which Manon convinces des Grieux to remain in the house of her second lover, M. de G.M., and to play the role of her little brother. The scene has no purpose but to give the lovers "the fun of the comic turn [des Grieux] was to put on as Manon's student brother" (54). Manon has so much fun that she almost betrays them through her irresistible laughter: "Manon, who was in a gay mood, nearly upset everything several times by shrieking with laughter" (55). Later in the novel she stages her own little comedy and forces des Grieux to participate unknowingly in a joke she organizes: she attracts a potential lover, the Italian Prince, to their home only to mock him in a well-prepared *coup de théâtre* by confronting him with the man she truly loves. She enjoys the scene and both men's surprise so much that, again, she cannot contain her laughter: "the room re-echoed with her peals of laughter" (92). Finally, when des Grieux finds her in the house of the young G.M. and bitterly reproaches her for her betrayal, she convinces him to stay there with her and have dinner and sleep between the young G.M.'s sheets because the scheme delights her (114).

The comedy at the old G.M.'s house and the joke played on the old G.M. are essential to the plot: they cause the deceived character's rage, which leads to the lovers' arrest and exile to America. The episode with the Italian Prince, however, which Prévost added to the 1753 edition of the text, has no consequence within the plot itself. Some critics have suggested that this anecdote serves to add an element of comedy to the tense atmosphere of tragedy in order to relax the reader, as well as to make Manon's character more noble by showing that she is capable of tenderness and fidelity. It is true that Manon does not betray des Grieux with the Italian Prince as she does with M. de B. or M. de G.M.; even so, this episode is more revealing of Manon's character than of her love for des Grieux. This is a very significant anecdote: it shows that Manon's inclination for pleasure is free; it is an inclination for theatrical game and not only for material goods. Manon's pleasure is that of a theatrical scene of which she is both the producer and the spectator. She treats both men in the same way: "She had sent the Italian Prince a flattering reply, giving him free permission to come and see her, and had given herself a second pleasure by making me participate in her plan without having the slightest suspicion" (93). She manipulates not only the Italian Prince, whom she entices to her house only to revel in his disappointment, but also the puzzled des Grieux, whom she displays like a puppet, holding him by his hair.

The scene with the Italian Prince has no purpose outside of Manon's pleasure: "thinking we might get some fun out of it, she had not been able to resist the vision her imagination had conjured up" (93). She is seeking a pleasure not of the body but of the imagination. Imagination is an intermediate faculty between the sensitive body and the intellect that gives both physical and mental pleasure. It is a pleasure that cannot be subjected to moral judgment, an egalitarian pleasure that does not concern itself with social distinctions. Des Grieux is quite embarrassed to see a man of good breeding offended in such a way in his presence: his criticism of Manon, however, has no power to reduce her delight in the success of her scheme. Even though des Grieux chooses to interpret this scene as a triumph of love and says that he "was touched to the heart by a sacrifice which [he] could ascribe only to love," there is a playful duplicity in Manon's laughter that has nothing to do with love and even derides the authenticity of grand feelings.

Manon plays with des Grieux as if he were a doll; she combs and manipulates him, and she has enough strength to drag him across the room. Des Grieux's own passion for Manon feminizes him. This feminization is revealed symbolically in a scene in which des Grieux helps Manon escape from the Hôpital and gives her his own breeches because he has forgotten to bring some for her: "There was only one thing to be done, and that was for me to leave my own breeches for Manon and get out somehow without them" (78). The scene after Manon's death in which des Grieux breaks his sword and buries it with Manon has also been read as a scene of symbolic castration and destruction of aristocratic identity.

The greatest danger of this inclination for pleasure may be its communicability. The joke played on the Italian Prince seems "a trifle overdone" to des Grieux. Yet he immensely enjoys playing the role of Manon's brother, an inexperienced country lad, in the house of the old G.M., and he reveals a real talent as an actor; in the house of the young G.M. he spends with Manon "one of the most delightful evenings of our lives" (116).

Because of his love for Manon, des Grieux continually transgresses the social and moral order to which he belongs by his birth and education. Transgression comes from the Latin verb *transgredior*, "to go beyond." Transgression is indeed expressed spatially in this novel in which transportation and change of place play a major role. Des Grieux escapes his father's house to run away to Paris with Manon, he follows Manon in all her successive moves, and eventually he leaves his fatherland to live in exile with Manon in America. From this one could easily conclude that the novel's subject is the conflict between the social and moral code des Grieux inherited from his father and his passion for a "harlot," which transgresses the code by refusing to be subjected to social or moral law. Step by step, we see des Grieux moving further and further away from the social and moral rules of his upbringing, giving up his "good and regular life" and transgressing the aristocratic ethics.

Des Grieux not only follows Manon everywhere; he also becomes more and more like her. As soon as he meets Manon he starts lying to Tiberge in order to run away with her; later, he escapes like a thief from the Saint-Sulpice convent. He plays his role with pleasure in scenes destined to deceive the lovers who Manon wants to "fall into [her] clutches." He does not hesitate to deceive Tiberge exactly as Manon deceives him in order to extort money from him. And des Grieux's betrayal is much more serious since he, unlike Manon, knows the code of honor. Des Grieux becomes a professional gambler, a swindler, at the Hotel de Transylvanie so as to keep his hold on Manon by giving her the goods necessary to her pleasure. In order to save Manon from the Hôpital, he deceives the Father Superior at the Saint-Lazare prison, who had treated him like a son, and kills a guard. Guilty of murder, he neither expresses a single remorse nor accepts responsibility for his crime; rather, he reproaches Lescaut for giving him a loaded pistol. Just like Manon, des Grieux seduces men from whom he tries to obtain favors or money; just like Manon, he counts money with precision; just like Manon, he betrays those who trust him; just like Manon's, his conduct is guided only by his interest; just like Manon, he transgresses the moral code.

Yet at the same time des Grieux blames Manon's inclination for pleasure as the only cause for all his misfortunes, and he remembers regretfully the mythical places of his lost innocence: "My thoughts turned wistfully towards Amiens, home, Saint-Sulpice and all the places I had lived in as a clean, self-respecting being. What an immense gulf lay between me and that happy state!" (51). Although des Grieux commits for Manon all the same crimes, villainies, and misdemeanors that Manon commits for pleasure, he still keeps the privilege of noble sentiments in his address to an old aristocrat. One would be right to conclude, as readers of younger generations often do, that des Grieux's accusations of Manon and his ignorance of his own responsibility are simply signs of his "bad faith."

Des Grieux's Sublime Sentiment

The novel's conflict is not simply between love and the social and moral code. Even though Manon and des Grieux commit very similar crimes, the difference between them remains radical. The narrative's noble value is not the aristocratic control of passion in the name of generosity and reason but passion itself, des Grieux's love for Manon. Which is why the hero does not fight his love in the name of more noble values. The novel's conflict lies between Manon and des Grieux—between love and pleasure.

The difference between love and pleasure is first a difference of intensity. Throughout the novel des Grieux uses the same metaphor to designate the violence of his passion for Manon: he calls it "transport." The word *transport* becomes a key word in the novel. Even though the French word *transport* was not yet used in 1731 to mean "transportation," its etymological

meaning is nonetheless a change of place, a carrying beyond. Manon embodies movement. Throughout the novel the lovers move from one place to
another because of Manon. She goes to Saint-Sulpice and takes des Grieux
away from his peaceful refuge. Unable to find satisfaction in the quiet
country life of Chaillot, she wants to return to Paris. For Manon, however,
movement is primarily physical and geographical. For des Grieux, transport
is a spiritual move: in the eighteenth century *transport* designated a violent
feeling of passion that carried a person beyond reason. It is not the same
thing to be "pleasure mad" and to be "mad on her [i.e., Manon]" (36).

Whereas Manon's pleasure can be calculated and obtained through
material means such as a change of place, des Grieux's transport is an internal movement over which he has no control: "I was carried away by an over-
mastering passion [*transport*]," he says of his first encounter with Manon.[11]
A sudden and violent physical reaction characterizes transport. Either it
produces aphasia—"I experienced such overpowering emotion [*une espèce de
transport*] that for some time I could not utter a sound" (15)—or it unleashes
physical strength, as when des Grieux falls upon M. de G.M. and tries to
strangle him after learning that Manon has been imprisoned in the Hôpital
like a harlot: "Even if at that moment I had been faced with imprisonment
for life or death itself, I could not have restrained my fury [*transport*] at this
terrible news. I flung myself upon him with such uncontrollable rage" (61).
Transport refers to extreme joy and love as well as extreme pain and fury: "I
found myself thrown from the peace of mind I thought was mine into a
terrible outburst [*transport*] of rage" (103). When des Grieux and his father
break, the word *transport* justifies the hero's lack of respect for his father,
inconceivable within the limits of aristocratic etiquette: "'Good-bye, cruel
and unnatural father!' I shouted back in a transport of fury" (132).

Three features characterize transport: its extremism, the total lack of
rational control it causes, and the fear it inspires in its witnesses, particularly Manon, who is scared by a violence of feeling she does not understand:
"She was so frightened by this outburst [*transport*]" (108). Des Grieux uses
the word *transport* almost exclusively to describe his own reactions, except
once when he uses it in reference to Tiberge and twice in reference to
Manon. The use of the word *transport* to describe Tiberge's gesture of affection towards Des Grieux is quite suggestive: "The warmth of his affection

[literally, "the transport with which he kissed me"] quite took me by surprise" (27). The word *transport* in the context of Tiberge's friendship for des Grieux implies that Tiberge too can be suspected of being passionate and that his desire to take des Grieux away from the diabolical Manon is not solely rational, charitable, and disinterested, as if Tiberge himself were acting under the influence of the same passion he tries to calm in his friend. The word *transport* is used twice to describe Manon's reaction, once when she rises in "un transport" of passion to embrace des Grieux in Saint-Sulpice (32) and once when she seems "transportée" by the pleasure of seeing him in old G.M.'s house, where des Grieux has come to reproach her for her betrayal. The use of the word *transport* in these circumstances is paradoxical: Manon expresses a passionate feeling precisely when des Grieux least expects it, that is, after betraying him coldly. Manon's transports, then, have nothing in common with those of des Grieux but confirm only the contradiction she embodies in des Grieux's eyes. The other characters' feelings, be they joy, love, anger, fury, or passion, are never called transports: the word is reserved for des Grieux.

When des Grieux describes the moral upheaval that seizes him upon seeing Manon in Saint-Sulpice, he uses a spatial metaphor that allows him to represent his fear as a transport into a new order of things: "I was horror-stricken at the contrast between the serenity of but a few moments ago and the wild stirrings of desire I could already feel within me. I was shuddering as you do when you find yourself alone at night on some desolate moorland, when all familiar bearings are lost [literally, "when you believe you are transported into a new order of things"] and a panic fear comes over you that you can dispel only by calmly studying all the landmarks" (32). The extreme feeling called *transport* is the very opposite of the humanist dream des Grieux expressed earlier in the novel, that of peaceful retirement in "a sequestered cottage with a little copse and a babbling brook at the end of the garden, a library of choice books" (29), where he could have been delightfully happy if only Manon had lived there with him. The feeling Manon inspires in him, however, is not this peaceful dream but a "horror" and "a panic fear" that makes all landmarks disappear. This feeling of horror and panic fear and the sensation of complete loss recall the sentiment of the sublime described in the eighteenth century by Burke, Shaftesbury, and Kant. As Kristin Ross suggests, des Grieux's feeling comes close to what Burke calls the "delightful horror" of the sublime.[12] This immoderate passion for Manon in which des Grieux himself sees a sacred path of suffering is a sublime sentiment.

Manon, however, neither deserves nor shares such transports. Des Grieux describes her as an "extraordinary creature" precisely because she does not experience suffering and passion as he does. Whereas des Grieux shows a violent jealousy and anger upon seeing Manon again, she simply enjoys his presence and expresses tenderness. Manon cries only when she becomes terrified by des Grieux's outburst of passion. She contrasts absolute passion with a material and concrete reality, that is, the bread to eat and the pleasure to find. Des Grieux makes an absolute of Manon and of the pleasure of the senses, which he even compares to Christian paradise, an analogy that horrifies Tiberge, who then accuses his friend of speaking like a "libertine."[13] Manon's inclination for pleasure is not an absolute but a moderate and changing feeling that is relative to material circumstances and escapes the moral categories that condemn it. Des Grieux's very passion for Manon contradicts Manon's being.

The ontological incompatibility between des Grieux's passion for Manon and Manon's inclination for pleasure is the novel's subject. Des Grieux has only one desire: to possess Manon, to be sure of her heart, to rely on her, to make her a sublime object of desire that deserves his love in an aristocratic system of values and makes the narrative more noble. Manon, in contrast, embodies the mobility of a feeling that cannot be possessed, nor stopped, nor restrained—a feeling on which one cannot rely because its essence is freedom and inconstancy. There is a contradiction between the Chevalier's extreme feelings and Manon's light quest for amusement. The object of the novel is not so much des Grieux's transgression of the fathers' order as it is his attempt to subject pleasure, a fleeting, changing, light feeling, to the law of sublime feelings such as Passion and Desire.

The metaphor of a "desolate moorland," which des Grieux uses to describe his extreme feeling at the moment when he sees Manon again after a long absence, seems to anticipate the geographical exile the lovers experience in the last part of the novel, when they are forced to go to America.

Louisiana, indeed, is also a lonely and desolate land with no familiar bearings. Paradoxically, the lovers' geographical "transportation into a new order of things" excites no fear and no horror in des Grieux and even seems to resolve all the novel's conflicts. Des Grieux escapes the paternal order and manages to stop Manon's quest for pleasure. Des Grieux and Manon suddenly reach peaks of stable love and happiness. In America they discover unexpectedly a land free of social restraints. For the first time des Grieux is *carried away* without experiencing an extreme and terrifying feeling: "I did not hanker after Europe, but, on the contrary, the nearer we came to America the more I felt my heart open into tranquillity" (141). Des Grieux is being assured, at last, of Manon's heart: "'Oh, God!' I cried, 'I have nothing more to ask. I am assured of Manon's heart. . . . My felicity is established for ever'" (144).

Accordingly, throughout the American episode we no longer find the word *pleasure*. For the first time we hear Manon, not estimating the price of the pleasure she gives, but rather avowing her guilt for being too capricious and frivolous: "I have been frivolous and fickle, and even while loving you passionately, as I have always done, I have never been anything but graceless. But you cannot imagine how I have changed" (144). Manon herself now uses des Grieux's moral vocabulary. "The true sweetness of love" replaces inconstancy and pleasure: "'New Orleans is a place to come to,' I often said to Manon, 'if you want to taste the true sweetness of love. Here love is free from self-interest, from jealousy and inconstancy'" (144). A process of sublimation takes place: material goods such as comfort and pleasure, of which Manon has been forcefully deprived, are replaced by expression of a sublime feeling, love, or one's devotion to the other. Manon repudiates pleasure.

But it is in America that Manon dies. One can easily enumerate the many successive causes that lead to Manon's death: des Grieux's desire to be reconciled with religion and to marry Manon; the fact that paternal authority reigns in America as in the old world, allowing the Governor's claim to take Manon away from des Grieux; Manon's beauty, which awakens Synnelet's desire in spite of her wishes; the duel between Synnelet and des Grieux; the lovers' flight into the desert; or the six-mile walk, which exhausts Manon. Yet they are not the real causes of Manon's death, which happens, in fact, without a concrete cause except her exhaustion after the walk. She literally becomes extinct: "She . . . murmured faintly that she thought her last hour had come. At first I took these words for the sort of language ordinarily used in misfortune. . . . I lost her, and . . . I received tokens of her love even as she was passing" (152). The spark that until then motivated all Manon's actions, the inclination for pleasure, is extinguished: in America there is no pleasure. When Manon becomes a "wonderful alchemist" whose mere presence changes a miserable hut into gold, when she claims her guilt, when, finally, she becomes a lover with a "matchless devotion" (151), she is no longer Manon. A fearful and shy Manon takes the place of the joyful and bright woman with whom des Grieux fell in love at first sight. She barely dares to express her desire for a marriage she had rejected up to then: "I have kept the wish locked up in my heart for fear of displeasing you, for I do not presume to aspire to the position of being your wife" (146). Her essence was movement: she no longer exists in stability, in an "established felicity." Manon had to die, because she was already dead. Manon's death in the utopian land of America has an allegorical meaning, namely, the impossibility of sublimating pleasure. Once sublimated, pleasure loses its essence and disappears. Manon's sublimity leads to her death. Pleasure exists only at the moment when it is felt. There can be no transcendence of pleasure because pleasure is a purely immanent feeling.

One could say that Manon's death has a narrative rather than ontological necessity since it allows des Grieux to retain a sacred image of his redeemed lover. But as I mentioned at the beginning of this chapter, des Grieux's narrative does not do justice to Manon's final redemption. From beginning to end, except in the few pages describing the lovers' life in America, des Grieux never stops accusing the "fickle" and "frivolous" Manon, the woman of pleasure. It is as if her death and her final avowal of guilt did not count; or, rather, as if des Grieux could not keep the image of a *sublime* Manon because this woman was not the one he passionately loved. The novel mourns the unfaithful, not the redeemed woman. Why is that?

The Allegorical Triumph of Pleasure

Before answering this question, let us remember how the novel starts. The Man of Quality, who is on a small trip to help his daughter resolve a legal problem, passes through the town of Passy and sees an uproar outside a shabby-looking inn. Curiosity makes him stop and ask a soldier what is happening. The soldier answers that prostitutes are being taken to Le Havre to be deported to America and that the peasants' curiosity has probably been excited by the fact that some of them are quite attractive. The incident might have stopped there since the Man of Quality is not frivolous enough to be curious about a pretty face. But his own curiosity is excited by an old woman emerging from the inn and yelling at him: "Oh, come and see, Sir! I tell you, it's enough to break your heart!" (7). If he is too noble and dignified for his curiosity to be excited by the vulgar desire to see pretty women, he yields to another kind of pleasure, that of having his heart touched, even broken, by a moving sight.

The instinct, however, is the same, even though it is now hidden behind a moral pretense. Prévost, indeed, uses the same word: *curiosité*. "My curiosity was now thoroughly aroused and I dismounted, left my horse with my man and forced my way through the crowd. It was certainly a pathetic sight that met my eyes" (8). Inside the inn, the vision of Manon and the contrast between her beauty and her situation intensify the Man of Quality's "curiosity" because this contrast seems to contain an interesting story. The women to whom Manon is chained are also miserable; the Man of Quality, however, does not inquire about them because their faces are not as interesting or beautiful as Manon's. The Man of Quality questions one of the guards: "I took the one in charge aside and asked to tell me something about this lovely girl. But he could give me nothing but a few bare facts" (8). His frustrated curiosity leads him to disturb des Grieux, who is "unconscious of everything around him" and looks like an "arresting picture of grief": "Could you satisfy my curiosity? I should like to know that charming person over there. She does not look as if she were made for the sorry plight she is in" (8).

If we have the story of *Manon Lescaut*, it is only because the Man of Quality yielded to curiosity, to the desire of gaining pleasure from an interesting story. There is something almost indecent and certainly not moral in a desire that leads him to disturb a man absorbed in his grief precisely because this grief contains the promise of an exciting story. Curiosity, the driving force at the beginning of the narrative, is neither a sublime feeling like des Grieux's love for Manon nor a moral principle like those taught by the Man of Quality, the noble and wise father, throughout his *Memoirs*. Curiosity is an instinctive, voyeuristic desire to see, to know, and to control things through sight. Curiosity, therefore, is nothing but an instinct of self-satisfaction, an "inclination to pleasure," a "pleasure-loving tendency." It seems fair to conclude that this pleasure-loving tendency Manon embodies throughout the novel is at the very origin of the narrative, in the very framing of the story.

Curiosity also plays an important role in the plot. In des Grieux's story, curiosity is the only motive that attracts des Grieux and Tiberge to the Arras coach that carries Manon: "We had no other motive than curiosity." Curiosity, therefore, determines des Grieux's destiny. It is also curiosity that allows Manon to find des Grieux in Saint-Sulpice after he has decided to forget her: "Her curiosity was aroused by a name so similar to mine" (31). Manon's curiosity is linked to her playfulness and her inclination for pleasure, as the episode with the Italian Prince shows: "She was looking at me with an avid curiosity" (91).

The Man of Quality is an old aristocrat, des Grieux is a young aristocrat, and Manon is a young woman of common birth. Despite their age and social origin, their motive is the same: curiosity. The Man of Quality's curiosity gives birth to the narrative; des Grieux's curiosity leads him to meet Manon; Manon's curiosity leads her to des Grieux after he has given up his passion.

If there is no moral conclusion to the novel, if the Man of Quality remains silent at the end of his *Memoirs*, is it not because his curiosity about Manon has forced him into the space of pleasure—the very space into which Manon's charms drag des Grieux? That space of wandering, which carries heroes and readers away from established rules, does not allow for a final word of closure. By yielding to his own desire to hear des Grieux's story and transcribing this story in a separate addendum after the last volume of his memoirs, the Man of Quality himself enters a space of wandering, of pleasure of the imagination. That space of pleasure is fiction—the telling of, and listening to, stories.[14]

MANON LESCAUT contains a double discourse. On the one hand there is the social and moral discourse of order and repression, which forces the noble heart to sacrifice his violent desire as well as his fleeting pleasure in order to resume a "good and regular life." On the other hand, the narrative's framing, the ambiguous role played by the Man of Quality as the one who first listens to the story, and des Grieux's mourning of the woman of pleasure introduce another discourse. Whereas the first discourse condemns wandering and des Grieux's love for Manon, the second, which is more subtle and must be read only as the subtext of the first, says that pleasure, be it sensual or imaginary, is more powerful than its repression, even though the repression of pleasure and the return to order seem to win out in the end.

Pleasure is a feeling everyone can share regardless of class and gender. As a character embodying sensual and material pleasure, Manon is the cause of des Grieux's misfortunes and the victim of the social forces that exclude her. But as an object of curiosity and a curious person herself, as a character embodying the pleasure of the imagination, she represents the driving force that determines des Grieux's and the Man of Quality's acts. She is the allegory of the narrative's pleasure. In spite of their moral condemnation of any base feeling and their belonging to a social class whose code is based on the repression of sensual instinct and the respect of honor, the Man of Quality and Chevalier des Grieux both yield to curiosity, to the pleasure of listening to narratives and telling them. The Man of Quality is "full of impatience to hear the detailed story of his misfortunes and his journey to America" (11). The only interruption of des Grieux's narrative is a comment about the pleasure given by the story: "He knew that we had enjoyed listening to him because our interest had never flagged, and he promised us that we should find something still more interesting in the sequel to his story," the Man of Quality says at the end of part 1. Des Grieux's grief has become "something interesting" in his own words, something the Man of Quality will enjoy listening to. The narrative of mourning and grief produces pleasure. The pleasure given by the story cannot be limited by moral censorship. It cannot be framed. It simply follows the free path of imagination, the desire to wander, a "vagabond life." Manon, then, dominates the narrative as an allegory and a woman of pleasure in spite of her death as a redeemed lover. *Manon Lescaut* represents allegorically the triumph of pleasure. In that sense, *Manon Lescaut* is the story not simply of a social conflict between two antithetical worlds, as most critics argue, but, rather, of an ontological conflict between two contradictory feelings that can be found in every human being, man or woman, aristocrat or commoner.

Manon Lescaut, however, is still an ambivalent "libertine" novel and therefore can be read simply as a love story, which is what Montesquieu does: "I read today, 6 April 1734, *Manon Lescaut,* a novel written by Father Prévost. I am not surprised that readers like a novel whose hero is a swindler and the heroine a harlot taken to *La Salpétrière:* for all the bad actions of the hero, the Chevalier des Grieux, are motivated by love, which is always a noble motive even when behavior is base. Manon loves him too: which makes us forgive her the rest of her character."[15]

Such a reading, however beautiful, does not do justice to Manon's "extraordinary" character and to the novel's ambiguities. Five years after *Manon Lescaut* was published, another novel drove in the nail of *libertinage.* Crébillon's *Les Égarements du coeur et de l'esprit* shows that given the superficial nature of man and his "pleasure-loving tendencies," love is not always sure to win the conflict between love and pleasure.

Three

1736-1738 ∿ Mme de Lursay, or Vanity

IN HIS preface to *Les Égarements du coeur et de l'esprit* Crébillon indicates what he sees as the aim of fiction: "painting men as they are."[1] He declares his intention to reach the truth, for "truth alone always survives," and he says that he does not yield to fashion: "An author constrained by the base fear of not pleasing his own age rarely survives into those of the future." Then he describes his project:

> You will see in these memoirs a man such as nearly all men are in extreme youth, simple at first and without art, and knowing nothing yet of the world in which he is obliged to live. The first and second parts deal with this ignorance and with his first experiences of love. In sections that follow, he is a man full of false ideas and riddled with follies, who is still governed less by himself than by persons whose interest is to corrupt his heart and mind. You will see him finally, in the last part, restored to himself, owing all virtues to a good woman. There you have the object of *The Wayward Head and Heart*. (19)

This project consists in narrating an education in three steps that form a kind of dialectical process: the first step is ignorance and naiveté; the second, corruption, or what one could call *égarement* (wandering); and the third, the return to virtue, in which the reader finds the hero at last "restored to himself, owing all virtues to a good woman." The expression "restored to himself" implies that there is a genuine self that can be found once the process has passed through corruption and wandering.

The novel's title too suggests such a moral amendment. Indeed, it is impossible to conceive of *égarement* without the idea of a straight path, as

Jean Sgard remarked in 1969: "The notion of wandering is interesting on two levels: it expresses an ambiguous and disconcerting state, a *loss*, a *frenzy* which leads analysis astray; it implies a norm at the same time, because there is wandering only in relation to a straight path."[2] The 1771 *Dictionnaire de Trévoux* defines *égarement* as "everything that swerves from the rule we have to observe, from customary principles and holy doctrine."[3] The word *égarement*, because of its moral connotation, implies knowledge and consciousness of that rule, be it moral, social, religious, or spiritual, from which there is deviation: the word *égarement* can be used only when the error or swerving from the rule has been recognized as such.[4] The very title of Crébillon's novel makes us imagine that the narrator, who recounts his adventures retrospectively, has stopped his wandering and returned to the right path. The novel's beginning reinforces this expectation: "When I entered society the idea of pleasure was the only one I had in my head." The temporal clause "when I entered society," which marks the novel's spatial and temporal starting point, makes us expect a resolution in which the idea of pleasure will no longer be the hero's only concern.[5]

Our expectation is never fulfilled: we do not witness the corrupted hero's moral transformation, and the novel ends instead with "wandering" and a scene of pleasure. In his preface Crébillon announces more than three parts, since he mentions "the first and the second," "sections that follow," and "the last part." But there are only three sections in the novel. Does this mean that Crébillon did not have time to finish his novel, or that he lost interest in it? Is this an unfinished novel, and are we allowed to imagine the hypothetical conclusion to which the novel leads logically: the hero finally "restored to himself" and happy thanks to a "good woman"?

This is the interpretation of Jean Sgard and many later critics. Jean Sgard wrote in 1969: "In the unpublished end of the novel, the hero would have been restored to himself thanks to a good woman, probably Hortense de Théville; the wandering of a young man, an almost conventional theme, would have ended with a conversion to love, with a radiant blooming of sensibility."[6] Raymond Trousson expressed the same hypothesis in 1993: "The last part Crébillon had announced was supposed to show the accession to truth, which is itself a return to lost values: the novel can be appreciated only in the light of what has not been written, and the absent conclusion is necessary for understanding it."[7] Both Sgard and Trousson base their analyses of the novel on a conclusion Crébillon promised but did not write.

The legitimacy of adding a conclusion in order to understand the meaning of a novel seems to be questionable. My interpretation is closer to that of Thomas Kavanagh, one of the rare critics to consider the absence of an ending meaningful, who writes: "Crébillon's refusal of narrative closure, his preference for dialogue, and his delight in interruptions of all kinds contribute to the strong sense throughout his work of an always changing and unpredictable present, of life lived *sur le moment*."[8] I shall go one step further and examine the missing end not merely as a meaningful part of the novel but as the very key for understanding Crébillon's initial claim to "truth."

Mme de Lursay: Object of Desire and Irony

Seventeen is the age when Meilcour enters the world and starts his social existence; it is also the age at which he starts having sexual desires: "I desired a felicity of which I had no very distinct idea, and for some time I did not understand what sort of pleasure it was I stood in need of" (4). At the beginning of the novel the narrator describes the confusion he experiences, a kind of mechanical state of desire that is merely linked to the development of his body and to the longing for an object. This object will be a friend of his mother whom Meilcour sees every day, Mme de Lursay.

Mme de Lursay, who is forty years old, is far from indifferent to the young Meilcour. At the twilight of a gallant life she is ready for a first passion. Her only problem is that Meilcour is completely ignorant of the code of seduction: he idolizes Lursay and respects her so much that he does not dare to declare his love. He is unable to interpret signs. "We . . . were of the same mind without being any the better off for it" (11), the narrator says, and "anyone less ignorant than I would have seen a thousand signs that he was loved" (19). Even though Meilcour and Lursay share a tender interest in each other, the young hero's extreme ignorance and continual mistakes may prevent things from progressing, for the social code of gallantry forbids Lursay from taking the steps the shy Meilcour does not dare to undertake. Mme de Lursay is reduced to giving her young lover clearer hints, even to the point of arranging a date.

How can a forty-year-old woman and a seventeen-year-old man who meet in society and whose hearts secretly commune manage to communicate their love without either compromising the woman's reputation or ruining the young man's chances of being heard? What kind of emotional and social trajectory can lead them to each other? This could be the subject of the novel. It could be the educational process Crébillon promised in his preface. Meilcour, who enters the world naive and ignorant, slowly learns how to use social and sentimental codes and to decipher signs. He learns, for instance, that sentiment is only "a conversation topic in the world," and love, "a kind of commerce that they entered into often without inclination" (5). One could think, then, that the "égarement" mentioned in the novel's title is nothing but the romantic enthusiasm of a young man made ridiculous by his social ignorance. It would be a deviation from the social code, which would then represent the straight path, or the norm. And the woman in charge of putting the young man on the right path by providing his social education would be Mme de Lursay, the "good woman" with whom Meilcour is indeed sexually united at the end of the novel.

Two elements, however, make the plot more complicated and contradict this interpretation, which has been defended by several critics.[9] Mme de Lursay cannot be the "good woman" mentioned by Crébillon in his preface because the narrator's tone and retrospective comments throughout the novel reveal his misogynous contempt for her. When Meilcour derides his own ingenuousness, he mocks the respect he had for Mme de Lursay, calling it "ridiculous." In spite of all of Lursay's convoluted and elegant discourses, she clearly desires only one thing: to put an end to the hero's respect for her, that is, to be seduced by him. This desire, which is certainly not inherently despicable, becomes so in the narrator's presentation of Mme de Lursay. Whereas the seventeen-year-old hero is sentimental and believes it impossible for him to interest such a dignified lady, the disillusioned narrator describes Mme de Lursay as if she were a mechanical toy. He continually accuses her of having manipulated him with clever stratagems. He ironically describes her desire to inspire less respect in the young hero: "Mme de Lursay, weary of her torment and the profound veneration in which I held her, resolved to deliver herself of the one by curing me of the other" (11). And although he does not deny that Mme de Lursay may actually be in love with him, he decreases the value of her love by proposing a mechanistic vision of "passion"; he explains Lursay's feelings as the result of age, arising out of a fear of loneliness and an attraction to young flesh: "She was not yet old, but she had become conscious that she would be, and for women in this situation no conquest is to be despised" (67). The narrator draws misogynous generalities from his analysis of Mme de Lursay's case: "Should she be arrived at that age when her charms begin to decline, when men, already indifferent to her, foretell by their coldness that they will soon see her only with disgust, she tries to think how she may prevent the solitude that lies in wait for her. . . . Made constant by the thought of what she would lose if she were not, her heart gradually learns to feel" (21). This reduction of their feelings to fears of old age, loneliness, and rejection by men does not give a very positive picture of worldly women. If respect for the codes of gallantry is the norm from which the hero must learn not to deviate, then such a norm appears despicable from the start.

The narrator's irony is one of the elements that show that Mme de Lursay is not the "good woman" mentioned in Crébillon's preface. The second element is the hero's encounter with another woman, Hortense de Théville, first referred to as the "stranger." This meeting takes place in the opera, where Meilcour has gone for distraction from his deep sorrow after desperately seeking Mme de Lursay and not finding her at home. Upon meeting the "stranger," Meilcour makes an important discovery: he understands that his feeling for Mme de Lursay is not true love. "I had just learned from my meeting with the beautiful stranger that I loved only her, and that for Mme de Lursay I had only those fleeting sentiments that one has for any woman the world calls handsome" (49–50). From that moment in the novel we know that the true object of the hero's desire is not Mme de Lursay but Hortense de Théville, and we expect to see a change in the plot, which until then had focused on Meilcour's naiveté and his gallant exchange with Mme de Lursay.

The Physical and Social Contrast between the Two Women

Nine characters appear in the whole novel. Mme de Lursay and Hortense de Théville, first designated as "the beautiful stranger," are the only ones who are present from beginning to end. Between Mme de Lursay and the other coquettes, Mme de Senanges and Mme de Mongennes, the difference is only one of degree since their means (conversation), their way of being (coquettishness), and their ends (seduction) are the same. There is, however, a radical difference between these women and Hortense de Théville, who remains unique.

Mme de Lursay and Hortense de Théville are different from each other in every possible respect—physical appearance, social behavior, and the effect they produce on the narrator. Lursay "does not neglect ornament" because "she . . . took care to repair the losses that nearly forty years had inflicted on her charms" (8). The pejorative connotation of the verb to repair is clear in the narrator's description of Mme de Senanges at her toilette: "Mme de Senanges was still at her toilette. This was not very surprising: the more a woman's charms diminish the more time she must spend in trying to repair the loss; and Mme de Senanges had much to repair" (126). In the context of libertinage, the theme of the toilette is very important. It is indeed at her toilette that the libertine or worldly woman artificially fabricates the mask that allows her to dissimulate her true being and manipulate others.[10]

Hortense, in contrast, has nothing to "repair." She shows herself as she is. She radiates "freshness and brilliance," looks "extremely young," and is dressed simply: "She was dressed simply but nobly. Indeed she had no need of decoration; could there be an ornament so brilliant that she would not have eclipsed it, or so modest that she would not have beautified it?" (26). The narrator first describes Hortense in negative terms ("no need of decoration"), which highlight the physical contrast between the two types of women.

The contrast is also social and psychological. Mme de Lursay has a worldly experience in the social and cultural sense of the word world:[11] thanks to her knowledge of the arts of love and conversation, she manages to manipulate the young hero. She knows how to fill an embarrassing silence and to give a conversation the orientation she wishes. Hortense, in contrast, seems not to feel at ease in the world and her behavior is not according to the social rules.

All the verbs Meilcour uses to designate Mme de Lursay's actions at the beginning of the novel refer to knowledge and will: "She had applied herself to the study alike of her own sex and of ours, and knew all the springs that moved them both" (9). The notions of knowledge and study are easily linked to those of dissimulation and manipulation. Meilcour most often uses the word *stratagem* (*manège*) to characterize Mme de Lursay's clever and artificial behavior when she attempts to seduce the seventeen-year-old young man without compromising herself. From beginning to end she appears as a manipulator to whom the young and innocent hero becomes victim: "I have since come to appreciate all Mme de Lursay's skill, and the pleasure she derived from my ignorance" (23), Meilcour writes toward the beginning of his memoirs. The end echoes the beginning: "For the rest, it was quite natural that Mme de Lursay, who joined to great beauty a thorough knowledge of the heart, should have led me imperceptibly into the relation I was now in with her" (201).

Hortense de Théville, on the other hand, neither manipulates nor even tries to seduce the other characters. She speaks very little in a novel in which conversation represents the dominant narrative mode (almost two-thirds of the text is dialogue). We see Hortense in a social setting only twice, once at Mme de Lursay's and once in her mother's salon. Except for one conversation with the narrator and one with a lady in the Tuileries, Hortense is silent. She remains melancholic in society and makes the narrator himself silent: "I tried in vain to begin a conversation, but her melancholic reverie increased my timidity" (85).

On Melancholy As a Sign of Truth

Not only does Hortense stay silent but she manifests her melancholy and lets herself be absorbed by her reverie in a way that does not fit the rules of aristocratic society. She thus astonishes other characters, who try to understand the cause of her sadness in order to integrate her into the social circle: "Versac . . . was talking to her about her melancholy and how to overcome it" (105). The few times Meilcour reminds us of Hortense de Théville's presence in salon conversations in which he, not she, takes part serve to highlight her strange silence and reverie: "Mademoiselle de Théville sank into a deep reverie" (96). She appears radically different from other characters and even from her mother, who, although "unsuited by nature for society and despising it" (84), nonetheless respects the rules of aristocratic society and is the first to worry about her daughter's asocial sadness: "'I know not what it is,' said Mme de Théville, 'but for some time I have noticed in her a melancholy that alarms me, and that it seems nothing can remedy'" (104). Hortense's only expression is that of melancholy, which she even communicates to the narrator: "The melancholy I observed in her made me sad too" (102). Like the narrator, we wonder about the cause of her melancholy throughout the novel.

Can we say that the value of silence and melancholy is superior to that of conversation and social rules in a novel written between 1736 and 1738? Would it not be anachronistic to place a libertine novel in a Rousseauist perspective? By focusing the interpretation on Hortense, does one not risk a ridiculously sentimental reading of *Les Égarements*, exactly the kind of reading that Crébillon seeks to avoid by setting his story in the world of the salons?[12] We need to remember Versac's mockery of Meilcour, who is frightened by Mme de Senanges's attempt to seduce him, as a warning addressed to sentimental readers: "'Your heart!' said he. 'Novelists' jargon. What makes you suppose that is what she is asking for? She is incapable of so ridiculous a pretension'" (158).

Crébillon describes a purely aristocratic society in which good taste and custom prevail. One would suppose, therefore, that Hortense's melancholy and asocial behavior would be ridiculed from an aristocratic point of view, which is the view of the novel's characters. A silent, serious, and sad Hortense in the middle of a loquacious, gallant, and joyful society should become the laughingstock of the novel, like Molière's misanthrope, whose bitter critique of human beings at last reveals his inability to behave properly in society and interact with young women. It is precisely because the comic sense of ridicule does not serve a universal sense of morality but only helps to form aristocratic manners that Rousseau, a champion of republican values, violently criticizes Molière's comedy in his *Lettre à Monsieur d'Alembert sur les spectacles* (1758). Crébillon, however, escapes a Rousseauist criticism since Hortense, in spite of her social ineptitude, is the only character in *Les Égarements* never to appear ridiculous.

Though her presence in the novel is relatively scarce, Hortense's role is essential precisely because she is the only character not to appear ridiculous

in a novel so concerned with good taste and the ridiculous. Hortense serves
as a counterbalance or even an "antidote," as the narrator says, to the novel's
other characters: "At last I reproached myself for paying so much attention
to someone whose worthlessness was so patent, and in spite of the coldness
I met with in Mademoiselle de Théville I turned my eyes toward her as an
antidote. . . . I reflected with astonishment upon the enormous distance
between her and Mme de Senanges; upon those touching charms; upon
that noble mien, reserved but without the least awkwardness, which was
enough in itself to ensure respect" (88). The respect Hortense inspires in
the narrator through her coldness and reserved attitude contrasts with the
contempt all the other characters (except for the mothers) inspire in both
her and the narrator: Mme de Senanges and Mme de Mongennes because
of their impudence; Mme de Lursay, whose stratagems and artifices are
revealed by Versac; Versac, who tries desperately to attract Hortense's attention by showing his legs and teeth as if he were a horse in a market;[13] and
Meilcour himself, who interprets Hortense's silence as a sign that she despises his superficiality: "Now and then she looked at me, sometimes with
a sort of scorn which I took much exception to, and which incensed me
against her more every moment. My only consolation was her determined
disregard of Versac, who was put almost beside himself by such an
unheard-of occurrence" (96–97).

Throughout the novel Hortense serves as a criterion of value, a sign of
truth, and a point of reference the narrator uses to judge himself and the
other characters. Without her the title *Les Égarements du cœur et de l'esprit* would
not be possible. She personifies the fixed point from which the hero swerves
in his *égarements* and which he seemingly tries to approach so as to end his
wandering. Indeed, Hortense's resistance to Versac's charms, which is much
noticed by the narrator, implies a set of values that is different from the
one Versac teaches Meilcour, whose principle is the art of pleasing. Versac's
system of values is certainly at work in the novel, since we find the words
please, displease, pleasure, and *pleasant* more than 170 times in a two-hundred-
page novel, that is to say, on almost every page. Unlike Mme de Lursay,
Mme de Sénanges, or Mme de Mongennes, Hortense does not want to
please. In contrast to Versac's values, hers are not theorized or disclosed: her

very silence gives them a certain consistency since, as an "antidote" to the other characters' conversation, they serve to reveal the superficiality and vanity of social chatter.

Vanity and True Sentiment

The contrast between the two types of women is echoed by a contrast between two feelings the hero experiences: inclination (*amour-goût*) and passion. Mme de Lursay awakens a superficial feeling in Meilcour that he refers to as a "passing desire" or "inclination": "It was a passing desire that died almost in the instant it was born. . . . I felt for her that inclination [*goût*] that is commonly called love" (31). Hortense evokes a violent commotion in his soul that he calls "passion": "The sight of her, even the love I supposed her to feel for another, had rekindled my passion" (50).

From the first encounter in the opera, seeing Hortense always produces a violent effect on the narrator's body: "I cannot describe the strange and sudden emotion that seized me at the sight; struck by so much beauty I stood dumbfounded. My surprise was so great I was transported. I felt a disorder in my heart that spread through all my senses" (26). The shock of this first encounter is described in terms reminiscent of those chosen by Prévost in *Manon Lescaut* five years earlier; they belong to the romantic topos of love at first sight, which is evoked each time Meilcour meets Hortense. It is notable that he never finds Hortense when he actively seeks her; he meets her always by chance, and her vision strikes him when he least expects it. The shock of surprise deprives him of any control over his body: "I was seized with such a trembling that I had scarcely the strength to walk" (48), Meilcour writes about the Tuileries meeting. "I can but feebly express the turmoil I was thrown into at the sight of her, and what love and ecstasy and fear were renewed in my bosom" (83), he writes about the third encounter at Mme de Lursay's, when he discovers Hortense's identity. If seeing Hortense provokes such violent disorder in Meilcour, then touching her makes his body almost hysterical, in a way that reflects the commotion in his soul: "Only I was left to escort Hortense. I offered my hand, but no sooner had I touched hers than I felt all my frame begin to tremble. My emotion became so extreme I could scarcely stand. I dared neither speak nor look at her, and we reached her carriage in the most absolute silence" (107). In a novel of social education, in which the hero learns good manners and good taste, love is defined as an impulse that unites the body and the soul and defies self-control and social propriety.

We also find the words *transport, trembling,* and others that usually describe Hortense's effect on Meilcour in passages in which the narrator describes scenes with Mme de Lursay. The feelings Mme de Lursay inspires in Meilcour are not very different from love but are differentiated from love in a subtle way: "I felt all the perturbations of passion with as much violence as if I had truly suffered them" (25). The difference is made evident by the words "as much . . . as if," which distinguish the real from its simulacrum: the physical emotion produced by a circumstantial passion greatly resembles that of love, but precisely because it only resembles it, it is not an emotion of love. The circumstances of Meilcour's meetings with Mme de Lursay also differ from those of his encounters with Hortense, for all of his meetings with Mme de Lursay either are anticipated by him or occur precisely when he is trying to avoid her. Mme de Lursay sets the time of the meetings, invites Meilcour to her house, leads him to remote corners, and questions him about his feelings in order to push him to declare himself.

The novel continually plays with the contrast between the two women and the two contradictory feelings they awaken in Meilcour. As we saw earlier, it is only when Meilcour meets Hortense for the first time that he understands the nature of his feeling for Mme de Lursay. Thanks to his encounter with Hortense, the hero establishes the distinction between two kinds of love: one is superficial and temporary; the other is deep, true, and eternal. Meilcour defines his desire for Mme de Lursay as a mere inclination and pleasure of vanity. In the *world*, having an affair with a beautiful woman also means making it known that one has had an affair because the pleasure of the senses is linked to the pleasure of fame, which is also, in a way, a sensual and superficial pleasure. At the beginning of the novel Meilcour still manages to reconcile his two contradictory feelings: "I went to sleep attributing mere desire to Mme de Lursay, and I know not what more delicate feeling to my fair unknown" (41). This harmonious combination does not last; as the novel progresses the antithesis gains strength. Although Meilcour lets himself be attracted to Mme de Lursay, his thoughts return to Hortense and he contrasts pleasing with love: "In order to enable myself to continue to please her I had to forget how much I loved my fair unknown" (56).

Pleasure, then, serves as a substitute for love. It becomes the distraction that makes the narrator deviate from his true desire—his love for Hortense—and thus it places this desire at the heart of the narrative: "I tried to distract my thoughts from her by fixing them upon the pleasures that awaited me" (56). Pleasure is devalued because it highlights a void that it is unable to fill: "If vanity alone could have satisfied my heart it would doubtless have been less agitated" (107). Vanity, the pleasure of pleasing ladies of the world and of acquiring a reputation as a seducer, cannot satisfy the hero's heart. The use of the word *heart*, which refers to true sentiment, already indicates that vanity and superficial feelings cannot be satisfactory. Hortense, on the other hand, represents the object that could satisfy the hero's heart; his love and desire for her have nothing in common with the senses' fleeting and superficial satisfaction: "The heart that seemed to oppose itself to my desires was the only one that could occupy my own" (107).

Meilcour's love for Hortense, a love at first sight that is confirmed by every encounter between the two characters, appears throughout the novel as the only counterweight to the fleeting desires awakened by Mme de Lursay and the disgust evoked by Mme de Senanges or Mme de Mongennes and, finally, as the only value not subject to the law of pleasure that Versac articulates: "Like me, all men seek only pleasure: fix that for ever in the same object and we should be constant too. Believe me, Marquise, no one would ever engage himself, even with the most charming creature, if it meant being bound for ever" (76–77).

Toward a Theory of the Moment

A contrast between two concepts of time adds to the contrast between two types of woman and two sentiments in the hero. We find an echo of this contrast in the only conversation between Hortense and Meilcour. This conversation, whose starting point is a love story Hortense is reading as

Meilcour arrives, concerns the definition of unhappy love. For Hortense, any love that is opposed by circumstances is unhappy even if the lovers really do love each other. Meilcour, in contrast, exalts the "moment" that lovers can shelter from outside obstacles: "Do they see each other for a moment? What delight is in that moment!" (118). Although this sentence comes in the middle of his speech, it is the first one Hortense addresses: "'What you say may be true,' she replied, 'but for every moment such as you have described, how many days of anxiety and pain!'" (118). This brief answer shows that Hortense truly is the philosophical counterpoint of Versac in *Les Égarements*.

For Meilcour as for Versac, the only other male character, whose role consists in teaching the young hero the philosophy of pleasure, the "moment" has intrinsic value. Hortense does not discuss the happiness of the moment itself, but she contrasts that moment with a duration that is weightier than the single instant, that is, with "many days of anxiety and pain." By denying the pleasure of the single moment in one of her rare conversations in the novel, Hortense takes a position against libertine temporality, which is composed entirely of moments.[14] As we shall see, it is indeed in the realm of the moment that Mme de Lursay has the power to exert her charms on Meilcour.

The moment, also called the "occasion," is a critical concept in Crébillon's vocabulary throughout his work.[15] The word appears in the title of a fictive dialogue written shortly after *Les Égarements* and published in 1755, *La Nuit et le moment ou les matinées de Cythère*,[16] and the concept is defined in another dialogue written around 1737–40 and published in 1763, *Le Hasard du coin du feu*: "Célie: 'What is the moment, and how do you define it? Because I must say in all good honesty that I do not understand you.' The Duke: 'A certain disposition of the senses, as unforeseen as it is involuntary, that a woman may conceal, but that, should it be perceived or sensed by someone who has an interest in taking advantage of it, places her in the greatest danger of being a little more complacent than she believed she either should or could be.'"[17]

The moment is not simply a brief period of time; it is defined by a set of circumstances, "a certain disposition of the senses," that applies specifically to women. The moment, or its equivalent in Crébillon's vocabulary, the *occasion* (opportunity), is a woman's state of sexual excitation, which allows a man to take advantage of her: the body (*nature*, in eighteenth-century vocabulary) becomes an active subject and follows the autonomous law of pleasure. The moment designates a physical and psychological state that separates the body from moral and social identity. The moment contains no past and no future; it produces a rupture in time, a suspension of any temporal and moral dimension.[18]

The moment is not only a temporal and psychological notion but also a concept in mechanics: it designates "the product of a (specified) force, mass, volume, and its perpendicular distance from its axis, fulcrum, or plane."[19] The mechanical meaning of *moment* is important. If the moment indeed pertains to a law of mechanics, then it has nothing to do with subjectivity or, more specifically, with sentiments. The moment can be experienced with anyone and at any time since it depends merely on a set of circumstances and on an encounter between bodies that obey physical rather than moral laws.

The moment, however, should not be confused with a wild impulse of the body. The laws it obeys are also social to the extent that, in the world described by Crébillon, social behavior has become second nature. Patrick Wald Lasowski describes Crébillon's libertine characters as social seducers who act mainly out of *politeness*.[20] Far from contradicting each other, social politeness and sensual pleasure are on the same side because both involve only external surfaces—appearances and skin—as opposed to internal feelings such as love. Crébillon contrasts the superficial part of human beings, which includes social vanity and the pleasure of the senses, both experienced in the moment, with a deeper part involving sensibility and sentiments, which require duration and a transcendence of immediate sensibility.

The moment plays a very important role in *Les Égarements du coeur et de l'esprit*, in which the narrator uses the words *moment* and *occasion* whenever he needs to justify the weakness that draws him to Mme Lursay in spite of himself: "I seemed to feel my contempt for her increase. But we were alone, she was handsome, and I knew her to be amorous. . . . At that age prejudice cannot withstand *opportunity* [*occasion*]" (79–80, my emphasis). Since he is caught between his romantic love for Hortense and his sensual desire for Mme de Lursay, Meilcour experiences the moment in its female version, as it is described by the Duke in *Le Hasard du coin du feu*. He is the one who tries to resist. It is for him, paradoxically, and not for Lursay, that the moment is dangerous, as Mme de Lursay ironically reminds him: "If I may say so it was you, not I, who, as you put it, saw fit to offer a fine resistance" (192). The moment is desired by Mme de Lursay more than by Meilcour; she plays the role of the masculine rake who, in the moment, knows how to take advantage of the other: "A sigh or two that she allowed to escape her completed my overthrow: *at this critical moment* she benefited from all my love for the mysterious stranger" (51, my emphasis). Meilcour, then, is in the position not of the seducer but of the innocent victim whose resistance is overcome by the power of the moment and Mme de Lursay's sense of opportunity.

The plot of *Les Égarements* is based on a dichotomy at all levels: between social behavior and melancholy, conversation and silence, pleasure and seriousness, worldly politeness and violent emotion, stratagems and simplicity, fleeting desires and passion, vanity and true love, the moment or occasion and duration, and finally the plural (Lursay, Sénanges, Mongennes) and the singular (Hortense). The contrast, ultimately, lies between a libertine temporality, which favors pleasure, lightness, play, and theatricality, and a temporality that is built by the narration, that is, by the tension of a desire that is not yet satisfied. Hero and reader share this desire; both expect a denouement in which the conflict between contradictory values will be resolved and truth will triumph. In addition, since the novel is replete with hints that Hortense may after all be interested in Meilcour, it seems that Meilcour will triumph only if he understands Hortense's love and at last decides to sacrifice superficial and temporary pleasures for a single and lasting love.

Throughout the novel love is represented as Meilcour's ultimate goal in his quest for real and stable happiness. It is this quest that generates the dramatic interest of the novel. The constant parallel between Hortense and Lursay not only contrasts two separate relations to time, desire, and society but also reveals that one is superior to the other. The final union of Hortense and Meilcour appears to be the object of the novel.

But the expected resolution does not occur.

No Resolution to the Conflict

The last scene of the novel takes place at Mme de Lursay's home, first in her salon, then in private. Initially Meilcour rushes to Mme de Lursay's in hopes of finding Hortense and not the former: "I went to Hortense's house, and was told that she and Mme de Théville had returned and gone out again. I assumed, I know not why, that they must be at Mme de Lursay's and I flew there directly" (175). Meilcour's impulsive desire to see Hortense will never be satisfied since Hortense is not visiting Mme de Lursay, and the novel ends with a scene that brings Meilcour and Lursay together. Readers are deprived of the scene the narrative had made them expect, in which Hortense and Meilcour would have cleared up their misunderstanding. But this last scene also represents an ironic reversal of the scene in which Meilcour met Hortense at the opera, where he was thinking of Mme de Lursay and simply trying to distract his attention from her. The last scene symmetrically mirrors the scene in which Meilcour realized that he did not truly love Mme de Lursay.

After a bitter confrontation in which Meilcour feels that his contempt for Mme de Lursay is stronger than ever and Mme de Lursay denounces Meilcour's ridiculous lack of manners, she finally gives herself to him, and he finally takes advantage of her, thus ending the ridiculousness of his "fine resistance."

The novel may have no other object: Crébillon, from the beginning, offered Mme de Lursay to Meilcour's cherubinistic desire and depicted her as intending to seduce, initiate, and fix the young man. In the resolution she reaches her goal: she initiates him sexually.[21] It seems that we have a complete story, that of the sexual and social initiation of a future *petit-maître* who, thanks to his double education by a gallant woman and an experienced libertine, finally understands the rules of the world he entered at the beginning of the novel. Such is, indeed, Michel Foucault's interpretation of the novel in his 1962 article "Un si cruel savoir": "The lesson was not useless since it procures us the narrative in its form and irony. Meilcour, narrating the adventure of his innocence, perceives it only in the distance, where it is already lost: between his naiveté and his imperceptibly different consciousness of it, Versac's knowledge insinuated itself with this custom of the world in which *the mind and the heart cannot help being spoiled*."[22] For Foucault, the object of Crébillon's novel is to deliver what he calls "une théorie de la fatuité," which is taught by Versac and Lursay and finally learned by Meilcour. Interestingly, Foucault does not even mention Hortense, as if the whole story involved only Lursay, Versac, and Meilcour. Why Hortense, then? Why is Meilcour continually drawing a parallel between Hortense and Mme de Lursay? *Les Égarements du coeur et de l'esprit* is the most complex and most interesting of Crébillon's novels, one that contradicts Kavanagh's suggestion that Crébillon's novels were condemned as superficial and frivolous from the eighteenth to the twentieth century precisely because "his cast of characters includes no real representation of any Other challenging the fundamental values these novels share with their audience."[23] *Les Égarements* represents otherness. Hortense, or at least Meilcour's view of her, challenges the social values of Crébillon's world. As we saw earlier, allusions to Hortense serve to counteract the worldly game and reestablish a moral dichotomy the libertine system pretends to ignore. This does not imply that a matured Hortense would not have become similar to Crébillon's other female characters, even though the novel gives no hint of her future evolution. But the point is that throughout the novel she represents different and better values than the social code of gallantry.

The pleasure Mme de Lursay and Meilcour share in the end implies the triumph of superficiality over the values embodied by Hortense. Meilcour, indeed, is drawn to Lursay by vanity and sensual desire, and not by love. Still hesitating to seduce Mme de Lursay, he suddenly thinks of his social image: "I had a clear remembrance of the ridicule Mme de Lursay had poured on my fears" (199). And finally he yields to the power of the moment: "The work of my senses appeared to me the work of my heart. I abandoned myself to all the intoxication of *that fatal moment*, and rendered myself at last as guilty as I was capable of being" (199, my emphasis). In this last scene we witness the triumph of Mme de Lursay, or of the feeling she has awakened in Meilcour, this fleeting desire that is satisfied in the moment.

Mme de Lursay, however, or rather the feeling she inspires in Meilcour, does not win entirely. Indeed, after the lovers have shared several moments of sensual pleasure, Hortense's name reappears in the text as the very proof that sexual pleasure does not suffice to make the narrator happy and that the dangerous moment lasts for only a moment. The moral vocabulary used ironically by the narrator seems to condemn the superficiality of pleasure. He calls sensual pleasure "illusion" and "crime." The first sign of disillusionment he describes is a feeling of emptiness, which reveals the vanity of sensual pleasure: "Without knowing what I lacked, I felt a blank in my heart" [*Sans connaître ce qui me manquait, je sentis du vide dans mon âme*] (292). This image of a "blank" devalues pleasure, which does not have enough substance to fill the soul once the senses have been satisfied. Hortense's name immediately comes to fill this blank in the hero's heart as well as in the text: "Hortense—Hortense, whom I adored though I had so utterly forgotten her, resumed her sway over my heart" (200). The hero may mock his late remembrance of Hortense, but it is still the thought of her that puts an end to the pleasure of the moment.

One may think, then, that the novel ends with an implicit condemnation of sensual pleasure since pleasure does not fill the soul and even leaves place for remorse. Meilcour is caught between contradictory feelings that alternately accuse and justify him and do not let him enjoy his pleasure in peace: "Torn away from pleasure by remorse, snatched from remorse by pleasure, I could not be sure of myself for a moment" (201–2). Pleasure is sensual, and remorse is moral. Pleasure happens in the moment when it is experienced, whereas remorse, which is a sign of memory, establishes a continuity with the past. A moral feeling such as remorse should negate pleasure and prevent the hero from experiencing sensual enjoyment, that is, from forgetting past and future, but this is not what happens. Remorse has little effect on the hero since his only consolation consists in drowning his feeling of guilt "in new frenzies" [*dans de nouveaux égarements*] (202). Wandering (*égarement*), instead of leading to the straight path, in the end leads only to more wandering. On the last page the young hero describes himself as more wayward than ever: "Some hours had passed in these contradictions: dawn was beginning to break, and I was still far from resolving the conflict within me" (202).

The Choice of Ambiguity

Instead of resolving the conflict of feelings in the narrator and the conflict of values in the text, the novel ends with the contradiction described by Meilcour. The confusion of feelings at the end gives a strong argument to the critics who argue that the novel is simply incomplete. Since Meilcour narrates his story from a retrospective point of view, one would expect him to finally take a position and give the final word. He does, actually. Indeed, although he keeps describing the terribly confusing contradiction in which he is caught, there is one single instance toward the end of the novel in which the narrator speaks "today," that is, at the moment when he is writing, and comments on the contradiction. This passage starts with the words "ce que j'en puis croire aujourd'hui," which Barbara Bray translates as "the conclusion I draw today." This translation clearly invites us to interpret this passage as the "conclusion" the narrator, at the moment when he writes, draws from the events and gives to the novel. "The conclusion I draw today is that if I had had more experience she would merely have reduced me the sooner, since what is called knowledge of the world only makes us wiser insomuch as it makes us more corrupt. . . . Instead of banishing the thought of Hortense from my mind, I should have found pleasure in dwelling on it. . . . I should have saved my heart from the disorder of my senses, and by these delicate distinctions, which might be called the quietism of love, I should have enjoyed all the delights of the moment without incurring the risk of infidelity" (201).

This is the only passage in the whole novel in which the contradiction between pleasure and love, between the moment and duration, is resolved. It is resolved not because one feeling is sacrificed to the other but simply because it is dismissed as a contradiction. Crébillon describes the possibility of experiencing enduring love for one person while experiencing fleeting pleasure with another and of reconciling superficial and deep feelings, vanity and truth, "the disorder of the senses" and "the thought of Hortense." Meilcour's suggestion comes close to Manon's attempt to combine love and pleasure when she tells des Grieux: "The fidelity I expect of you is that of the heart."[24] There is, however, an important difference between *Manon Lescaut* and *Les Égarements*. In Prévost's novel the division of heart and body is suggested by Manon, a woman who acts as a courtesan and transgresses social laws. In *Les Égarements* the division is proposed as the very rule of good social behavior. Des Grieux represents Manon as an extraordinary character and expresses his shock upon hearing her vulgar proposal. In Crébillon's novel such a moral perspective is lacking. Meilcour, and not Hortense, both as the narrator and a character, suggests a solution to the contradiction between love and pleasure. Crébillon's critique of sentimental and moral dichotomy is more radical than Prévost's.

This passage, however, is not the real conclusion of the novel: it is not the final paragraph and, above all, it is written in the past tense of the conditional mode, the mode of the unreal. Jean Sgard even considers the use of the conditional mode to imply a moral condemnation: "What is condemned here under the name *quietism* is a kind of libertine naturalism, whose bad faith Crébillon perceives."[25] Crébillon, however, gives no hint of such a condemnation. Meilcour does not say that he rejects the "quietism," and what he calls afterwards the "convenient metaphysics" of love, in the name of higher values. Rather, he only says that he did not know "these delicate distinctions" at the time of the scene with Mme de Lursay because he was lacking one primary requirement: experience ("if I had had more experience"). We are quite free to think that Meilcour has this experience as he writes his memoirs. This would mean, then, that if the scene were replayed, Meilcour would quietly "enjoy the delights of the moment without incurring the risk of infidelity" and that he would no longer be caught in a contradiction he cannot resolve.

But this is not what Crébillon writes either. Meilcour does not describe a new scene in the present tense. The only resolution of the conflict is in a passage written in the past tense of the conditional. There is no clear conclusion. The end of the novel remains in the limbo of ambiguity and leaves us free to interpret and choose our own conclusion. This explains why Crébillon's novel can lead to the two contradictory interpretations mentioned in this chapter: on the one hand, the interpretation of Jean Sgard, who reads *Les Égarements* as a novel of sentimental and moral education whose end is lacking; on the other hand, that of Michel Foucault, who considers this a novel of social and immoral education, delivering simply a "théorie de la fatuité." Ambiguity, which characterizes Crébillon's style, as Bernadette Fort has shown remarkably in *Le Langage de l'ambiguïté dans l'oeuvre de Crébillon*, is the novel's final word. This is why the story stops abruptly: we do not see Meilcour "restored to himself" through his union with a good woman because this is not the object of the novel. Instead, Crébillon's novel replaces such a moral concept of the self with a libertine concept of the non-self, of the divided, playful, and ambiguous self.

This paragraph in the conditional mode requires a careful reading and more attention than it has previously received. It is the only passage in which the narrator reconciles the two contradictory poles of the dichotomy, composed of genuine love and the pleasure of the moment. In that sense it represents the true resolution of the novel, its denouement. Yet, because this passage is written in the past tense of the conditional, it remains a mere hypothesis, not a clear statement, and readers can easily misread it. If, indeed, Crébillon did condemn the "convenient metaphysics" of love, the text would then lose its irony and Crébillon's vocabulary would likewise lose its ambiguity. Such a condemnation does not exist in the text; critics or readers project it onto the novel because of the expectation created by the plot, the title, and the preface. It is easier to endow the novel with a moral meaning, which can be clearly stated, than to accept ambiguity. In a sense, ambiguity is an esthetic choice analogous to pleasure: ambiguity does not suffice to fill the void we feel in our *souls*, which is a desire for meaning.

Ambiguity remains Crébillon's moral and narrative choice, as we can see in the novel's final sentence. Remorse has so little power over Meilcour that he promises Mme de Lursay that he will return the next day. The final sentence expresses nothing but irony and ambiguity: "Thanks to the proprieties that Mme de Lursay observed so strictly, she dismissed me at last, and I quitted her, promising, in spite of my remorse, to see her early next day, and firmly resolved, moreover, to keep my word" (202). This sentence mocks the moral value of keeping one's word by associating it with the pleasure of the moment, that is to say, with the very proof of infidelity. The expressions "firmly resolved" and "keep my word" indicate a moral determination and a respect for moral values, but they are used in a context in which they have a contradictory meaning, since they come to signify Meilcour's incapacity to resist carnal pleasures and to be faithful to his genuine love for Hortense. Instead of resolving the conflict of values, Crébillon embeds the contradiction into language itself and accumulates ironical antiphrases so as to confuse categories that were clearly divided until then.[26]

The novel is therefore complete since it completely baffles the reader's expectation. The last sentence derides both the aristocratic values of honor and fidelity to one's word and the bourgeois values of constancy and fidelity to one's self. It also mocks the very notion of an ending, since it opens onto a future that will undoubtedly resemble all the days and nights described in the novel, without resolving the contradiction between love and pleasure, the unique (Hortense) and the plural (Mme de Lursay and other coquettes). *Les Égarements* makes us expect an end, only to deprive us of it. If, as Peter Brooks writes in *Reading for the Plot*, "the ultimate determinants of meaning lie at the end, and narrative desire is ultimately, inexorably, desire for the end," [27] what, then, is the meaning of the suspension of an ending in Crébillon's novel?

Paradoxically, Crébillon's novel abstains from favoring true love over vanity after showing the moral superiority of the former. In the end, Meilcour simply observes that vanity, as superficial, erroneous, and deceitful as it is, represents a motive as strong as, or even stronger than, true desire, and in a way this observation is also his conclusion: "I have come to the conclusion since . . . that it is far more important for a woman to flatter a man's vanity than to touch his heart" (55).

As we saw in the introduction, vanity is a concept that traditionally has negative moral connotations. By using moral values that belong to the tradition of Western metaphysics and not resolving a contradiction between them, Crébillon's novel demonstrates that the dichotomy between vanity and truth has no moral and metaphysical validity. There is a truth of vanity and, similarly, a vanity of truth. If remorse tears Meilcour away from pleasure, and pleasure snatches him from remorse, the endless alternation of pleasure and remorse indicates their equivalence in their relation to time: like pleasure, remorse lasts only for a moment. Remorse, which has a moral meaning since it is a sign of Meilcour's betrayal of his love for Hortense, assaults the hero and then leaves room for new pleasure; remorse is therefore as superficial and light as pleasure itself and cannot claim any moral or ontological superiority. Crébillon, by suspending the end of the novel, ironically recognizes that superficiality is as deep as depth, and depth as superficial as superficiality. Crébillon's deliberate lightness can be read as the very consciousness of the superficiality of depth.

LES ÉGAREMENTS du coeur et de l'esprit does not reach the end suggested by the title, promised by Crébillon's preface, and built by the plot. At the end of the novel the hero, far from being "restored to himself," is more than ever lost in his wandering and contradictions. Crébillon leaves his readers in a state of suspension that does not satisfy their desire for an end, in a state of ambiguity that does not allow them to decide what is the moral, social, and sentimental norm from which the hero's mind and heart have deviated.

I suggest that *Les Égarements*, in spite of its apparent incompleteness, should be read as a well-finished novel that achieves its aim. Far from being incidental, the absence of an ending is essential: it is the very object of the novel. I would call this object *irony*, the ability to deride seriousness and reject morals while using seriousness and moral values as the central axis from which the hero deviates in his wandering.[28] By showing that one's acts may contradict one's most sincere sentiments and moral values, the suspension of the end represents the very end of Crébillon's novel.

Crébillon's irony is directed toward his readers, whom his ambiguous style invites to laugh at themselves—at their self-deceiving metaphysical and sentimental tendencies. Crébillon's irony reveals a fundamental suspicion toward the moral and metaphysical concept of the self. By stating, in his preface, that his novel's object is to reveal the moral transformation of his hero, at last "restored to himself," and by not offering the expected ending, Crébillon deceives his readers. Rather than *deception*, however, it would be more appropriate to speak of *self-deception*. Crébillon's novel does not so much deceive readers as it reveals to them that they deceive themselves when they express a moral contempt for superficiality and frivolity. The pleasure of the text lies in this ironic lesson, which teaches readers that vanity—the superficial, fleeting, and sensual feelings Mme de Lursay inspires in Meilcour—motivates them as strongly as do deep and enduring sentiments. Deception is both a narrative strategy that deprives readers of the end they had the right to expect and a psychological device that teaches them not to trust their idealistic, moral, and sentimental impulses.

The narrators of the novels analyzed in the next two chapters, unlike des Grieux in *Manon Lescaut* and Meilcour in *Les Égarements*, men who tell readers the mistakes of their youth, are young women, one of whom recounts the story of her education, the other the story of her misfortunes, who address a male reader: *Thérèse philosophe* and Diderot's *La Religieuse* only reinforce the strategies of deception that serve to lure readers in order to teach them a lesson about their own desire.

Four

1748 ∾ Thérèse, or Reason

IN *Thérèse philosophe*, one of the most famous eighteenth-century pornographic novels, a young woman narrates her sexual and philosophical educations from her childhood to her free and happy union with the Count, the man to whom she addresses her story. "What, Sir, you seriously want me to write the story of my life? . . . You are asking for an orderly and detailed description from a girl who has never written a word before? You would like an account in which the scenes . . . should be rendered in all their lasciviousness?"[1] Thérèse's exclamation at the beginning of her narrative highlights her addressee's voyeuristic expectation. If she finally accepts to undertake this task "beyond my capacities," it is only to propagate the knowledge that has made her happy: "But, you say, if their example and their argument have brought me happiness, why wouldn't I try to bring happiness to others by the same means—by example and by argument? Why be afraid to write useful truths for the good of society? Well, my dear benefactor, I will resist no longer" (39; 249–50).

This beginning reveals the paradox of the pornographic novel in the Enlightenment: it claims to be both erotic and pedagogical. Like every pornographic novel, *Thérèse philosophe* aims at exciting readers in the privacy of their bedrooms—at producing a physiological effect that leads them to abandon the book, as Jean-Marie Goulemot observes in *Ces livres qu'on ne lit que d'une main*. Although the title of Goulemot's essay comes from an expression in Rousseau's *Confessions* that Rousseau himself attributes to "a lady of the world,"[2] it is generally admitted that readers of pornographic novels in the eighteenth century were men rather than women; pornographic novels, in the eighteenth century like today, seem to feed a male fantasy of power and violence and to transform readers into voyeurs by giving them a show of female sexuality.

Thérèse philosophe, however, like many other pornographic novels, also claims to be useful for society and even for humanity. Descriptions of physical acts alternate with philosophical discourses that comment upon and justify those acts; the novel also contains technical lessons on mastur-bation and contraception that seem to be addressed principally to women rather than to men because women were supposedly more ignorant than men in the eighteenth century. One could speak, then, of a philosophical or enlightened pornography. Eighteenth-century pornographic novels would bring pleasure and reason into harmony and fully participate in the Enlightenment project, which consisted in unveiling truth and fighting social, moral, and religious prejudices.

Andrea Dworkin and Katherine McKinnon have launched a rather vio-lent attack against pornography in recent years. In their view, pornography is only an instrument of oppression and violence that incites men, its main consumers, to commit acts of violence against women; it reduces women to the status of used, enslaved, and humiliated objects. Robert Darnton, in *The Forbidden Bestsellers of Pre-Revolutionary France*, and Lynn Hunt, in *The Invention of Pornography*, have recently shown that it is necessary to historicize pornogra-phy instead of reducing it to such a Manichean structure.[3] Before the eighteenth century there were very few pornographic texts aside from Aretino's *Sonnets* in sixteenth-century Italy, Brantôme's *Les Dames galantes* in seventeenth-century France, and Chorier's *L'Académie des dames* at the end of the seventeenth century. It was in eighteenth-century France that porno-graphic writing developed as a genre, and it cannot be taken out of the philosophical climate in which it was born: the category "philosophical books" referred both to materialist pamphlets and to pornographic novels, which also contained philosophy.

The very title *Thérèse philosophe* refers to this "philosophy," which occu-pies a limited part of the narrative but builds a coherent system of thought. The discourses uttered by various characters are borrowed from or inspired by contemporary philosophers. As Robert Darnton shows, some pages are simply copied from an anonymous 1745 nonpornographic pamphlet, *Exa-*

men de la religion dont on cherche l'éclaircissement de bonne foi.[4] This was a usual practice in the eighteenth century, a period in which the notion of plagiarism did not yet exist; Sade, for instance, borrowed many pages from philosophical texts for his novels at the end of the century. Thérèse's narrative starts with an "Address to the Theologians on the Liberty of Man" (50; 250) and ends with "A Curious Reflection by Thérèse to prove that the Principles contained in her Book should contribute to the Happiness of Men" (189; 298). Every sexual scene is followed by a discourse in which the determinist argument is reiterated. Twenty-five pages out of 150—a sixth of the narrative—are devoted to philosophical discourses on God, freedom, nature, jealousy, and so on.

For Robert Darnton, *Thérèse philosophe* is a veritable treatise on feminine liberation: it teaches its readers, men or women, means of contraception and liberates women from serious threats to their health and reputation. Darnton considers the Count, Thérèse's lover and addressee, to be a truly enlightened man, the ideal of "man master of himself," of "the sensible man, the *philosophe.*" Darnton also considers Thérèse an enlightened woman whose lessons are addressed to all women: "She takes the château and the two thousands livres, adding a codicile of her own: mutual masturbation, yes; sexual intercourse, no. . . . The decision remains hers. She retains her independence to the end. Even if she is the creation of a male fantasy, Thérèse speaks for the right of women to pursue their own pleasure."[5]

Although Lynn Hunt also recognizes the philosophical dimension of eighteenth-century pornography and its link with materialism, she nonetheless argues that pornographic novels, in the eighteenth century like today, are addressed primarily to men. Lynn Hunt criticizes Robert Darnton and Jean-Marie Goulemot for dismissing this fact and for ignoring this important gender difference, which specifies the voyeur as male and the object of voyeurism as female: "Men wrote about sex for other male readers. For their own sexual arousal, men read about women having sex with other women or with multiple partners. The new fraternity created by these complex intersections of voyeurism and objectification may have been democratic in the sense of social leveling, but in the end it was almost always a leveling for men."[6] The narrator in *Thérèse philosophe* is a woman, and she recounts many scenes in which she was the voyeur, not the object. But her addressee, the ultimate voyeur, is a man. Thérèse describes not only the scenes she has witnessed but also the effect of these scenes on her. Through her innocent and philosophical gaze the narrative focuses the reader's eyes on a specific object—"that part which distinguishes us from men" (42)— which is referred to by different names according to its misfortunes. A recurrent metaphor throughout the narrative also seems to confirm Lynn Hunt's interpretation: the male sex is named "dart," "arrow," or "bolt," words suggesting a male fantasy in which the male member is the active agent and the female genitals are the object of conquest.

The opinion that voyeurism, the main strategy of pornographic novels, establishes a division between a passive female spectacle and a male voyeur who controls the spectacle is widely held. The issue of gender leads to another: the philosophical issue of the relation between reason and imagination. The eye is the voyeur's organ: sight, which is the only sense that preserves a distance between the object and the body, makes control of the object possible. In Western metaphysics the eye has traditionally been the organ of knowledge, and sight is the sense that embodies rationality, as Peter Brooks points out in *Body Work*. The word *idea* comes from the aorist of the Greek verb meaning "to see": *eidon*, "I saw." Brooks reminds us that the division between the male gaze and the female object of the gaze covers a traditional epistemic distinction between knowledge and the object of knowledge: "The epistemic principle, and the point from which vision is directed at the world, have largely throughout the Western tradition been assumed to be male. . . . That which is to be looked at, denuded, has been repeatedly personified as female: Truth as goddess, as sphinx, or as woman herself."[7]

The recent interest of American critics in eroticism, pornography, and voyeurism goes hand in hand with a deconstruction of the Western male gaze, and often with feminist claims, because it seems that voyeurism allows the voyeur to "master" the other.[8] It is tempting to use the Freudian analysis of the scopophilic instinct developed in *Three Essays on the Theory of Sexuality* to establish an equivalence between the desire to see, the desire to know, and the desire to master. Such a desire for mastery appears to be specifically male and Western: all the books dealing with this issue published in the past ten years insist on the gender imbalance and conclude that voyeurism is a phallocentric structure.[9]

How, then, should we read *Thérèse philosophe*—as a text in which the female narrator and philosopher is used only as bait for the readers' excitement or as a narrative that liberates women by propagating knowledge? What kind of relation between men and women, knowledge and the object of knowledge, does this text establish? Is the model of mastery through the gaze—through voyeurism—it proposes a model of enlightened or perverse mastery?

The Attack against the Church

The entire first part of *Thérèse philosophe* contains an attack against the Catholic Church.[10] Using transparent anagrams, the novel's subtitle, "Memoirs about the Affair between Father Dirrag and Mademoiselle Eradice," refers to a scandal in Toulon in 1731, when a young devotee, Catherine Cadière, accused her confessor, Father Girard, of seducing her.[11] The text is both erotic and ideological and delivers a clear message: through its hypocrisy and prohibitions Catholic discourse on flesh and sin can lead to dangerous abuses. The pornographic novel kills two birds with one stone: it denounces the hypocrisy of Catholic taboos and uses these same taboos as the obstacles whose transgression makes the text exciting.

The attack against the Church starts with the heroine's birth. Thérèse's mother, who had lived happily for ten years between her husband and her lover, suffered an accident while giving birth that forced her to give up carnal pleasures forever. This is how her sudden conversion is described: "Everything changed face in my father's house. My mother became a devotee, the monk who was the Capucins' door-keeper replaced the frequent visits of the Marquis de ———, who was dismissed. My mother's natural tenderness only changed its object: she gave to God by necessity what she had given to the Marquis by inclination and temper" (41–42). God is only a substitute who serves to replace natural pleasures and allows the mother to place her "tenderness" somewhere else.[12]

The second attack against religion is launched soon thereafter, when Thérèse recounts two practices from her childhood: that she used to caress herself instinctively and to give herself pleasure in her sleep at the age of seven and that she and other children her age used to show their intimate parts to each other and to whip each other's "little bottoms," the little girls playing with the "guiguis" of the little boys, making dolls with them and kissing these "little instruments" (45). The repetition of the word "little" stresses Thérèse's innocence and the instinctive character of the pleasures experienced at such an early age. The notion of sin appears only at the moment when adults start paying attention to the children's games. Italics emphasize the words used by her mother that are not her own words but words borrowed from her confessor: "I cried and answered her that . . . I didn't know what she meant by the terms *touch, impudicity* and *lethal sin* which she used" (45). These words designate carnal pleasure as evil, but the periphrasis Thérèse chooses afterwards to describe her pleasure as a child denounces religious hypocrisy by suggesting that nuns are submitted to precisely the same natural needs as she was: "There was no doubt that it was the strength of my temper which made me do in my sleep what relieves so many nuns when they are awake" (45). The notion of sin is developed a little later when Thérèse goes to a convent and recounts her confessor's words: "Avoid above all listening to the demon of the flesh" (46). Thérèse discovers the idea of evil, which makes her blush at her innocent childish games and confess everything. Here we find the third attack against Catholic religion, an indirect attack against the ritual of confession as a voyeuristic perversion: "I told him everything. What details didn't he require from me!" (47). Details make the scene visual; requiring details turns the confessor into a voyeur.

The pornographic novel launches a double attack against Catholicism. On the one hand, it attacks the interdiction against carnal pleasure as being unnatural and impossible to respect. The proof is that nuns and priest are the first to transgress this interdiction, as Father Dirrag's behavior will reveal. If the prohibition is respected, then it can have dangerous consequences for health. In the eighteenth century many believed that masturbation made people sick, and this belief appears in *Thérèse philosophe* when the heroine attributes the weakness of her youth to masturbation: "My vivacity was lost, my legs could barely sustain me" (42). But the text immediately counterattacks by showing that the illness resulting from a lack of masturbation is far more dangerous: "I fell in a state of debility that was visibly leading me to the grave, when my mother removed me from the convent" (49–50). If solitary pleasures are forbidden in the name of health—of

nature—it is also in the name of health that the text tries to undo the prejudice against masturbation: "I resembled a living skeleton. The practice of
religion had almost dispatched me. . . . This divine liquid which affords us
physical pleasure . . . had flowed out of its customary channels and into
unfamiliar ones, all of which had produced disorder throughout the
machine" (54; 253). The novel recommends the practice of masturbation by
giving the reader an ostensibly scientific explanation about the functioning
of the body.

The second attack against Catholicism concerns its metaphoric language. The idea of sin is expressed through metaphor: "Never put, he said,
either your hand or even your eyes on this infamous part through which
you pee, and which is nothing but the apple which seduced Adam. . . . It is
inhabited by the demon. . . . Stay away . . . from this piece of flesh in young
boys your age. . . : it is the serpent, my girl, which tempted Eve, our common mother. Do not let your glances or your touch ever be soiled by this
villainous beast; for it shall sting and devour you without fail" (47–48).
With this metaphor the priest addresses Thérèse's imagination, not her
reason, and seeks to scare her instead of explaining things to her. The
Christian myth of hell and paradise acts on the imagination. The confessor
tries to inspire two feelings in Thérèse: the fear of the other sex and repulsion for her own sexual parts, represented as a disgusting object. But at the
same time the pornographic text shows that it is precisely the metaphor
expressing the interdiction that makes the interdiction erotic.

Throughout the first part of the narrative the text plays with the erotic
power of the biblical image of the serpent. Scared by the priest's speech,
Thérèse replies: "He seemed so sweet to me! He bit none of my friends. I
assure you that it had the smallest of mouths and no teeth at all; I saw it
well" (48). Thérèse's innocence focuses the reader's gaze on the intimate
parts the priest had just forbidden her to ever touch again; and it is precisely her innocence, that is, her ignorance of the metaphoric sense of the
image, that forces the priest to pursue the metaphor, in order to lend more
urgency to the danger and therefore to the image of the beast: "The ser-
pents you dared to touch were still too young and too small. . . . They will
lengthen, grow, and leap at you: then you should dread the effect of the
venom with which they are accustomed to dart with a kind of furor" (48).

Thanks to these details, the banal image of the snake becomes the most erotic of images, separating the member from the rest of the body and focusing the listener's gaze on the male erection; in addition, the repulsion expressed in the image becomes the very sign of desire. The mere word *member* would not be as exciting as the violence expressed by the priest's words "grow," "leap," "dread," "dart," and "furor." The result is that the fantasy soon fills Thérèse's imagination; she forgets the prohibition and the fear the priest tried to inspire in her and remembers only the "charming serpent": "This charming serpent always painted itself in my soul. . . . Sometimes, when aroused, I believed I was putting my hand on it, I caressed it, I admired its noble and haughty look and its firmness although I was still ignorant of its use" (49). Through the phantasmatic power of the image the Christian interdiction turns against itself and naturally invites transgression: it produces pleasure. *Thérèse philosophe* thus reveals in a subtle and ironic way the perverse effect of Catholic discourse, or the equivalence between interdiction and desire.

The most anti-Catholic episode in the novel involves Father Dirrag and Eradice. This episode, which recounts the seduction of a young, ingenuous penitent by her confessor, stages not only a sexual act but the use of a language: the most exciting and comic element of the scene is the language used by Father Dirrag, who persuades Thérèse's friend Eradice that she is becoming a saint. The sanctification is performed by means of the insertion into Eradice's body of a "piece of the cord of St. Francis" (the belt of his robe): "With the venerable cord of St. Francis I'm going to purge you of all impurities that remain in you" (62). This "venerable cord" is, of course, the sexual organ of the priest.

The text plays with clichés and literary allusions. "Stop! Stop! Cover your bosom with this handkerchief" (58; 256), says Father Dirrag to Eradice as she uncovers her left breast, and one recognizes Tartuffe's famous line in Molière's play, "Cover that bosom, which I must not see."[13] Other stereotypes include the priests' taste for fustigation and their passion for sodomy. Eradice presents two orifices to Father Dirrag, and the priest hesitates a moment, "but prudence, finally, won out over his natural inclination": "It must be said, in fairness to him, that I distinctly saw His Holiness's ruby red member take the canonical path after he delicately opened its purple lips with the thumb and index fingers of each hand" (65; 260).

The text provides readers with a voyeuristic pleasure by focusing their attention on the actors' intimate parts, described by Thérèse with an accuracy of detail that highlights her position as a voyeur: "I saw that approximately a thumbnail's width of the holy instrument was always held back, deprived of a role in the festivities. I saw also that with each backward movement of the father's rump, as the cord withdrew and its head appeared, the lips of Eradice spread open, revealing a crimson hue wondrous to behold. I saw that, in the next moment, as the father thrust forward, these same lips, of which one could now see only the short black hairs covering them, grasped the arrow so tightly that it seemed all but swallowed up" (66; 261). The pleasure of the text comes both from this precise and pornographic description of sexual acts and from the language used by the characters, that is, from the contrast between the priest's sexual acts and his religious discourse. Thérèse conveys to the reader-viewer the confusion engendered by the layering of sexual and mystical registers. The denunciation of the eroticism of religious language reaches its climax at the moment of orgasm, when the passive Eradice speaks for the first time: "Purge me of all impurities. I . . . see . . . the . . . an . . . gels. Push forward . . . Push now . . . Ah! . . . Ah! . . . Good . . . St. Francis! . . . I'm dying!" (69; 262). By showing that mystical ecstasy and carnal pleasure can be expressed in exactly the same terms, the pornographic novel both pleases readers and mocks religious mysticism.

In the first part of the novel voyeurism has an epistemological function: it unveils "truth" by denouncing the hypocrisy of Catholic discourse and showing the potential dangers that can result from the priests' hypocrisy and from the ignorance they try to preserve for the sake of their pleasures. The danger of ignorance is made apparent by the effect the scene has on Thérèse. Back in her room, Thérèse dreams of the scene she witnessed, and she instinctively finds a way of duplicating that pleasure: "This ruby red member entering Mademoiselle Eradice's part could not get out of my imagination. . . . Mechanically I placed myself in the position in which I had seen Eradice, and, mechanically again, . . . I slid on my stomach down to the bedpost which served as a support for the part in which I felt an inconceivable itching" (76). Thérèse finds pleasure in this instinctive way, but the rubbing against her bedpost makes her genitals extremely sore. Her subsequent difficulty walking attracts the attention of Mme C., a friend of her mother's, who then questions her, teaches her how to soothe the pain by "bathing the sore parts with red wine," and worries about Thérèse's "poor little wounded parts" (83).

Mme C.'s concern for Thérèse's well-being leads to the second part of the novel, Thérèse's philosophical education by a friend of Mme C., the abbé T., who reveals to Thérèse the cause of her itching and explains how to appease it without pain or danger.

A Lesson in Materialist Philosophy

The abbé T.'s discourse confirms what the reader understands from the first episode: pleasure is natural, but the girls' ignorance and the priests' hypocrisy can lead to far more dangerous consequences than a simple genital inflammation. The abbé T. is an enlightened priest who preaches a secular morality founded on respect for natural instincts and social order. He reveals to Thérèse that Father Dirrag endangered the life and reputation of her friend Eradice by exposing her to the risk of pregnancy. The abbé T. thinks that only a rational education can give women the means to protect themselves from abuse.

The abbé T.'s introduction into Thérèse's narrative marks the beginning of a new type of discourse: materialist, concrete, and nonmetaphoric. During Thérèse's lessons he labels things by their proper names and not with images expressing desire or disgust. He calls the female sex "the natural part," the male sex "the natural member of man, which is used for procreation," sexual desire "a temperamental need as natural as hunger and thirst," and the sexual act "the mechanism for the production of the human race" (85–86). He teaches Thérèse that sexual pleasure is natural but that penetration must be avoided because it could compromise her health or reputation—her health because pregnancy and mainly delivery often caused the mother's death in the eighteenth century, her reputation because human beings who live in society are forced to respect the rules and prejudices of that society and eighteenth-century French society precluded any sexual relationship for women before marriage. The confessor's moderate and tolerant discourse rationally analyzes and deconstructs the prohibition, not in order to lead to its transgression, but to explain why it ought to be respected. The abbé T. suggests masturbation as a remedy for Thérèse's itching, but in the name of a social ethics that holds virginity sacred he forbids her to "insert the finger inside the opening there" if she does not want to "arouse doubts in the mind of the man you will marry": "There's nothing wrong with using your hand, or your finger, to assuage that body part with the rubbing necessary for its relief. However, I expressly forbid you to introduce your finger inside the opening there" (85; 265).

After listening to these rational precepts, which charm her soul, Thérèse thinks about this "careful reasoning," proceeds to "examine in detail that part of the body which makes us women" (87), and, as her finger "traveled up the length of the opening," she discovers "a little protuberance" that causes her to shiver: "What a happy discovery for a girl who had within her an abundant quantity of the liquid which is the principle of pleasure! For six months thereafter I bathed continually in a river of voluptuousness" (87; 267).

Until then the novel brings the pleasure of voyeurism and enlightened pedagogy into harmony. Every voyeuristic scene serves to unmask the hypocrisy of Catholic taboos and to reveal that the prohibition only increases the pleasure of the senses by producing fantasies. Every pornographic scene brings pleasure to Thérèse and teaches her something: a practical knowledge of her body and of the means to find pleasure, as well as a philosophical knowledge of social and religious hypocrisy and of the necessity of pleasure. Thanks to the abbé T.'s lessons, Thérèse gets to know herself. She learns the functioning of her body and the way to satisfy her temperamental needs while remaining in control of herself, of her health and reputation.[14]

Thérèse philosophe, however, is a pornographic novel and not a treatise on the education of women. The novel's first aim is to excite readers. Is this compatible with pedagogy?

Pornography needs obstacles; the pleasure of the text comes from the transgression of limits. The abbé T. utters an interdiction: "I expressly forbid you to introduce your finger." The restriction is rationally explained, but in the context of a pornographic novel the erotic power of interdiction matters more than its rational legitimacy. This prohibition is accompanied by the necessity to hide from Thérèse reasonings that she is too young to understand. This restriction of her knowledge immediately awakens her desire to know more: "I resolved to do all in my power to discover what they were trying to hide from me" (88; 268). The pornographic novel reveals the link between the desire to know and sexual desire; Thérèse's desire to learn everything leads to new scenes of voyeurism.

Thérèse catches sight of the abbé T. giving Mme C. some practical lessons. The man she sees is no longer the wise and enlightened priest preaching self-control, the respect of the other, and moderate pleasures. This is a man in a state of desire. Having just demonstrated to Thérèse that this act was dangerous for women, he now tries to convince Mme C. to let herself be penetrated by him. The abbé T.'s language now mixes scientific terms with metaphors: "The lover . . . finds himself in the state necessary for the act of procreation: his blood, his spirits, and his erecting nerve have together caused his dart to swell and become hard. . . . The arrow of the lover is thrust into the quiver of his mistress" (95; 273). The irruption of metaphor in the abbé T.'s speech allows us to perceive the loss of self-control that results from desire. The image of "dart" or "arrow" is not neutral like that of "natural member of man which is used for procreation" but expresses an aggressive fantasy that is the very voice of desire. The abbé T. himself recognizes his contradiction after the orgasm and tells Mme C. that she was right to resist him: "In truth, my good friend, after thinking it over, I think you were right in refusing me the enjoyment I asked from you. I felt a pleasure so great, an arousal so powerful, that I suspect that the dam would have broken if you had let me have my way. One must admit that we're very weak animals indeed and very seldom able to master our urges" (97; 274–75).

In the face of the abbé T.'s contradictions, Mme C. seems to embody reason—the faculty to know, judge, and act conforming to rational principles. She firmly denies the abbé T. and finds another way to "teach this little upstart a lesson" [*mettre ce petit effronté à la raison*] (96; 274). By calling the abbé T.'s erect member "this little upstart" she shows that she accepts a part in her friend's fantasy; the words "to teach . . . a lesson" [*mettre . . . à la raison*], while suggesting the abbé's pleasure, also indicate that Mme C. remains in control of the situation. Mme C. is both reasonable and tolerant—the ideal of the Enlightenment. The word *raison* refers to both the abbé's plea-sure and Mme C.'s control.

But the following scene reverses the power relationship between the protagonists: it is now Mme C. who is begging and the abbé T. who is resisting. Mme C., who almost died giving birth and for this reason is determined never to be penetrated again, suddenly forgets her principles and her own interest because of a book the abbé T. lent to her: "'Reading your awful *Portier des Chartreux* has set me all on fire. . . . Put it to me today, abbé, I beg you,' she added. 'I'm dying of desire, and I'll even risk the worst'" (102; 279).[15] Confronted with Mme C., who is offering herself, the abbé T. now embodies reason and reminds Mme C. of the motives that should keep her from asking for penetration: "I love you and I'm too much of a gentleman to risk your reputation and your justified reproaches by this imprudence" (102; 279). Is this the voice of Enlightenment? We must remember that the abbé T. was previously saying just the opposite. He now adds a second reason for his refusal: "Monsieur the doctor is not, as you see, at his most brilliant today, I'm not a Gascon, and . . ." (103; 279).[16] Mme C. interrupts him: "I can see that very well. . . . The latter reason is so com-pelling that you actually needn't have troubled to flatter yourself with the first one" (103; 279).

What is played out in this little exchange between Mme C. and the abbé T. and in this double role reversal is important: when the abbé T. wants to penetrate Mme C. she resists in the name of her own interests and seems to embody reason and self-control in pleasure; but reading a pornographic novel the abbé T. lent her is enough to make her lose control in front of him, and he then resumes his role of reasonable preacher. If, however, he does not take Mme C. up on her offer, it is, among other reasons, because "Monsieur the doctor is not at his most brilliant." The verb *to see*, which is used once by the abbé T. ("as you see") and once by Mme C. ("I can see that very well"), now attracts the reader's gaze to the abbé T.'s member, which is in a state that cannot satisfy Mme C.'s desire, which was his own desire the day before. Mme C. names this state of impotence ironically as a "compelling reason" [*raison énergique*]. In its Aristotelian meaning, *énergique* actually means "in act."[17] The reason "in act," the reason that determines the abbé's acts, is his impotence; here the text suggests that the state of the member is stronger than any rational reason. The abbé T.'s rational princi-ples are thus but a mask covering the only real reason, his temporary impo-tence. In this brief scene, for the first time in the novel, reason is derided.

The contradiction between rational principles and desire and the defeat of reason in its struggle against desire are even more apparent in the effect the scene has on Thérèse: "I began mechanically to mimic everything I saw. My own hand did the work of the abbé's hand; I imitated all the move-ments of my good friend" (104; 280). The scene between Mme C. and the abbé T. echoes that between Eradice and Father Dirrag. Mme C. expresses her pleasure in almost the same way as Eradice: "Push hard, push, my little one. Ah! what bliss! I'm melting . . . I'm faint . . . ing!" (104; 280). "Mechan-ically," Thérèse says. At the time when *Thérèse Philosophe* was written, in 1748, one year after La Mettrie's scandalous essay *L'Homme machine*,[18] the adverb had a much stronger meaning than it does today: it truly identified the body with a machine, functioning independently of the mind. After Thérèse has been educated by the abbé T., voyeurism still has the same powerful effect on her as it had when she witnessed Father Dirrag abusing Eradice. The mimetic effect of voyeurism is irresistible: "Continuing still to imitate exactly what I saw and without a thought for my confessor's interdiction, I stuck my finger in, in my turn" (104; 281). Why does she need to remind her readers of the confessor's interdiction, which she forgot, if it is not because there is no interdiction, even a rationally justified one, that can resist trans-gression when erotic desire is concerned? Mme C.'s cry of pleasure and the ellipses that leave holes in her words are far more efficient than all the abbé T.'s lessons: this disrupted language expresses a state of rapture that com-municates itself to Thérèse, who then forgets her own reasoning, and even the "slight pain" she feels, to reach orgasm "mechanically."

The episode with the abbé T. is the most philosophical in the whole novel. The abbé T. develops the principles of materialist philosophy. To Mme C. he explains "why jealousy is ridiculous" (91–92), he gives "instruc-tions for the women, the girls and the men who wish to travel safely through the pitfalls of sexual pleasure" (93–95), he "proves that the plea-sures of the little goose are entirely lawful" (96–98), he gives a "definition of what we should understand by the word *nature*" (98–99), he explains "why evildoers should be punished" (100), he makes an "examination of religions by natural light" (107–12), he compares "a man's life to a throw of the dice" (113–14), and he explains why his philosophy should not be communicated to the public (115). The whole philosophy of the novel, all the determinist arguments that Thérèse repeats from beginning to end, can be found in the abbé T.'s speeches. We learn that his thoughts are "the fruit of twenty years' meditation and study and burning the midnight oil" (114; 287).

This philosophy cannot be democratic: religions are a necessary evil to preserve social order. If, however, the abbé T. is not a democrat, he is certainly a feminist: his concern for women's pleasure, health, and reputation is greater than is usual in pornographic novels. The novel does not merely contain a male fantasy of voyeurism; it also contains practical recipes that the abbé T. recommends to women. For instance, the abbé T. says that he cannot reason well when he feels "the goading of the flesh" and that he therefore always had "a little girl *ad hoc* like a chamberpot for peeing" (93; 272) to whom he "stuck it once or twice" when he lived in Paris and spent his time reading and studying. The abbé T.'s recommendation to "any man of letters, any studious fellow," and even to "any gentleman conscious of his social obligations" seems quite misogynous, all the more so since this practice is not reversible: it would be much more difficult for a woman to satisfy her sexual need with a little boy ad hoc, used like a chamberpot. But this objection is immediately raised by the abbé T. himself: "Now, Mme, perhaps you will ask me . . . what women and girls should do. They have the same needs, you'll tell me, as men; they are made of the same stuff. They do not, however, have the same resources at their disposal. Concern for their good name, fear of an indiscreet or clumsy partner, fear of pregnancy— these do not permit them to have recourse to the same remedy as men. Moreover, you'll say, where could they find these available men like your little ad hoc girl?" (94; 272). At this point the abbé T. recommends masturbation to women, the use of a dildo, "a rather good imitation of the real thing," and imagination—fantasy.

A pornographic novel that gives advice to both men and women, fights prejudices, and increases its readers' sexual and philosophical knowledge for the good of society truly participates in the project of the Enlightenment. But it is also during the episode with the abbé T. that a contradiction first appears between pornography and enlightenment, aside from the fact that moral pedagogy limits sexual excitement. In this episode reason serves as a stimulant. Reason, like the Catholic interdiction previously, becomes the discourse that must be transgressed to bring pleasure to the reader. What makes the text exciting is not the abbé T.'s philosophical discourses but the voyeuristic scenes that reveal a contradiction between rational principles and desire. The episode with the abbé T. contains the materialist philosophy of the Enlightenment, but it is also the place in which the power of reason is questioned. Reason is shown to be nothing but the effect of desire or of a lack of desire, as the philosopher Thérèse herself says when commenting upon Eradice's adventure: "But whichever path he chooses, there will always be a reason, a desire, which will lead him invincibly to the decision that reflects it" (52; 251). The words "reason" and "desire," simply separated by a coma and both subjects of the verb *to lead*, are equivalent in this sentence: desire is a reason, and reason is nothing but a way to justify either desire or its lack.

For the needs of the pornographic novel the abbé T., in spite of all his philosophy, is finally not worth much more than Father Dirrag: the discrepancy between his words and acts makes him the interesting hero that he would not be if he were simply a philosopher. From this discrepancy in the second episode stems a representation of male sexuality that is developed in the novel's third episode, with Mme Bois-Laurier.

Women's Laughter

The third episode, very different from the preceding two, has often been said to be interpolated. This is the opinion of Robert Darnton, who chooses not to translate the episode and analyzes it very briefly: "this part does not harmonize well with the rest of the book" (97). It is easy to understand such reticence: Bois-Laurier's narrative breaks with the tone of the former two, in which Thérèse was the narrator and heroine, and resembles instead a kind of catalogue of sexual tastes, which are not even perverse enough to be interesting. In addition, the anecdotes introduce many characters who play no role in Thérèse's sexual and philosophical education.

The third episode occurs between women. The sapphic scene is a stereotype in the eighteenth-century pornographic novel, as if the representation of two women making love were one of the primary male fantasies, the fantasy of a pleasure from which men are excluded but which they control through voyeurism.[19] Does the episode with Bois-Laurier satisfy the Count's voyeuristic fantasy? *Thérèse philosophe* does not escape the stereotype, for Thérèse and Bois-Laurier do indeed share a physical intimacy: "As soon as we were in bed, our follies took the place of reason" (170). Thérèse, however, does not describe at all what happens between them: their "follies" remain in a discreet silence. Likewise, we learn that Thérèse is for the first time in the role of teacher, instructing Bois-Laurier in the principles of materialist philosophy: "She was very surprised to see how enlightened I was in moral, metaphysics, and religion. . . . 'You just opened my eyes to mysteries that produced the misfortunes of my life'" (127). But during this episode we never hear Thérèse reasoning. Her lessons seem to matter principally by their effect, which is to inspire Bois-Laurier's trust: "I owe you confidence for confidence, lesson for lesson" (128). The "lesson" the text transmits to readers in this third episode is the one Bois-Laurier teaches Thérèse in exchange for her materialist philosophy.

Instead of giving a philosophical speech, Bois-Laurier recounts her sex life as a prostitute. In these anecdotes she is the protagonist: she depicts her own body. But Bois-Laurier is also the voyeur: unlike Eradice and Mme C., she never faints from pleasure and loses conscience. Her body is insensitive because of a physical particularity: her vagina is obstructed by a membrane that makes her impossible to penetrate, a membrane she never wanted to have surgically removed: "A nervous membrane closes the avenue so exactly that the sharpest arrow Love ever had in his quiver never could reach its aim" (135). Bois-Laurier occupies the best position as a voyeur since her own body is the site of the spectacle and she remains a distant observer. The object of the show is the male member.

"The sharpest arrow," Bois-Laurier said ironically when describing her impenetrable body. Throughout her narrative, however, we do not see many "arrows," "darts," or other images glorifying male erection. On the contrary: Bois-Laurier is interested in the member not in states of glory but rather in states of humiliation. The President who bought her virginity does not even try to take it; she sees him "shaking between his thighs something black and flaccid which all his efforts could not hoist up" (138).

Shortly thereafter the madame of her brothel calls the President's organ an "old, rusted, wrinkled and used instrument" (139). Bois-Laurier relates the case of a man who needs to hear his mistress sing for his "machine" to be "moved": but one false note and "the *metronome* was not just a limp rag" (143). "The most lascivious touch could not give back the languishing part its elasticity" (143). Bois-Laurier then speaks of a bishop who must squeal like a pig in the moment of pleasure, of a wealthy gentleman who gets his pleasure by threatening her with a whip and running after her while holding his "bundle" in his hand, of a man who enjoys himself while watching her masturbate, of an old physician who will not give "any sign of virility before receiving a hundred lashings," which she applies to his buttocks, and of a voluptuous courtesan who holds his "flabby instrument" in his hand and enjoys himself only while watching his valet, who is endowed with "one of the most brilliant," make love to another woman. Finally she describes three Capucins with "enormous instruments" pointed at her who argue about who will get her first: "Their robes, raised above their heads, revealed their wretched tools which, although they had looked salient before, were now reduced to the shape of dish-mops" (159).

Bois-Laurier recounts only scenes of impotence or scenes in which the male member appears ridiculous or disgusting. She describes either genitals of aristocrats that nothing can "hoist up" or the erect organs of monks that suddenly lose their erections and cannot regain them once "reduced to the shape of dish-mops." The image reveals a definite contempt for male desire. This spectacle has the same effect systematically on Bois-Laurier: she bursts into laughter. "Throughout this peculiar scene, I didn't stop laughing until I couldn't breath anymore" (143), she says about the man with the penchant for singers. Even the rare sight of a man who manages to penetrate her companion makes her laugh: "I continued laughing to the point of crying while watching with all my attention the labour which was taking place behind me" (144). One of the Capucins who tries to penetrate her is ironically called "Father Hilaire"; he does not laugh much himself, but he causes the young woman's hilarity: "I threw myself back onto the bed, ready to die from laughter and completely lacking strength, while he rummaged around my charming parts" (159). The scene in which the Capucin and the old Dupuis vomit on each other after trying to make love provokes Bois-Laurier's "immoderate laughter." Finally, Bois-Laurier's last adventure aims only at making her listener burst into laughter as well: she says that she "let go a mellow wind right in the man's face" and the man had to flee. Thérèse is delighted with this last scatological anecdote: "Here Mme Bois-Laurier was forced to interrupt her narrative by the immoderate laughter that this last adventure provoked in me. To keep me company she also laughed with all her heart" (168).

As Philippe Roger observes in his preface to *Thérèse philosophe*, "Au bonheur des dames sensées," in all these adventures there is "neither copulation nor perversity": "One is therefore surprised to hear Sade's Juliette praise a sister who is not especially interested—this is the least one can say—in the *bizarre inclinations inspired by nature*" (23). But if there is perversity in *Thérèse philosophe*, it is not in the pornographic, that is, sexually arousing, quality of the text, which decreases as the story moves forward. The perversity, which is the strength of the text, lies in the women's laughter, in the derision of male desire and male power.

Thérèse heard Eradice and Mme C. say that they were dying (*se pâmer*) of the pleasure brought by St. Francis's cord or the abbé T.'s finger; the impenetrable Bois-Laurier is ready to die (*se pâme*) of laughter. This is where perversion lies, in the reversal of the text against its premises. The "dart," the "inflamed bolt," and the "arrow," which appear to be glorious in the fantasies of aroused men, are only "soft dish-mops," "rags," and "miserable tools" in Bois-Laurier's narrative. Her physical impenetrability gives Bois-Laurier the power to ridicule and humiliate male sexual desire. A role reversal takes place in this episode, not because Thérèse is now the teacher and listener instead of the pupil and narrator, but because the female body objectified by male voyeurism now becomes a gaze that focuses the readers' attention on the male genitals and transforms them into ridiculous objects. The episode with Bois-Laurier must have particularly struck the eighteenth-century imagination, because it was published again, with other names, under the title *La Courtisane anaphrodite ou la pucelle libertine* in 1787, nearly forty years after *Thérèse philosophe*. It may also have been the invention of this character that struck Sade and made him say of an otherwise rather innocent book that "the charming work of the Marquis d'Argens had shown the goal, without however quite attaining it."[20] Indeed, in *L'Histoire de Juliette*

Sade gives la Durand, Juliette's last lover and the only other woman who survives at the end of the novel, the same physical characteristic as Bois-Laurier: her vagina is obstructed. Sade also gives her a very long clitoris, which allows her to make love with women as if she were a man.[21] One could argue, as Lucienne Frappier-Mazur does in *Sade ou l'écriture de l'orgie*, that a phallocentric model dominates even the sapphic episodes of pornographic novels.[22] Yet, what matters here is not the illusion of being a man or with a man but the *as if*, the game of illusion, the imitation, the playfulness of women who change gender and identity and who take all roles.[23] The sapphic fantasy, in *Thérèse philosophe* and in many other pornographic novels, is not merely the expression of a male, voyeuristic desire to *penetrate* and control the unknown terrain of female sexuality; rather, it serves to project an ironic light on male sexuality through the woman's gaze and to transform the male member into a mechanical object that appears ridiculous and disgusting.[24] The phallus-god portrayed in pornographic novels is most often handled, depicted, and manipulated by women. The female gaze that focuses on the phallus separates the male member from the rest of the body, objectifies it, and considers its function and usefulness before its belonging to a human being. In most eighteenth-century pornographic novels the "member above all others" is treated like a toy and the god of pleasure is used as a dildo. In Nerciat's *Le Diable au corps* a heroine calls the limp male member an "inanimate toy." In Nerciat's *Le Doctorat impromptu* Erosie mentions the "baby toy" of the young man who seduces her. Before seeing Solange's sex, she amuses herself by comparing it, in her imagination, with the dildo she is holding: the male member looks ridiculous in comparison with its copy, the dildo. In *Le Portier des Chartreux* Monique describes the male member as "the original of a thing of which the copy had given me so much pleasure" (59). The original not only is not always enhanced but is often ridiculed as a source of frustration in comparison with the dildo, which never disappoints women. A fantasy, indeed, haunts erotic novels: male impotence. Heroines have no pity for withering heros. The sapphic fantasy is also that of an omnipotent, devouring female desire that is never frustrated.[25] One could say that the representation of an omnipotent female desire is a male sexual fantasy, but it would be difficult to consider the humiliation and derision of male sexual power as part of the same fantasy. What manifests itself through the episode with Bois-Laurier in *Thérèse philosophe* is the fear of impotence that threatens male sexuality (mainly the sexuality of aristocrats) and a derision of the male desire to see, to know, and to penetrate.

If, however, the text of this third episode so radically mocks male desire —the desire for penetration and power symbolized by sexual desire— which had already been questioned in the previous two, one wonders why it ends with such a timid and traditional scenario: a heterosexual and happy relationship in which Thérèse, now a kept mistress, yields to the reasonable and moderate desires of her lover, a man of the Enlightenment.

Coïtus Interruptus, or the Morals of the Story

The novel ends with practical advice about coïtus interruptus and a happy love story that enhance both pleasure and self-mastery: "Afterwards we began again, and have continued to renew our pleasures in the same manner for ten years, without a problem, without a worry, without children" (186; 298). Such a conclusion seems to confirm the abbé T.'s philosophy and allows Robert Darnton to comment that

> *Thérèse philosophe* is not just a sex book and not only a philosophical tract; it is a treatise on contraception. To be sure, coïtus interruptus subjects the woman to the goodwill and self-mastery of the man. . . . However willingly, Thérèse lets herself be manipulated and seduced. She might be considered as the ultimate target of the book's pervasive voyeurism—that is, as a sex object. But she emerges in the end as the true hero of her story. Unlike Mademoiselle Eradice, who accepts Father Dirrag's injunction to be passive—"Forget yourself and let yourself go"—she takes charge of her life and lives it on her own terms, making her own decisions.[26]

The Count, Thérèse's lover, is a man of the Enlightenment. When Thérèse and the Count first met, they were attracted to each other's philosophies: "They joked about my moral principles. You appeared to be curious to explore them, and then, charmed to know them thoroughly" (169). The Count is completely honest with Thérèse, even more than the abbé T. He hides nothing from her and respects her freedom. If this relationship of mutual respect and tender love still has a legitimate place in a pornographic novel, it is only because it preserves one last obstacle: Thérèse refuses to be penetrated by the Count. This refusal has been prepared and justified by the whole novel: Father Dirrag's perversity, the abbé T.'s lessons, Mme C.'s experience, and, above all, Bois-Laurier's contempt for male desire.

The question of penetration establishes an erotic continuity from one episode to the next. In the last episode we see fantasy reappear through Thérèse's fear of penetration: "I trembled at the sight of the bolt with which you were threatening to pierce me. How would it be possible, I asked myself, for something of this length and this width, with a head so monstrous, to be inserted into a space where I could barely fit my finger? Moreover, if I became pregnant, I felt, I would surely die of it" (177; 293). The argument of pregnancy, which is the most important in the novel's second episode, here is only secondary and comes as an afterthought. What matters is the fantasy of disproportion and Thérèse's imaginary representation of penetration, which expresses an aggressive and sadistic fantasy that makes the text exciting again by giving a tactile consistency to the male sex and focusing the reader's eyes on its length, width, and head. In Thérèse's resistance to penetration in the fourth episode we see the martial image of the "bolt" reappear and the male member celebrated again in a state of triumph. But the third episode provides Thérèse with enough strength and distance to resist her lover. So the question now is, how will this last obstacle be overcome? How will an enlightened man manage to convince an enlightened woman who is as strong, as wise, and as knowledgeable as himself to do something she does not want to do, namely, let herself be penetrated by him?

The Count's first strategy is "the force of reasoning": "I remarked that, once the knife of desire was whetted, under the pretext of catering to my taste for moral and metaphysical issues, you employed the force of reasoning to help me decide in favor of that which you desired of me" (178; 293). Then we find three pages of the Count's moral reflections on self-love, "which determines all the Actions of our Lives," "on the Soul's Inability to act or think independently in One Manner or Another," and on "the Meaning of the Spirit." But reasoning is not that efficient: Thérèse is not convinced, and the Count is beginning "to be a little tired of my refusals"

(180; 295). He changes his strategy: he sends to Paris for his library of erotic books and pictures. He loans them to Thérèse for one year on the condition that she promise "to refrain for two weeks from touching that part of the body which should, by rights, today be within [his] domain," and he makes a bet with her: "Let's make a wager, which you'll no doubt win: I bet my library and my paintings against your virginity that you will not practice abstinence for two weeks, as you have promised" (182; 295). These conditions seem fair, but it should be noted that they are decided by the Count, not by Thérèse, who can only accept the wager since it touches a very sensitive point for her, the question of self-mastery: "'In truth, Monsieur,' I answered, with a slightly offended air, 'you have a very curious idea of my temperament, and you attribute to me very little self-control'" (181; 296).

Thérèse resists four days while looking at lascivious paintings and reading the classics of pornography, including *Le Portier des Chartreux*, which had set Mme C. on fire. But "the fifth day, after an hour of reading, I fell into a kind of ecstasy" (182; 296). Here again we find something that Sade borrowed from *Thérèse philosophe* and describes in *Histoire de Juliette* as Juliette's "secrecy": the secret consists in fifteen days of abstinence while the imagination fills with the most elaborate fantasies; this is the way, says Juliette, to prepare oneself for the most atrocious crimes and the most powerful orgasms. *Thérèse philosophe* does not go to this extreme but nonetheless reveals the irresistible power of fantasy. The sight of two paintings, *The Feast of Priapus* and *The Love Affair of Venus and Mars*, like the living scenes Thérèse witnessed in the previous episodes of the book, produces a mechanical effect on her: "I set myself to imitate all the postures that I saw. . . . Mechanically, my hand ventured where that of the man was placed, and I was on the point of inserting my finger there when reflection held me back" (182). "Mechanically," Thérèse says again. In this last struggle between the "mechanical" and the "reflective," the mechanical finally wins out when Thérèse turns her gaze to the second painting, *The Love Affair of Venus and Mars*: "I admired the striking attitude of the god Mars. The fire with which his eyes, and especially his lance, seemed to be animated passed directly into my heart. I slipped under the sheets. My buttocks rocked lustfully as though they would bear onward the crown destined for the conqueror. . . . 'Ah! dear lover! I can resist no longer. Come forward, Count, I'm no longer afraid of your dart. You may pierce your lover. You may even strike where you will!'" (185; 297). This demand is immediately followed with a magical effect: "You appeared all of a sudden, more proud, more brilliant than Mars in the painting" (185; 297). The novel ends with this apotheosis of the male member, which now is not only a "dart" and a "bolt" "piercing" the lover, but also Mars's inflamed "lance" or even the god himself. The Count calls his member Thérèse's "conqueror." Once again we find the principal cliché of pornographic novels, that of the male member as god and conqueror. *Thérèse philosophe*'s conclusion seems to glorify both the male member and the enlightenment embodied by the Count, who attains his end, penetrating Thérèse.

We should, however, notice that the Count gives up reasoning in order to convince Thérèse. The enlightened man trusts the persuasion of pornographic novels and erotic paintings more than reason. "You'll no doubt win," he tells Thérèse, but the bet serves only to offend Thérèse so as to make her accept the challenge. The Count knows that she cannot win. The Count, in using the power of the image as his main argument, is the first enlightened and "wise" protagonist to admit, almost openly, that the power of the image is stronger than that of reason. The Count therefore recognizes the failure of the Enlightenment, or at the least of rational argument, in the domain of desire.

Thérèse philosophe is the story of Thérèse's sexual as well as philosophical education. One might believe that these two educations went hand in hand, and this is Robert Darnton's interpretation. But in fact we are witnessing a double movement: on the one hand, a philosophical enlightenment of Thérèse's mind; on the other, and conversely, a "mechanical" persistence of the body's desire, which demonstrates philosophy's impotence. The mimetic power of voyeurism manifests itself even more strongly when Thérèse yields to desires produced by images in spite of her rational concern about her own health. The Count's final wager is the very stake of every pornographic novel: it shows that the effect of voyeurism is stronger than self-control and the rational desire for knowledge. When voyeurs are confronted with an erotic spectacle, or readers with the description of lascivious scenes, they feel desire, which is only a mimetic and mechanical reproduction of what is seen. The Count's bet reveals the power of fantasy;

imaginary representations, inspired by images seen in books, paintings, or living scenes, suddenly become more real than reality. Thérèse gives herself to the Count neither because she is convinced by his rational arguments nor because she is in love with him; she simply yields to the mechanical power that images exert on her body and will.

The issue at stake in *Thérèse philosophe* is not only one of gender but also a philosophical question about the relation between reason and imagination, as I mentioned at the beginning of this chapter. Both female and male voyeurs are subjected to the same power of the image. One could say that in the final episode Thérèse yields to the Count's desire and is manipulated by him; but it is equally true that the Count must finally resort to the power of the image and forsakes reasoning to let the image act. By acknowledging the power of imagination over reason, the pornographic novel concedes a failure of the Enlightenment, or at least stresses its limits: reason educates people but does not determine the course of events. This is precisely Thérèse's philosophical conclusion: "Reason enlightens us, but cannot determine our actions" (189; 299). The pornographic novel uses the word *Enlightenment* in its proper meaning and acknowledges its limited function: it can only enlighten us. The use of reason can only be limited. Reason, finally, consists in recognizing the very limits of reason. Through voyeurism and its *mechanical* effect, which transforms the voyeur's distant gaze into a sexual organ, the eighteenth-century pornographic novel shows that the Enlightenment is useless from the moment the film of fantasy has begun. Acknowledging the power of the image is probably the pornographic novel's strongest intuition. *Thérèse philosophe*, like most pornographic novels, derides the rational optimism of the Enlightenment by transforming it into an erotic obstacle whose transgression the text, by its very genre, invites.

The male member in *Thérèse philosophe* is represented as a toy used as a doll by little girls, as a disgusting or charming serpent, a dart or an arrow, a dish-mop, a divine lance or even a god. After being depicted in Bois-Laurier's narrative as a "miserable tool" that can inspire only laughter in women, the member reappears in the end as Mars's brilliant lance. It seems impossible to ignore the text's irony here since in the former episodes the fantasy of male power was shown to go hand in hand with impotence, or at the very least with a great fragility. The text ironically denounces men's desire to take their own member for a god, to penetrate the impenetrable (Bois-Laurier), and to control everything through the eye of reason.

At the beginning of this chapter I mentioned that the eighteenth-century pornographic novel inherited the traditional distinction between the female, passive object of voyeurism and the male principle of knowledge; although *Thérèse philosophe* seems to respect and finally reaffirm this dichotomy, it also plays with it and subverts it. The novel undermines the male fantasy of omnipotence with female laughter, a complicity between two women, and, finally, Thérèse's skillful hand, which envelopes her "conqueror": "When I had seized his member, I pressed it lightly in my hand, which enclosed it like a case" (186; 298). The conqueror remains silent, conquered by pleasure, letting his mistress "handle" the situation and, more precisely, oust him: Thérèse "seizes" her conqueror and forces him to "withdraw." The use of martial metaphors in *Thérèse philosophe* and other pornographic novels reveals the text's awareness of a power reversal. In a later pornographic novel, *Lettres galantes et philosophiques de deux nonnes*, the heroine exclaims: "The Abbé, who had promised to spare me, was bound to his promise. His *doctor* had warmed up in the height of the fray. . . . I seized him, completely foaming, and . . . my hand forced this rebel to capitulation. Soon he laid down his arms as you can imagine. . . . Proud of my victory, I stayed in control of the site and I left with all the honours of the war" (273).[27] The words "seize," "force," "rebel," "capitulation," and "victory," which ordinarily apply to the male role in the sexual act, are ironically displaced to the female partner's side. The practice of coïtus interruptus, which lovers in the pornographic novel have been forced to take up because of the risk of pregnancy, leaves the woman "in control of the site": she is at the same time the "site" (the inert space) and the one in control (the active principle) in an unexpected expression of autonomy.[28]

FROM *Thérèse philosophe* to Sade's *L'Histoire de Juliette*, pornographic novels display the same irony toward gender relationships and mock the male fantasy of power. By associating pornography and philosophy, the pornographic novel shows the link between the male fantasy of sexual power and the Enlightenment's encyclopedic project—the project of knowing everything. Because voyeurism links together the desires of seeing, controlling, and penetrating the other, pornography, while ridiculing the male fantasy of sexual power, also mocks the desire for rational control. In the first episode the pleasure of the text comes from unmasking Father Dirrag's perverse hypocrisy; in the following episodes the pleasure of the text comes from humiliating both reason and the member that pretends to embody it.

If, then, *Thérèse philosophe* participates in the Enlightenment project, it is not because it propagates philosophical knowledge and gives practical advice to sensible men and women. The novel's message is more subtle: by revealing the contradiction between sexual acts and reasonable discourses, by showing the power of image through the mechanical effect of voyeurism, and by representing male sex as an instrument manipulated by its own desires, fears, and fantasies, *Thérèse philosophe* redefines the power of reason as the knowledge of its own limits. The pleasure of the text comes from the very limits that impose themselves independently from the will of its reasonable characters.

Diderot's *La Religieuse*, written twelve years later, is not such an explicit and graphic novel. Yet we will see the same issues—the negative role played by the Church, the question of innocence, the relation between reason, the body, and the imagination—resurface in a novel that originated as a collective joke and goes much further than *Thérèse philosophe* by wandering into the dark realm of madness and sending its readers a subtle message about what it takes to be human.

FIVE

1760 ∾ SUZANNE, OR LIBERTY

IN 1770 Jean-François La Harpe, a writer whose name today is not as famous as Diderot's, published a successful play full of good intentions, *Mélanie ou la religieuse*, which denounced the cruelty of a social system in which daughters without dowries were imprisoned for life. Melchior Grimm seized this occasion to publicly "confess," in his *Correspondance littéraire*, "the horrible plot" in which he had taken part ten years earlier.

The origin of Diderot's *La Religieuse* is well known. In 1760 Diderot, Grimm and their friends were missing their charming friend Croismare, who, after a life of pleasure in Paris, had recently retired to an estate near Caen and suddenly thrown himself into a life of great religious devotion. The conspirators invented the character of a beautiful and young nun whose unfortunate fate was supposed to awaken the marquis's pity and convince him to return to Paris to help the miserable orphan; once he was there, they would reveal the deception to Croismare. The idea so excited Diderot that he wrote the nun's memoirs.[1] This was the genesis of the novel, which was published for the first time in a 1780 issue of *Correspondance littéraire*, twenty years after being written and ten years after the public revelation of the plot. Meanwhile, the joke acquired a higher status: in 1760 Diderot referred to the novel as a "tale" or "my nun"; on 15 March 1770 Grimm mentioned it as "the most cruel satire ever made of cloisters"; on 27 September 1780 Diderot himself described it as the "most dreadful satire of convents," thus stressing the ideological content of a novel fighting for social justice.[2]

116

The novel's subject—a nun's unhappy fate—and frame—the joke played on a friend—led to two readings of *La Religieuse*. One is a historical reading that focuses on the ideological content and historical context of the novel;[3] the other, more recent, examines the relation between the novel and the *préface-annexe* and demonstrates that *La Religieuse* is an illustration of Diderot's esthetic principles.[4] The reading I propose here is concerned neither with the historical context nor with the esthetic debate about fiction but, rather, with the ethical issue that is at the heart of Diderot's work and is raised by Suzanne Simonin's story: liberty and its relation to the law, to reason, and to the body.

The heroine's only desire is liberty: All I ask is freedom"; "I am seeking to be free because the sacrifice of my liberty was not freely made" (70). The subject of the novel is Suzanne's quest for liberty, yet this novel, more than any other, seeks to seduce readers and, to that extent, to restrain their freedom of mind. Although the novel is full of slight inconsistencies, which have been highlighted by many critics,[5] the plot nevertheless produces an effect of make-believe, as if the power of imagination were stronger than that of reason.[6] Because the convent is a prison that drives the nuns mad, Suzanne's struggle for freedom is a fight not only against the convent's walls but also, and above all, against mental alienation. Suzanne fights to keep her reason, yet Diderot uses her as a bait to excite the reader's imagination, mostly in the second half of the novel, which becomes openly erotic. Is there not a contradiction between Suzanne's rational quest for freedom and the novel's increasing eroticism? The novel seems to have two different purposes, one ideological, consisting in denouncing an inhuman institution in the name of reason, the other erotic, consisting in arousing the reader's imagination. This chapter questions the apparent contradiction between eroticism and ideology and examines the definition of liberty that results from this contradiction.

The Language of the Body: Hysteria as a Woman's Fate

"At last you know who you are" (39), her mother tells Suzanne after the latter learns the secret of her illegitimate origin. For her mother, Suzanne's identity is defined only by the fault that results in her birth. The sacrifice of her freedom to God must be payment for the mother's sin: "God preserved both you and me so that the mother might atone for her sin through her child" (40). Her birth, for which she is not responsible, forces Suzanne to become a nun. The novel challenges this fate: Suzanne starts her narrative by telling her addressee, the Marquis de Croismare, that she will reveal who she is: "Why should he resolve to reshape my destiny without knowing who I am" (21). For Suzanne, her identity is not determined by her birth: a whole narrative is necessary to define it. Her identity results from the recollection of her individual story, and this story is precisely that of a fight against her destiny as a woman, against a destiny that condemns the illegitimate daughter to become a nun.

Suzanne dreads imprisonment in the convent less than the alienation for which the convent becomes the metaphor, namely, madness. Before discovering that the convent drives people mad, she feels no violent repulsion toward the monastic life, which the nuns at Sainte-Marie even make attractive to her by a "course of the most carefully calculated seduction": "There were times when I actually longed for the day when I should make the final sacrifice" (26). It is not life in the convent but a specific event that sets off her desperate struggle for liberty: a vision of a mad nun who has escaped from her cell. "She was all disheveled and half-naked, she was dragging iron chains, wild-eyed, tearing her hair and beating her breast. . . . She was . . . looking for a window to throw herself out of. I was seized with panic. . . ; seeing my own fate in that of this unhappy creature, and thereupon a vow was made in my heart that I would die a thousand deaths rather than expose myself to it" (27).

As Walter Rex observed in *The Attraction of the Contrary*, the vision of the mad nun is a fundamental scene.[7] This vision, in which Suzanne sees her own fate, makes her determined to fight the risk of madness by any means. What is this madness? It manifests itself through a bodily disorder that transgresses social norms ("all disheveled and half-naked"); through the wild eyes, which reveal the loss of the mind; and through the screams and the beating of oneself, which express an excessive suffering and a desire to kill oneself. This vision contains something excessive, dissolute, disordered, and animal-like that strikes Suzanne to the point that she recognizes herself in it, whereas her present condition is extremely far from it since the nuns in her first convent take good care of her. The mad nun in Sainte-Marie embodies the female fate Suzanne thereafter promises herself to escape. This fate is not merely the passive acceptance of social exclusion but also, most importantly, the disorder of the body, what Diderot calls "hysterism." In 1772, in a brief essay on women written as a review of and an answer to Mr. Thomas's cold and academic eulogy of women, Diderot describes the influence of the uterus on female temper: "Woman carries inside herself an organ susceptible of terrible spasms, commanding her and provoking ghosts of all kinds in her imagination."[8]

From the beginning to the end of La Religieuse all the women are hysterical.[9] As Robert Mauzi wrote in a preface to La Religieuse, the novel's three mother superiors, the mystical Mother de Moni, the sadistic Mother Sainte-Christine, and the sensual Mother Superior of Sainte-Eutrope, represent three figures of female hysteria.[10] Imprisonment inside the convent only strengthens what is, for Diderot, a main component of feminine nature. After the scene of the mad nun in Sainte-Marie the first case of hysteria involves Suzanne herself in the carriage where she sits with her mother when the latter brings her home after the scandal she deliberately provoked in the convent: "I flung myself at her feet and laid my head on her knees, saying nothing, but sobbing and gasping for breath. She pushed me away roughly. . . . My nose began to bleed, I nevertheless seized one of her hands and made it wet with mingled tears and blood as I kissed it" (34). Suzanne expresses an emotional demand through theatrical bodily signs—a liquid loss of tears and blood and an incapacity to utter articulated sounds.

This incapacity to express oneself through rational language, this shaking and flowing of a body that suddenly escapes the control of symbolic language, characterize the hysterical woman for Diderot. When the body speaks, it does so in an excessive, disordered, and violent manner that results in the fear and rejection by the person to whom the emotional demand has been addressed. Hysteria is not only linked to monastic life, for Suzanne's mother is also described in a similar state at the moment when she reproaches her daughter for being born: "Her expression hardened, her eyes began to blaze. . . ; she wanted to say something but could not frame the words for the quivering of her lips. She . . . buried her head in her hands to prevent my seeing the violent spasms shaking her. She remained . . . holding back the tears that were forcing themselves out of her eyes. Then she said: 'The monster!'" (40). We find once again the same signs—wild eyes, quivering of the lips, shaking of the body, tears, and incapacity to speak.

Upon learning the secret of her birth Suzanne discovers a division between two kinds of language. Her mother's physical disorder expresses not only a meaning but also a violent emotion. The mother does not simply tell her daughter that she is an adulterous child; she makes her guilty of her own crime: "Your sisters have by law a name you only have because of a crime" (41). But there exists another kind of language, which Suzanne heard just previously from her director, Father Séraphin. She does not give a physical description of Father Séraphin but merely reports his words: "Your mother . . . has asked me to tell you that you are not Monsieur Simonin's child. . . . Now look, Mademoiselle, just weigh everything up and decide whether your mother, with or without your father's consent, can treat you in the same way as children whose sister you are not" (36–37). Father Séraphin does not accuse Suzanne of her mother's crime; on the contrary, he emphasizes Suzanne's positive, mental qualities, which are her own: "You are sensible, you are intelligent and have reached an age when you can be trusted with a secret even if it didn't concern yourself" (36). Father Séraphin's language is rational, not emotional, and this rationality appears through his choice of verbs, *weigh up, decide, consider*, all of which appeal to Suzanne's rational judgment. If Suzanne finally seems to accept her fate as an illegitimate child, if she lets herself be taken to a second convent after causing a scandal to escape the first, it is only because she hears an appeal to her free faculty of judgment: "I know now, I know who I am, and it only remains for me to live as befits my state" (39). The words "I know who I am" [*Je me connais*] refer to her illegitimate birth; but what matters here is the use of the verb *to know* in the first person and in the reflexive mode (in French), which implies a personal intervention of her consciousness. In Sainte-Marie Suzanne resisted the nuns' insidious seduction with all her strength. She opposed her own "firmness" to the nuns' sweetness. Paradoxically, she shows the same firmness of mind when she accepts her return to a convent after examining the new data the priest exposed to her.

The Firm and the Soft

Throughout the novel we find two contrasting dimensions: on the one hand hysterical language, softness, seduction, tears, blood, everything that is sweet and soft and that flows; on the other hand rational language, firmness, toughness, rule, everything that resists and does not bend. The body yields, abandons itself, becomes soft, and lets itself be manipulated or seduced like an object, even outside an erotic context. Suzanne distrusts seduction long before her arrival at Sainte-Eutrope. She names "seduction" even the mystical impulse of the Mother de Moni, the only one whom she loves, because this impulse is expressed through corporal signs such as the sound of the voice, the face reflecting ecstasy, the transport of passion, and the sweet tears: "Yet her object was not seduction, but that is what she achieved" (47). Suzanne resists seduction even unwillingly. Her cold reasoning interrupts the mystical exchange between the Mother Superior and heaven. She distrusts any form of body language that escapes her control. The body is her enemy since by becoming weak to the point of fainting it takes away her self-awareness.

This is how Suzanne becomes a nun at Longchamps: "I had almost reached the state of an automaton. I saw nothing, but occasionally little convulsive shudders ran over me. . . . I was merely a puppet all through that morning which was non-existent in my life, for I never knew how long it lasted, what I did, or what I said" (51). Fainting means a deprivation of consciousness and mental faculties; what she experiences in this state is nonexistent for her since she has no conscious knowledge of it and no rational control over it. To believe that she took her vows, she needs to see written and verbal proof of it: "I asked if it was really true that I had made my profession. I wanted to see the signature with my own eyes, and the witness of the whole community" (52). Between the state of softness and fainting that allows the community to dispose of Suzanne and the madness of the Sainte-Marie nun there is only a difference of degree. Madness comes to women through their body. Suzanne never stops distrusting the body because it is the source of disorder, wandering, and loss of the self.

Throughout the novel Suzanne contrasts women's hysterical language, the emotional language that comes from the body, with another kind of language, men's rational and clear language, which is also that of the law. From M. Simonin to Father Lemoine, all male characters, be they severe or sensitive, represent reason, justice, and the law. They are all lawyers, judges, or directors of conscience: Monsieur Simonin, Suzanne's supposed father, and Monsieur Manouri, who takes care of her defense, are lawyers; Father Hébert is an ecclesiastic judge; Father Séraphin, Father Lemoine, and Father Morel are directors of conscience. Men exert their power through words, and not just any kind of words but words ruled by a code of either human or divine justice—the least subjective, passionate, and hysterical words. The men's words serve neither to conceal or express feelings, nor to calumniate arbitrarily, nor to seduce people but rather to articulate the law. So it is not by chance that Suzanne, when she addresses the Marquis de Croismare, always places him in the legal role of judge or witness, thus focusing on his judicial power and sense of legal propriety: "I appeal to your judgment as I appeal to the judgment of God" (52), "You know, sir," "You can judge," "You will notice." Suzanne pretends to appeal more to the Marquis's moral and intellectual judgment than to his senses and feelings.

Likewise, when she stages and describes her own body she surrounds this description with rhetorical precautions that allow her either to deduce rationally her beauty from other people's comments, as if they were testimonies in a trial, or to use her own body as the proof of the persecutions she had to endure: "I . . . threw myself at the feet of the Superior and the Archdeacon. 'Well,' he said, 'what is the matter?' Displaying my head bruised in several places, my bleeding feet, my livid and fleshless arms, my dirty and torn clothes, I said: 'You can see!'" (98). The verb *to see* used by Suzanne does not simply mean an act of sensual perception but also a judgment. Although the exhibition of her body could be considered a sort of hysterical seduction, it is important to note that Suzanne gives it a legal frame. Her body does not speak for Suzanne, but she speaks for her body. Her body does not scare her when she uses it as a symbolical language and thus reverses her physical weakness into a legal weapon and a proof of her right. Before this exhibition she is careful to warn her reader that the Archdeacon is not the kind of man to let himself be moved by the sight of a body precisely because he is impartial, "just and wise" (87). The body she presents to him is not a seductive image but a body of evidence that she uses in her trial against her natural fate. She controls her body with words.

Suzanne finds in the law an ally against hysterical alienation and arbitrary passions. She trusts the civil law when she decides to protest her vows; but she also trusts the religious law, all the rules that structure life in the convent. These rules are called the *Constitutions*. In the section of the memoirs that recounts Suzanne's life in the Longchamps convent legal vocabulary dominates. The nouns *proof, testimony, judgment,* and the verbs *to prove, to judge, to allege, to cite,* and *to attest* can be found on almost every page. All her acts are justified by her will to respect the rule of her religious order: "I read and reread our regulations and knew them by heart, so that if I was directed to do anything which was either not clearly set out therein or not there at all, or which seemed to contradict them, I refused absolutely, but took up the book and said: 'Here are the promises I made, and I made no others'" (56).

Suzanne memorizes the *Constitutions* governing life in the convent not because of her religious faith but in order to place herself on the side of the law and thus regain the right she lost due to her illegitimate birth. She uses a book written by men in order to resist the arbitrary orders of another woman. Suzanne's strong sense of lawfulness even allows her to act as lawyer for other nuns in the convent. The word *lawyer* is not used by Suzanne, but her actions remind us directly of this profession, which was that of her legal father, M. Simonin: "I appeared before them, defended myself and my companions, and not a single time was I found guilty, so careful was I to have right on my side" (56). The decision to protest her vows, which suddenly gives Suzanne a reason to live, confirms her will to place herself on the side of the law through a written text. The memoir she has to write for a lawyer allows her to exert her mental faculties and protects her against the madness that could result from persecution. Suzanne places herself "under the protection of the laws" (69). She then gains a very important freedom, that of consulting with judges or lawyers; in the name of the law, this right cannot be denied her.

From Sainte-Marie to Longchamps, the first part of the novel stresses Suzanne's firmness. At Sainte-Marie Suzanne provokes a scandal by saying with a "firm" voice, "No, Sir, no." At Longchamps she uses the convent's regulations to "firmly" refuse any act contradicting the rules. When the Archdeacon comes and questions her, she answers "firmly." The Archdeacon's voice is also "firm and tough." Firmness is a positive value that represents the opposite of passive submission and yielding to one's fate. Being firm means not yielding. Firmness is a sign of a fairness of the soul that allows Suzanne to act not only as a lawyer but also as a judge. This is why she can call a "pantomime [*une mômerie*] typical of the weird mentality of the Superior" the mortification she endures from Mother Sainte-Christine when the latter makes her lie in a coffin in the center of the choir (81). It is her firmness of character that allows her to call monastic life "a tissue of puerilities" that she despises (109) and to claim her rights: "I am warning you that if I am refused food I shall be forced to make my complaint to those who have taken me under their protection" (83). Being firm, she can resist the arbitrary authority of Mother Sainte-Christine, who orders her to swear that she used for her confession all the paper she asked for: "'Swear to me, on holy obedience, that all of it was used for writing out your confession, and that you have none left.' 'Reverend Mother, I repeat, the second thing being no more important than the first, I cannot swear'" (63). Firmness of character again appears as a moral quality when Suzanne uses the word to qualify the behavior of her only friend at Longchamps, Sainte-Ursule, when the latter refuses to lead the punished Suzanne by a rope: "She had the strength of character [*fermeté*] to go to the Superior and protests that she would rather face death than perform this unspeakable and cruel function" (111).

Her firmness reveals Suzanne's mental superiority over the "weak heads" of the superstitious nuns who are haunted by Satanic imagination: "Their troubled imagination saw me with a hideous face, they crossed themselves when they passed me and fled shrieking: 'Satan, get thee hence!'" (85). Suzanne's cold and firm voice denounces the superstition that reigns inside convents.

The Mother Superior and her accomplices have no power over this firm Suzanne. They can torture Suzanne's body, but her mind does not yield. Suzanne's first movement is to let her hysterical body speak: "My first instinct was to put an end to myself; I tried to throttle myself, I tore my clothes with my teeth, uttering fearful cries and howling like a wild animal" (65). When she expresses her desire to kill herself, her first movement is followed by a second movement that puts the narrator in control of herself once more: "My mind grew more collected, I was more myself" (60). The self is the rejection of hysteria and the return to reason; it is control. Even when she learns that she has lost the trial that was her only incentive, Suzanne does not yield to despair. Instead of reflecting the abnegation of her will, her deliberate submission to the rule and her acceptance of punishment only reinforce her alliance with the law, as the use of reflexive verbs shows: "They had cut me off from church, so I cut myself off from refectory and recreation" (106). Whereas Suzanne has lost hope of a legal liberation, she remains free inside the convent by applying the rule to herself: her submission is a form of resistance because it implies a self-determination over which arbitrary authority has no power.

With Suzanne Simonin, Diderot invents a female figure who is different from those in his essay *Sur les femmes*. Suzanne's greatest quality is a firmness she demonstrates in the domain of moral and legal judgment. Suzanne has no passion, she distrusts women who yield to their instinctive reactions, and she places herself deliberately on the side of the law. The "organ" she carries inside herself does not dispose of her. She claims to stand outside any strategies of seduction and addresses her reader as if he were a judge. For Suzanne, claiming liberty means not only protesting the vows but also fighting the hysterical body and imagination. In the first part of the novel Diderot seizes every opportunity to highlight his heroine's rational attitude: through her voice he denounces the convents' superstitions, cruelties, and childishness. In the part of the novel that describes Suzanne's life at Sainte-Marie and Longchamps her character is consistent with Diderot's ideological argument. Diderot uses Suzanne's "firm" character to reveal the perversion and alienation that result from being imprisoned inside a convent.

The "Animal Functions"

In a central passage of the novel, just before we learn that Suzanne has lost her trial, we hear a philosophical voice denouncing the inhumanity of an institution such as a convent:

It seems to me that in a properly governed state it should be the opposite: difficult to enter in religion but easy to come out. . . . Does God, who made man sociable, approve of his hiding himself away? Can God, who made man so inconstant and frail, authorize such rash vows? Can these vows, which run counter to our natural inclinations, ever be properly observed except by a few abnormal creatures in whom the seeds of passion are dried up, and whom we should rightly classify as freaks of nature [*monstres*]. . . ? Do all these lugubrious ceremonies . . . suspend the animal functions? . . . Where is it that nature, outraged at constraint for which she is not designed, breaks down the obstacles put in her way and in a frenzy of madness throws the working of our bodies into a disorganization beyond all curing? . . . A vow of chastity means promising God continual breaking of the wisest and most important of His laws, a vow of obedience means giving up man's inalienable prerogative, freedom. (101–3)

This passage is very important because it is almost the only one to clearly state the ideological project of the novel. The "satire of the convents" is accompanied by a strong denunciation of the injustice and above all the inhumanity of such institutions. The convent is inhuman because it is incompatible with what Diderot calls "the wisest and most important of His laws," which is neither a civil nor a religious law but the law of nature, stronger than any law written by men. Several expressions in this passage refer to this law: "natural inclinations," "the animal functions," "nature," and "the working of our bodies" [*l'économie animale*]. All these words belong to the same semantic group, that of the body and sexual need. In this context the "law" designates "the animal function" of human beings, that is, their sexual activity, whether for mere enjoyment or procreation (the text does not specify). The law of nature is defined in opposition to chastity and affirms the necessity of sexual pleasure. The word "God" here means nature, in Spinoza's sense of the word (*Deus sive natura*), that is, everything that exists in nature. Diderot is clear: the freedom he is speaking about is not an abstract freedom but a very concrete and physical one, the freedom to satisfy one's sexual instinct. In this passage we recognize ideas that Diderot develops in many other essays and dialogues, such as the article "Animal" in the *Encyclopédie*, *Le Supplément au Voyage de Bougainville*, and *Le Neveu de Rameau.* The words "inconstant," "passion," "nature," "animal functions," and "working of . . . bodies" are key in Diderot's vocabulary; they refer to human beings' natural inconstancy, which nullifies eternal promises. "Is there anything, indeed, that seems more insane to you than a precept that proscribes the change that is in us; . . . than an oath of immutability of two beings made of flesh, in front of a sky that is never the same, under caverns that threaten to collapse; at the bottom of a rock that becomes powder; at the foot of a tree that cracks; on a stone that is shaky?" Diderot writes in *Le Supplément au Voyage de Bougainville.*[11]

The religious institution is doubly antinatural: it requires making eternal vows and giving up "animal functions." The repression of "animal functions," that is, of sexual activity, leads either to madness or to a breaking of the vows. The nuns' cruelty and madness in *La Religieuse* is explained by the perturbation of their animal functions, of the "working of [their] bodies." The questions asked in this short ideological passage imply that the repression of sexual instinct naturally generates hysteria and madness.

Who is asking these questions? Because of a lack of punctuation, it is not clear whether Suzanne is speaking in this passage, as the words "it seems to me" (101) seem to indicate, or Manouri, as the words "went on Monsieur Manouri in his argument" (103) later point out. The editors of the text make an interpretive choice according to their placement of the quotation marks: Jacques and Anne-Marie Chouillet, for instance, put the quotation marks just before the expression "Il me semble": they clearly attribute the thoughts to Manouri, not Suzanne. Tancock, in contrast, using H. Bénac's edition, does not put quotation marks before the expression "it seems to me" and attributes the thoughts to Suzanne. In spite of the ambiguity due to the missing quotation marks, the content of the questions makes it impossible for it to be Suzanne's. It is not because, being young and a girl, she could not ask philosophical questions using Diderot's terminology but rather because this passage expresses a claim that cannot be Suzanne's. She is, indeed, continually suspicious of the body. The words "passion," "nature," "animal functions," and "working of our bodies" could have no meaning for her. Why does she want to break her vows and leave the convent? Because she wants to follow the "general inclination of nature" and explore "animal functions," knowing that chastity is a violation of the wisest and most important of God's laws?

If *La Religieuse* was simply, as Diderot stated in 1780, a "dreadful satire of convents," it would be logical to describe a heroine who was the prey of repressed desires, a heroine who could not stand the unnatural rule and chastity of the convent. But this is not the case: there is no better nun than Suzanne; and above all, she has no physical desire, not even in her imagination. All the novel's characters are struck by this fact, and their surprise shows that this is not a natural phenomenon. One after the other, they all try to make her confess a specific desire that would justify her disgust for religious life. There is none. Suzanne tells Ursule, a friend in whom she can confide fearlessly: "It will not be alleged about me, as it is about many others, that I am driven to abandon my state by an uncontrollable passion. I see nobody and know nobody" (70). In front of the suspicious Mother Sainte-Christine, Suzanne swears: "I call God to witness that my heart is innocent and no shameful sentiment has ever dwelt there" (76). "It is difficult to believe," the Mother Superior replies. Even Suzanne's lawyer, Manouri, ends up suspecting a "secret motive" that would allow him to understand Suzanne's grief at losing her trial: "'Madame, dare I ask you a question?' 'Do, Sir.' 'Could there be some secret reason for such over-whelming grief?' 'No, Sir'" (108). Father Hébert, the wise and impartial Archdeacon, also comes to suspect Suzanne and Manouri's relationship: "Whether Monsieur Hébert's distrust was directed at me or my benefactor, I was hurt" (120). The person who is most surprised is obviously the Mother Superior of Sainte-Eutrope, who cannot understand this silence of the "heart": "'So it isn't some passion, secret or disapproved of by your parents, which turned you against convents? Let me into the secret, I am indulgent.' 'Dear Mother, I have no secret of that kind to confide in you'" (144). Suzanne's purity seems inconceivable to the novel's other characters, who also acknowledge that she is a good nun. Ursule, Suzanne's only friend at Longchamps, tells her: "But it is incredible that you should have such distaste for a way of life the duties of which you carry out so easily and so scrupulously" (70). Mother Sainte-Christine, who does not like Suzanne, tells her exactly the same thing: "Nobody fulfils her duties better than you do" (76). This is a fact: Suzanne properly observes the vows she protests;

far from suffering from a rule that represses the freedom of her body, she uses this rule to protect herself from anyone desiring her inside the convent. This is clearly the case in the Sainte-Eutrope convent, where Suzanne keeps reminding the capricious Mother Superior of the rule: "Dear mother, I told her, that is forbidden" (150). Suzanne cannot be accused of breaking any rule. In the above passage, however, in which Diderot or Manouri denounces the inhumanity of the institution of the convent, he says that the vows can never "be properly observed except by a few abnormal creatures in whom the seeds of passion are dried up, and whom we should rightly classify as freaks of nature [*monstres*]." Should we conclude that Suzanne is a monster?[12]

This paradox could meet an immediate objection: one could say that Suzanne's purity is just one more argument in Diderot's satire of the convent. Since she has no desire, it becomes impossible to say that a dissolute passion leads her to demand freedom. As she keeps saying throughout her memoirs, she wants nothing but freedom: "All I ask is freedom" (78). Neither her body nor her sensibility has any part in this claim. Suzanne longs for an abstract freedom that will exist in total harmony with the law. Far from condemning, however, even dissolute passions, Diderot uses them as the best argument against convents. The questions quoted above reveal that the religious institution is inhuman and vicious precisely because it ignores "human nature," that is, the necessity of sexual pleasure, and forces human beings to practice a chastity such as that claimed by Suzanne. Such chastity and purity, Diderot tells us through his satire of convents, are impossible. They are not human but monstrous. There is therefore an inconsistency, if not a contradiction, between Diderot's ideological argument against convents and Suzanne's fight for a pure and abstract liberty.

This inconsistency becomes even stronger in the second part of the novel, after Suzanne loses her trial and is transferred to Sainte-Eutrope. Until then good and evil were clearly separate. Evil was on the side of the institution and of the nuns who let themselves be perverted; good was on the side of Suzanne, Sainte-Ursule, or the men—of those who, thanks to the firmness of their character, knew to resist perversion and to remain human. At Sainte-Eutrope the situation is far more complex: we cannot say that there is on the one hand a fair and saintly character who suffers and on the other an unjust and cruel character who torments the former. From being a persecuted victim, Suzanne unknowingly becomes a persecuting tormentor. The relation between Suzanne and the Mother Superior of Sainte-Eutrope is not a relationship of power but one of desire.

Innocence and Eroticism

Sainte-Eutrope is a place where the feminine nature rejected by Suzanne reigns. In her first description of the Mother Superior, Suzanne portrays her as an agitated, disordered, contradictory, capricious, unbalanced, inconsistent, and illogical woman. Like the Mother Superior, the convent is full of disorder: "Her ever-changing expression indicates the disconnectedness of her mind and all the instability of her character. And so order and disorder succeed each other in the convent" (122). Suzanne's first comment on Sainte-Eutrope is a judgment that condemns this disorder and reveals once again her own firmness and her love for order: "You are very ill at ease with women like that and never know what will please or displease them, what to avoid or do; nothing is stable" (123). Life at Sainte-Eutrope is unruly, and this lack of rule is expressed by sweetness: sweetness of the fruits, marzipans, and preserves the nuns eat, of the coffees they serve and the little visits they pay one another, of the time they spend chatting and playing music, of the tears they shed for Suzanne's stories, of their innocent caresses. Confronted by this unruly nature, Suzanne reacts exactly as she did at Longchamps: she protects herself with the rules, which are stated here by the director.

At Sainte-Eutrope as at Longchamps, Suzanne's attitude is characterized by her submission to the rule and to the men who issue the rule. The confessor's moral authority replaces that of the civil law. She tells him everything: "He did question me and I kept nothing back" (161). In the conflict between the Mother Superior's and the confessor's authority Suzanne chooses that of the Father, who views carnal pleasure as forbidden and calls the Mother Superior "a wicked nun, a pernicious woman," and "a corrupt soul" (162). Suzanne protects herself with her confessor's orders. But the meaning of her attitude has changed. At Longchamps she used her alliance with the rule to fight arbitrary orders. At Sainte-Eutrope she uses her submission to the rule only to preserve her innocence. In the new context of Sainte-Eutrope's eroticism Suzanne's relation to the law is as strong as ever, but it becomes passive. The dominant vocabulary is no longer that of proof and testimony but that of obedience and submission. The words *allowed, forbidden,* and *to order* can be found very often in this part of Suzanne's memoirs. Even eroticism belongs to the logic of hierarchical respect: "She invited me to kiss her forehead, cheeks, eyes, and mouth, and I *obeyed*" (137, my emphasis).

We find the word *innocent* in every scene at Sainte-Eutrope in which the body plays a role. Everything the Mother Superior asks from Suzanne is said to be "innocent," and the Mother Superior herself keeps calling Suzanne "innocent": "What innocence! ah, dear innocent child!" (138); "How innocent she is!" (146). Suzanne's innocence has been often discussed. Many critics have observed that such innocence was impossible at the time when the memoirs were written since we learn toward the end of Suzanne's narrative that she now understands the meaning of these acts. This innocence is also incompatible with the rational and intelligent character Diderot has portrayed until then. At Longchamps Suzanne was not entirely innocent since she was able to denounce the "suspicious intimacy" between some of the nuns and between Mother Sainte-Christine and a young priest: "The Superior went in for long and frequent interviews with a young priest, and I had discovered the reason and the pretext for these" (57). At Sainte-Eutrope Diderot suddenly deprives his heroine of the intuitive intelligence with which he endowed her at Longchamps, and he makes her blind to the most obvious signs. Whereas Suzanne's references at Longchamps to the other nuns' imbecility revealed her judgment, her firmness, and her vivacity of mind, the insistence on her innocence at Sainte-Eutrope makes her almost an imbecile.

In the second part of the novel Diderot clearly plays with his heroine: he uses her to transform his ideological critique of the convents into an erotic novel. And he transforms the reader into a voyeur.[13] Through Suzanne's "innocent" eyes he describes scenes of sapphic pleasure. The scenes narrated by Suzanne—her undressing by the Mother Superior, the piano lesson during which the Mother Superior puts her fingers on Suzanne's breast and faints, the scene in which Suzanne's docile kisses cause the Superior's orgasm, the scene in which the Mother Superior listens to

Suzanne narrating her torments, the scene in which she asks to share Suzanne's bed—all lead to the Mother Superior's sexual pleasure, which produce both the text's eroticism and the heroine's physical confusion: "I don't know what was going on inside me, I was afraid, my heart was thumping and I breathed with difficulty. . . . My strength had left me and I was about to swoon" (138). It has frequently been said that Suzanne's "innocence" is a rhetorical device and an erotic strategy that allow Diderot to describe sexual scenes in meticulous and almost clinical terms.[14] In the context of collective pleasure obtained at the expense of a friend's religious devotion it is clear that Suzanne's innocence aims to trap the Marquis de Croismare, who finds himself in the position of a voyeur and is forced to give Suzanne's technical descriptions the erotic meaning she persists in ignoring: "Truly that hare-brained woman was incredibly sensitive and had the most exquisite taste for music, for I have never known anybody on whom it had such an extraordinary effect" (135). The Marquis, and every reader after him, is thus confronted by his own knowledge of sexual acts, and by his own desire aroused by Suzanne's "innocent" description.

The Triangle of Desire, or the Failure of Words

Suzanne's innocence, however, is not only sexual: it is also a psychological ignorance. At Sainte-Eutrope she enters a triangular dynamics of desire. Suzanne is not alone in front of the Mother Superior's desire. Another character interferes, sister Sainte-Thérèse, who plays a main role in each of the scenes with the Mother Superior. The structure of these scenes is almost always the same: Suzanne obeys the Mother Superior's orders, which cause both characters' physical confusion, a confusion that is soon increased by the arrival of Thérèse, whose violence in turn produces Suzanne's wonder. Suzanne then questions herself about Thérèse's strange behavior and finds a plausible explanation: "It occurred to me that this girl was jealous of me and was afraid I would steal the place she occupied in the good graces and favor of the Superior" (131). She confronts Thérèse and tells her that she should not be jealous since she, Suzanne, will do nothing to deprive Thérèse of the Mother Superior's friendship: "You can be sure I shall never use the confidence she places in me except to make her cherish you more" (131). Thérèse's answer, which shows no gratefulness, surprises Suzanne even more: "But will that depend on you?"

This brief exchange, which contains the whole dynamics of desire taking place at Sainte-Eutrope, undoes the logic of the novel's first part. At Sainte-Marie and Longchamps, a persecuted Suzanne used the symbolic power of written and spoken words to fight female arbitrariness. At Sainte-Eutrope, when Suzanne faces Thérèse's visible suffering she uses the same rational method: she thinks that speaking out will help relieve Thérèse's irrational jealousy and suffering. Suzanne is not mistaken: Thérèse is jealous of her. Suzanne is wrong, however, not in her interpretation of Thérèse's attitude but in her faith in the power of words. Thérèse's answer—"But will that depend on you?"—is significant: it means that rational will has no power in the domain of desire. This simple question, which Suzanne answers with the words "Why not?" since she cannot understand it, suddenly brings another dimension to the novel, a truth of desire, over which words have no power. Suzanne can name and analyze the process of jealousy, but she cannot stop it with words because it does not takes place at the level of words. Words can describe desire, but they cannot regulate it. The best intention in the world can do nothing about it, as Thérèse is the first to acknowledge: "It isn't your fault. I know that perfectly well and tell myself so every minute" (131).

Whereas Suzanne, while claiming her innocence, remains in a Manichean system of good and evil that is ruled by moral and judicial law, Thérèse goes much further when she recognizes that what happens is not Suzanne's fault: she states a law of nature that reigns beyond and against words, inside and outside the convent. In the brief exchange between Suzanne and Thérèse something essential happens: Thérèse's silent sadness defeats the symbolic order, which was the stronger until that point. Thérèse's suffering reveals that the liberty Suzanne claims through knowledge of rules and a mastery of language is incommensurable with that other dimension that is beyond symbolic language and imposes its own law.

Suzanne understands what happens with Thérèse or with the Mother Superior only in a rational and deductive way. When the Mother Superior exclaims, "Ah! Sister Suzanne, you don't love me!," Suzanne answers, "I don't love you, dear Mother? . . . Tell me what I must do to prove it to you." "That you will have to guess," the Mother Superior replies, and Suzanne says, "I am trying, but I cannot think of anything" (137). Suzanne gives a judicial meaning to the verb *to prove*, which Diderot chose ironically because it belonged to the libertine vocabulary of the time: in Crébillon's and other erotic novels the expression *to prove one's love* refers to sexual acts.[15] For Suzanne, proof is only a legal concept and must be clearly and rationally defined: "Tell me what I must do." Suzanne has no intuitive understanding of things; she cannot "guess." She speaks the language of the law, an efficient language in which ideally one word should have only one meaning and present no problem of interpretation.

The second part of the novel reveals the failure of words and rational interpretation when confronted with the truth of the body. Even when she sees the physical symptoms of Thérèse's suffering Suzanne keeps trying to master violent feelings with words: "'What have you got to fear from me?' No answer. 'Can't the Reverend Mother love us both equally?'" (135). The law of religious life and of Christian love requires such an equality. Suzanne is surprised by Sainte-Thérèse's violent answer: "'No, no,' she angrily replied, 'that is impossible. Soon she will loathe me and I shall die of grief'" (135). Like all the other women in the novel, Thérèse is described by Suzanne as a hysterical woman: "It was that crazy Sainte-Thérèse, her clothes in disarray, her eyes wild. . . . Her lips trembled and she could not speak" (135). Clothes in disarray, wild eyes, trembling lips, and incapacity to speak—here again we find the symptoms characterizing madness, in the face of which Suzanne remains calm and rational.

Trying to understand Thérèse's hysterical violence, Suzanne interprets it as an effect of monastic life: "There you have the effect of segregation. Man is born for life in society; separate him, isolate him, and his ideas will go to pieces, his character will go sour, a hundred ridiculous affections will spring up in his heart, extravagant notions will take roots in his mind like tares in the wilderness" (136). This is a famous passage, often quoted as Diderot's indirect attack against Rousseau, who, around the same time, emphasized the virtues of solitude and criticized life in society. One can also see here an allusion to the choice of Croismare, who had left Paris for the remote countryside.

Taken out of its immediate context in the novel, this passage can certainly be read as a philosopher's satirical comment about another writer or a friend. But in its local context the meaning of this passage is very different. Suzanne uses the expressions "ridiculous affections" and "extravagant notions" to allude to Thérèse's violent declaration that the Mother Superior will loathe her and she will die of grief. Suzanne calls this declaration ridiculous and extravagant only because she does not understand the logic of desire; to the reader, who better understands Thérèse's suffering, her bitter declaration appears as psychological and sexual truth. No deliberate act can change the Mother Superior's desire. Desire may be made more intense by life in the convent, but it is not the result of this life. It is precisely to defend the law of desire or the "general inclination of nature" that Diderot attacks convents. The novel shows that Thérèse, and not Suzanne, is right: the tragic fate Thérèse predicted for herself will be both hers and the Mother Superior's: the latter dies of not being able to stand Suzanne's indifference.

What happens here is important: the ideological passage against the convent and the attack against Rousseauist misanthropy must be read as the psychological mistake of a heroine who, instead of understanding desire, tries to master the situation with a few general statements. This double meaning of the text reveals the ambiguity of Diderot's position and invites us to read the text carefully: general and abstract statements may just be based on a misreading of human reactions and a misunderstanding of emotional truth since a passage in which one is tempted to read an ideological message of the text also reveals the heroine's ignorance of the Other. The more the novel progresses towards the end, the more Suzanne's "innocence" appears as a denial and an ignorance of the Other. This ignorance has important moral consequences: it transforms the victim into a tormentor.

If Diderot expresses himself in the second part of the novel, it is much more through the Mother Superior of Sainte-Eutrope or Sister Sainte-Thérèse, who acknowledge that they cannot control their passions and who follow "the general inclination of nature" until they reach madness and death. Suzanne's first physical description of the Mother Superior reveals that she is a typical Diderotian type: "She is short and quite plump, yet quick and lively in her movements, her head is never held straight on her shoulders, there is always something wrong with her clothes. . . . Should she want to speak, she opens her mouth before sorting out her ideas" (121). Suzanne's description of the Superior has often been compared to two other well-known texts by Diderot: his description in his 11 August 1759 letter to Sophie Volland of Langres's inhabitants, which resembles a self-portrait; and his similar depiction of the nephew in *Le Neveu de Rameau*.[16] This familiar Diderotian type displays a mobility and sensibility expressed by the face and gestures, revealing a life that transcends any kind of order or rule.

From scene to scene, the relation between Suzanne and the Mother Superior evolves and regresses. Even though Suzanne's body expresses some confusion and at times her will abandons her, she keeps asserting her innocence and "firmly" refuses to understand what happens to her own body: "'If you wished, my dear child, I would make myself clearer.' 'No, dear Mother, no. I know nothing, and I would rather know nothing than acquire knowledge which might make me unhappier than I am now. I have no desires, and I don't want to discover any I couldn't satisfy'" (145). The more Suzanne refuses to know, the more the Superior's desire transforms itself into suffering and then into madness because of the impossibility of even having her desire understood, much less satisfied. The first signs of the Superior's madness are her loss of "gaiety, freshness, and sleep" and her wandering about the corridors at night (147). Finally, when the Superior takes it upon herself to clearly express what Suzanne should do to relieve her, Suzanne replies: "But, dear Mother, that is forbidden" (149). Suzanne uses the neutrality of the law to fight the subjectivity of desire.

The Truth of Madness

The Mother Superior's desire, despair, madness, and death imply the existence of a force surpassing her will, which she acknowledges with humility: "That is not my responsibility . . . I cannot see how this Father Lemoine of yours can see my damnation all signed and sealed in such a preference which is difficult to avoid" (167). [*Cela ne* depend *pas de moi . . . je ne conçois pas comment votre P. Lemoine voit ma damnation scellée dans une* partialité si naturelle *et dont il est difficile de se garantir* (185, my emphasis).] For the Mother Superior, lack of control is due to a "partialité si naturelle," and in these words uttered in a moment of intense suffering we recognize Diderot's argument against an institution that aspires to curb natural inclinations.

Whereas the Mother Superior becomes a more human character through her suffering and madness, proving that she is a passionate being (and therefore unable to stand monastic life), Suzanne regresses and becomes less and less human in her persistent denial of the body's language. The scene in which Suzanne is terrified by the Mother Superior at night reveals this regression, since she now yields to the very same terrors she was deriding at Longchamps: "The picture the confessor had shown me of her inflamed my imagination, and I trembled, dared not look at her for fear of seeing a hideous face enveloped in flames, and said within myself: Satana, vade retro, apage, Satana" (164). The young nuns at Longchamps were screaming: "Satan, get thee hence!" (85). Suzanne shouts at the Superior: "Get thee behind me, Satan!" (165). It is not mere coincidence that Diderot chooses the same words on both occasions. It shows that Suzanne rejects the Superior's pleas not because she is following her own rational principles and reflection but because she suddenly remembers the imaginary fears implanted in her by her confessor's warnings. That Suzanne uses the same exorcising formula as the superstitious nuns of Longchamps reflects the triumph of imagination that she has long dreaded as the first step toward madness. The passage from French to Latin indicates a regression and an even greater submission to the interdictions of the Church.

In front of a terrified Suzanne who yielded to imaginary fears, the Mother Superior, driven mad by love, now embodies reason: "What is upsetting you? Stop. I am not Satan, I am your Superior and your friend" (165). Reason is no longer contradictory to the body and its disorders; reason is now the humble expression of suffering. The truth of the text is on the side of the Mother Superior. Suzanne can only testify to this truth that she does not understand, which she names *égarement*.[17] The final images of the Mother Superior recall the vision of the mad nun that terrorized Suzanne at the beginning of the novel and made her determined to win her liberty by any means: "One morning she was found barefoot, in her nightgown, shrieking and foaming at the mouth, running round and round her cell with hands clapped over her ears, eyes shut and body pressed tight against the wall" (181). The novel ends shortly after these scenes and after we learn about the deaths of the Mother Superior and Thérèse. Suzanne's narrative ends with these descriptions; the remaining text is composed of fragments.

In the second part of the novel the subject is no longer Suzanne's fight against arbitrary passions and for her liberty. Now the subject is arbitrary passion, Thérèse's and the Mother Superior's suffering, madness as a sign of humanity, alienation as an opening of reason. We discover that Suzanne has gained only one kind of power by fighting for her liberty and innocence, the power to ignore and reject the Other, a power her inflexible mother possessed in the carriage. The last scene between the Mother Superior and Suzanne reproduces the initial scene between Suzanne and her mother, but with an inversion of roles. Suzanne described the scene in the carriage thus: "I flung myself at her feet and laid my head on her knees, saying nothing, but sobbing and gasping for breath. She pushed me away roughly" (34). Here is the final confrontation with the Mother Superior: "She stopped me and began looking at me without saying a word, and the tears ran down her face. . . . She was my Superior and here she was at my feet, her head was on my knee which she was grasping. . . . Some instinct of aversion made me go on" (170).

This final scene is a mirror image of the first scene. "She" takes the place of "I," and "I" the place of "she." The scene in the carriage, the only one in which Suzanne tries to initiate physical contact with another person and express herself through an instinctive movement of the body, not through rational words, functions in La Religieuse as a kind of primary scene.[18] The aversion that makes Suzanne turn from the Mother Superior is as irrational as the horror she inspired in her mother as a child born of carnal sin. The law of the body expresses itself through this aversion. So we understand that Suzanne, the rational and firm character created by Diderot, also is determined by imaginary fears that her reason does not control.

The end of Suzanne's memoirs is not complete, as if Diderot did not finish the novel. But the fragmentation does not result from a lack of completion: unlike the story of her fight for liberty and innocence, what Suzanne discovers outside the convent cannot be recounted in a linear narrative. Fragments reveal the triumph of the dimension denied by Suzanne, that of the body and of imagination. What is her first experience after escaping the convent? A sexual aggression: "So there I was on the way to Paris with a young Benedictine. I soon realized from the indecent tone he took with me and the liberties he indulged in that he was keeping none of the conditions which had been stipulated" (184). Although we do not know whether this young Benedictine is Father Morel, Suzanne's director, with whom she had a transparent relationship established by dialogue, we can assume that the conditions for the escape were stipulated by him, since Suzanne had had contact with no one else. Her flight from the convent does not bring Suzanne the ideal liberty she longed for, one that would protect her from losing her reason. On the contrary, it delivers her into the hands of a nature that she refuses to acknowledge and dreads: "Then I regretted leaving my cell and felt the full horror of my situation" (184). The pleasure of the body and the arbitrariness of passions reign outside the convent just as they do inside, but with less repression and therefore less perversity. The only difference is that Suzanne cannot say to the young Benedictine, as she did to the Mother Superior, "But it is forbidden." Words and right have no power against desire; only a physical fight will suffice, and a few words that do not even form a sentence are enough to describe this act: "Violent set-to between the cabby and the monk" (184).

Outside the convent, Suzanne also discovers that the convent has become inscribed in her body in spite of her. She repeats mechanically all the gestures of a nun: "I have become accustomed in the religious life to certain behavior which I go through automatically. For example, if a bell happens to ring I either make the sign of a cross or kneel down. If somebody knocks on the door I say *Ave*" (187). This automatism again reveals the power of the body. And having at last won the liberty she longed for, Suzanne uses it only to beg for the Marquis's protection: "My ambition is not great, I should like a post as a lady's maid or even an ordinary servant, so long as I could live in obscurity in a place in the depths of the country . . . just security, peace, bread, and water" (188). She asks for nothing that she did not already have in the convent. From within the convent she claims liberty; from the space of liberty she claims walls that will protect her from the world.

The short fragments at the end of Suzanne's narrative serve only to contradict the claims she has uttered throughout the novel and to reveal her fear of liberty, of nature, of the Other, and of herself. Even the postscript to her memoirs represents a strange regression, especially when compared with the claims of autonomy and innocence she makes throughout the novel: "Supposing the Marquis . . . were to persuade himself that I am addressing myself not to his charity but to his lust, what would he think of me? This thought worries me. In reality he would be quite mistaken if he ascribed to me in particular an instinct common to all my sex. I am a woman, and perhaps a bit coquettish, who can tell? But it is a result of our nature, and not of artifice on my part" (189).

This closing paragraph attributes to Suzanne the instinct she was lacking until now, that of her sex, and unexpectedly dooms her to her fate as a woman, the fate of nature. Her memoirs, which recount her fight for reason and justice, end with a series of questions in which she suddenly doubts her ability to know herself and exert rational self-control, accepting the ambiguity that comes from the body's obscure motivations. Her last words reduce her identity to the very essence she was denying: "I am a woman."

LA RELIGIEUSE is a perverse novel in the etymological sense of the word *perverse*, a novel that turns against its own premises. These premises took the form of struggles for liberty, both a judicial fight for civil liberty and a rational fight for mental freedom. In the first part of the novel, at Sainte-Marie and at Longchamps, madness represents the alienation Suzanne struggles against in order to preserve mental freedom. In the second part of the novel, at Sainte-Eutrope, madness becomes the figure for the truth: Thérèse's and the Mother Superior's suffering and death are truer than the innocence of Suzanne, whose only goal is to escape madness and desire. The second part of the novel reveals that there is no liberty outside the alienation of desire. It is impossible to be free without recognizing a fundamental absence of liberty and accepting the determinism of the body, that is, the arbitrariness of desire and the "partialité si naturelle." This arbitrariness depends neither on the Superior, nor on Thérèse, nor on Suzanne, and it leads to madness only when it is repressed and denied as it is by Suzanne.

The novel of persecuted innocence fighting for the triumph of truth becomes a novel of persecuting innocence fighting to deny truth. Suzanne's innocence makes her a monster, whereas Thérèse's jealousy and the Superior's madness prove their humanity.

This novel thus goes well beyond the joke played on a friend who retired from a life of pleasure or the ideological context of a "dreadful satire of convents." Neither simply playful nor ideological, but both at the same time, *La Religieuse* presents a metaphysical reflection on liberty. Through Suzanne's innocent cruelty, the novel criticizes the use of rationality against the body and reveals that there is no pure liberty. The novel undoes the dichotomy on which Suzanne's fight is based in the first part of the novel, between the firm mind on the one hand and the soft body on the other, between reason on the one hand and hysterical madness on the other. The second part of the novel shows that reason and the body cannot be opposed, for there is reason in madness. Hysterical pain and alienation express a reasonable claim: the necessity of satisfying the "general inclination of nature." At the very moment when the novel seems to become more playful and more erotic, when the Superior's "illness" is described in detail, it also becomes more serious and deeper, showing that the force that escapes reason is stronger and truer than that which remains under the illusory control of reason.

How should we read this reversal, this perversion of the novel? Does Suzanne's failure reveal the misogyny of Diderot, who forbids women to escape a female nature that dooms them to hysteria and passion? Even if Diderot attributes to women a fate determined by their bodies, or even more precisely, by an "organ susceptible of terrible spasms, commanding them and provoking ghosts of all kinds in their imagination," we should not speak of misogyny and thereby give a negative meaning to Diderot's definition of femininity.[19] Diderot praises women for being capable of violence and passion, which are beyond the rational limits that education and culture impose on men. Diderot shows the same enthusiasm for "female hysterism" as he does for imagination and the pleasure of fiction. In *La Religieuse* not only does the convent becomes the metaphor of madness, which in the end appears to be the only form of liberty, but women— all the hysterical mothers, daughters, and sisters—become the metaphor of the power of imagination, which reveals the deception, not of reason in itself, but of a pure reason detached from the interests of the body.

Diderot's materialist morals impregnated the non-Rousseauist final third of the eighteenth century. Such materialist thought is to be found in the final text examined in this book, Vivant Denon's *Point de lendemain* (*No Tomorrow*), written sixteen years later. In this short story, however, *libertinage* is more calculated. The heroine is not an innocent tormentor but a very clever manipulator, prefiguring Laclos's Mme de Merteuil and Sade's Juliette, and yet, as we shall see, she is a very decent woman.

Six

1777 ∾ Mme de T——, or Decency

No TOMORROW (*Point de lendemain*): the title seems to announce clearly the stakes of the story, an affair without sequel and without consequences. The story is narrated in the first person by the man who had the affair. The opening words could have begun some great love story, full of torments and switches: "I was desperately in love with the Comtesse de —; I was twenty years old and I was naive. She deceived me, I got angry, she left me. I was naive, I missed her. I was twenty years old, she forgave me, and, because I was twenty years old, because I was naive—still deceived, but no longer abandoned—I thought myself to be the best loved lover, and therefore the happiest of men."[1] On the sixth line, however, the narrative breaks away from the model of the romance novel to introduce another woman, the woman who will be the heroine of the story: "She was a friend of Mme de T——."

The rapid succession of verbs and the play of repetitions give this passage the rhythm of a ballet, transforming sentiment into a mechanical round dance. In five lines the narrator disposes of months of suffering and amorous joy. He then produces a sudden slowing of time and describes in detail one single night. This is the way *libertinage* proceeds: the senses, pleasure, and amusement—not sentiment—impose their rhythm.

One evening at the opera the narrator meets by chance Mme de T——, his mistress's friend. Mme de T—— abducts him. The narrator does not really dare to hope that this might be the beginning of an affair because he knows that Mme de T—— already has a lover and she is not a frivolous woman. In the carriage that takes them away from Paris he learns the reason

143

behind the mysterious abduction: Mme de T—— simply wants to avoid dining alone with her boring husband, whom she is going to meet that night for the first time in five years. After they dine with the husband, the husband goes to bed and Mme de T—— invites her young companion for a walk in the gardens. The walk leads to confidences, the confidences lead to kisses, the kisses to a quarrel, the quarrel to a greater intimacy, until finally they consummate their sacrifice to love in a garden pavilion. The night of pleasure, however, does not end here: Mme de T—— invites her lover to follow her to a little room in the castle that is full of erotic resources. They spend the rest of the night there. At dawn the young man leaves the chamber in a hurry, and just when he finds himself alone in the gardens, Mme de T——'s official lover, the Marquis, suddenly arrives. The Marquis reveals that his friend has been manipulated: Mme de T—— used him to make her husband believe that he, and not the Marquis, was her lover. Now that he has fulfilled his function, he can leave. The Marquis offers his coach and the narrator climbs in, concluding: "I looked hard for the moral of this whole adventure . . . and found none" [*et . . . je n'en trouvai point*] (747).

This brief, rapid story of a one-night seduction has recently attracted much critical attention in France. New editions targeting a nonacademic audience have been published.[2] In his recent novel *La Lenteur* (1995) Milan Kundera uses *Point de lendemain* to criticize the contemporary reality of speed and forgetfulness. Philippe Sollers, who had already mentioned the short story in his novel on Watteau, *La Fête à Venise*, in 1995 published a biography of Vivant Denon, *Le Cavalier du Louvre* (Denon founded the Louvre Museum), in which one chapter, entitled "Une Leçon de nuit" (A night lesson), is devoted to *Point de lendemain*. *Point de lendemain* becomes, then, the pretext for a contemporary debate about pleasure. The stakes of the debate may be represented as follows: what is the meaning of the story—the value one should give to the notion of pleasure and to what Kundera calls the "hedonist ideal of the enlightenment"?

However diverse the critics' commentaries, all agree on one point: *Point de lendemain* captures the essence of the art and spirit of eighteenth-century hedonist thought. They all stress the mastery of style and irony. Yet the general, critical view of *Point de lendemain* is that it is a wonderful but perfectly utopian dream of pleasure.[3] *Libertinage* may be a form of liberation, for and through pleasure, from moral and social norms and prejudices, but such a liberation, which can be easily conceived in the realm of fiction, is not possible in reality. This is an old idea in Western metaphysics and literature: that the reality principle and the pleasure principle are contradictory and the reality principle must necessarily triumph at last over the pleasure principle. Probably only in the eighteenth century, with its tradition of *libertinage*, has there been an attempt to reconcile them. But libertine novels themselves seem to prove the failure of this attempt since in almost all there is an unhappy ending and the libertine heroes recognize that they were mistaken.

Point de lendemain is an exception: there is no unhappy ending and the moment of pleasure has no bad consequences. This is possible, the critics say, only because *Point de lendemain* is unaware of the consequences of the event it narrates. Michel Delon writes that love in *Point de lendemain* "is reduced to a desire, and decency to a mundane code"; the story "tells of a happiness that is only the good health of youth."[4] The reduction expressed here twice ("is reduced," "is only") contains an implicit moral judgment: that once we grow up, we learn that human reality is not reducible to what we find in *Point de lendemain*; *libertinage*, which cares only about the body, seems to forget that man is not simply a pleasure machine. For Raymond Trousson, pleasure in *Point de lendemain* is only a "rampart against interior emptiness."[5] In *La Lenteur* Milan Kundera asks a series of questions about the hero: "How will he feel after he leaves the castle? What is he going to think about? About the pleasure he felt or his reputation as a fool? Will he feel a winner or a loser? Happy or unhappy? In other words: is it possible to live in and for pleasure and to be happy? Can the ideal of hedonism be realized?"[6]

Kundera concludes that the story's "hedonism" is "hopelessly utopian." This is also Kavanagh's judgment in his chapter on Vivant Denon, "Writing of No Consequence," in *Enlightenment and the Shadow of Chance*: "As the story of a moment defined as inconsequential, this text describes a utopia—the impossible dream of a moment cut off from past and future, of a now with no tomorrow to extend its implications beyond the present of the event's occurrence."[7] Kavanagh reads *Point de lendemain* as the utopian dream of a moment of pleasure lived outside reality and made possible only by forgetting responsibilities and the meaning of consequences that are imposed upon us by reality and by our relationship to time. Kavanagh wonders what is going to happen in the unwritten sequel of the story: he is certain that this night of pleasure will affect the relationship between Mme de T——— and her official lover, the Marquis. Both Kundera and Kavanagh wonder what is going to happen to the story's protagonists in the future and deny that this story could be a whole without sequel. They see it as an episode of a longer narrative such as, for instance, *Les Liaisons dangereuses*. If the sequel to the one-night affair were written, it would lead necessarily to the characters' unhappiness. It is in the name of the tomorrow that the critics condemn *Point de lendemain* as a utopia. Tomorrow becomes synonymous with reality. Pleasure, obviously, is also a reality. But reality here means our social, moral, and psychological existence, which implies duration, continuity, and consequences, whereas pleasure is experienced only in the moment.

This judgment that pleasure and reality are incompatible is the starting point for my analysis of the story. First, it is wrong to think that *Point de lendemain* is not concerned with the day after. The first proof is the title. A title that contains the word *lendemain*, meaning "tomorrow," even if only to deny this word, is obviously not ignorant of the *lendemain*. Likewise, a story that ends with the affirmation that there is *no moral* to the story is not ignorant of the moral. No tomorrow, no moral—a double denial frames the story. Furthermore, the story ends with the very word that begins the title, *point* ("Point de lendemain," "je n'en trouvai point"). As Philippe Sollers points out in *Le Cavalier du Louvre*, the word *point* can also signify an affirmation in the French verb *poindre*, meaning "to dawn," "to break through." *Point de lendemain*, which starts with a *point* and ends with a *point*, is clearly a story that defines its limits with precision.

Chance, or the Process of Seduction

Tomorrow: we see it dawn also at the end of the first paragraph, where the narrator writes that Mme de T——— "seemed to have some designs on me yet did not wish to compromise her dignity. As we shall see, Mme de T——— possessed certain principles of decency to which she was scrupulously attached" (732). We learn here two things about Mme de T———: that she had designs on the narrator but also "principles of decency." The word *design* (*projet*) belongs to the libertine vocabulary and designates the manifest intention to seduce. The *projet* is that which can be seen, that which is put forward, projected. Decency, on the contrary, consists in not showing, in not allowing to be seen. The word *decency* comes from the Latin *decet*, meaning "it is proper" or "it is advisable." Diderot and d'Alembert's *Encyclopédie* defines *decency* as "the conformity of exterior actions with the laws, customs, usage, spirit, mores, religion, point of honor, and prejudices of the society of which one is a member." In eighteenth-century society a woman was not to draw attention to herself; any commotion was sufficient to make her lose her reputation, that is to say, her social existence. If scandal is the ruin of women, decency is the primary condition of their existence. They are constrained to submit to the rules of society. In contrast, for men any infraction of the rule can represent a true feat of prowess, for this infraction is itself a part of the social code. The contrast between these two words, *projet* and *décence*—found at the end of the first paragraph in both versions of the text (1777 and 1812)—contains the seeds of *Point de lendemain*'s entire story.

The stakes are clearly posed: how will Mme de T—— retain her dignity, and how will she respect her principles of decency while realizing her "designs" on the young man? This is precisely the question of the day after: how will she be able to appear still worthy and decent on the day after? The word "decency" refers to the social reality Mme de T—— can never allow herself to forget. By mentioning Mme de T——'s decency in the first paragraph of the story, the text raises the question of the relation between pleasure and reality.

It also answers this question, in a sense, by making decency an object of derision. The adverb "scrupulously" and the ironic interpolation "as we shall see" [*comme on le verra*], which appear in both versions of the text, already lead us to expect a spectacle capable of compromising the dignity of Mme de T——.[8] Decency is furthermore subjected to ridicule at the beginning of the second paragraph. While the narrator awaits his mistress, the Countess, in his theater box, another woman cavalierly invites him to approach: "I heard someone calling from the adjacent box. Was it not the decent Mme de T—— again?" (732). The narrator uses the adjective "decent" in the manner of a Homeric epithet, as if decency were the essential quality defining the very being of Mme de T——. Yet this quality is essential only because it is the object of derision of the narration since it is clear that Mme de T—— is not decent in the moment when she cavalierly talks to the narrator, who is waiting for another woman. The narrator's ironic insistence on the decency of Mme de T—— echoes that of Meilcour at the end of Crébillon's *Les Égarements du coeur et de l'esprit*: "Thanks to the proprieties that Madame de Lursay observed so strictly, she dismissed me at last" (202). Propriety and decency, both pure forms of respect for social customs, are ridiculed as empty shells. Libertine fiction laughs at the expense of the superficial social convention of propriety or decency, which is shown to be only a hypocritical semblance. This is indeed what *Point de lendemain* does in its first part.

How can seduction be decent? The answer to this question is simple: by not being visible. After abducting her young companion, Mme de T—— never appears to be trying to seduce him. The young man is not very happy when Mme de T—— reveals that she only intends to use him to keep her company during an evening reunion with her husband. It would be difficult to imagine a less erotic end, and he responds indignantly: "You would have me believe that I'm of little consequence" (733). To be "of little consequence" means that one does not have the power to compromise a woman, undoubtedly because one does not have the power to seduce her. In the context of the story, the use of this expression therefore has two implications: one, that a seduction always has "consequences" since a seducer is someone "of consequence"; the other, that there is no risk whatsoever of an amorous seduction between Mme de T—— and her companion.

The first physical contact between them is attributed to chance: "The lurching of the carriage caused Mme de T——'s face to touch mine. At an unexpected jolt, she grasped my hand; and I, by the purest chance, caught hold of her in my arms" (733). Only the bumps in the road seem to produce this "unexpected jolt," "the purest chance." Mme de T——'s reaction is severe: she becomes angry and accuses the narrator of having "designs" on her. He denies and invokes chance: "Designs . . . on you . . . I wouldn't dream of it! You would see through me too easily. But mere chance, a surprise . . . that can be forgiven" (734).[9]

Chance plays a large role in the first part of the story. The promenade during which Mme de T—— and the narrator gain a more intimate knowledge of each other is an effect of chance in the sense that it does not follow a predetermined route but rather winds along the sinuosities of a terraced garden next to the banks of the Seine. The promenade is conducive to the exchange of confidences and naturally determines the posture of their bodies: "She had at first given me her arm, then that arm somehow or other entwined itself around me" (735). At the moment when the protagonists begin to tire, the chance of the promenade provides them with the opportunity to rest: "A grassy bank appeared before us; we sat down on it without changing position, and in this posture we began to sing the praises of trust" (388). Even kisses, one may say, are the result of chance. Such a suggestion may seem rather strange since it seems rather difficult to exchange a kiss just by chance. But there is nothing erotic about the first kiss Mme de T—— and the narrator exchange. It is a symbolic kiss that the young man asks of Mme de T—— so he will know that she has forgiven him for the scene in the carriage. She gives him the kiss to show that she is not frightened of him, not frightened of being seduced by him: "'I need to be sure that you forgive me.' 'And for that, I would have to. . . ?' 'Grant me, here, the kiss that chance . . .' 'Very well, you would be too proud of yourself if I refused. Your vanity would convince you I was afraid'" (735). This kiss of pardon apparently seeks to ward off the imposing threat of chance; it is a matter of showing that their will is stronger than the chance that surprised them in the carriage: however, despite their attempts to ward it off, chance ultimately prevails over their will. Something happens, indeed, that was not planned: "Kisses are like confidences: they attract each other, they accelerate each other, they excite each other. In fact, the first had been barely given when a second followed on its heels, and then another; their pace quickened, interrupting and then replacing the conversation. Soon they scarcely left us time to sigh" (735).

Kisses have their own logic, over which the human will has no power. Here again we find a theme recurrent throughout all the novels analyzed in this book: that the body has its own logic, which in some moments is stronger than any reasoning and any memory of the past. The narrator and Mme de T—— stop kissing as soon as they "hear the silence," as soon as they become aware of what is happening and can then regain control over themselves. Like the grass bank and the arm, kisses become the subjects of verbs.

This syntactical function attests to their autonomy from the persons who give and receive them. It is no longer even clear which kisses are at issue, those of Mme de T—— or of the narrator; it is kisses in general. The law of the kiss is that it must be followed by another kiss and that kissing cannot therefore be stopped by an exercise of the will.

Finally, it is also by chance that the seduction is able to come to its conclusion. While the two characters are lost in a conversation about the charms of confidence and sentiment (a subject Mme de T—— takes advantage of to criticize the narrator's mistress), chance comes along to distract them from their "metaphysical reasoning." Mme de T—— draws the narrator's attention to "a pavilion that had witnessed the sweetest of moments" (738). She expresses her regret at not having the key because she would have liked to show the beautiful furniture to her companion. But chance intervenes once again: "Still chatting, we approached the pavilion. It had been left open" (738). Not only is the pavilion found to be open but it acts according to its own law, as the carriage, the garden, the grass bank, and the kisses had previously. The pavilion's law is to be the place of love and thus to induce those who enter to fall in love: "This was love's sanctuary. It took possession of us: our knees buckled, our weakening arms intertwined, and, unable to hold each other up, we sank down onto a sofa that occupied a corner of the temple" (738).

The scenario is repeated each time: whenever an erotic, physical contact occurs between the two protagonists, it is attributed to chance or to a logic that escapes their will. Places, physical acts, and body parts ("this arm," "a bank," "kisses," "the pavilion") become the subjects of active reflexive verbs (*to intertwine, to appear, to attract, to accelerate, to excite, to have been left open, to take possession*). Each time, Mme de T——'s decency leads her to react to this chance and to resist the slippage toward seduction. But then another chance event occurs and makes her slip further. The insistence on chance is clearly too strong for the narrator's irony not to be perceived. This irony, which from the beginning of the story is aiming at "that decent Mme de T——" and her hypocritical respect for the social code, makes us understand that chance is Mme de T——'s method. Each instance of chance thus has a determined function: it allows the seduction process to progress while decency is preserved.

The contact in the carriage, for instance, has a determined function: it makes the seduction possible by reversing the relationship of power between the protagonists. Even though Mme de T——— seems angered by this chance event and her reaction seems to forbid any further physical contact between her and the narrator, it is precisely this reaction that renders further contact possible. When she slips out of his grasp and appeals to his sense of honor, she recognizes that he holds a power over her and grants him the margin of maneuver he needs in order not to be too intimidated by her and to seduce her. If there is one social rule of seduction in the eighteenth century, it is precisely that the woman cannot make all the moves, and particularly not the first physical gestures, without displaying a brazenness that would incite the scorn of men, as Mme de Senanges does in *Les Égarements du coeur et de l'esprit*.[10] Likewise, the pavilion found open by chance is encountered at the precise moment when the hero can no longer have any suspicion of indecency because carnal possession, as it has been prepared by Mme de T———, now has value only through the exaltation of sentiment, spoken in terms of the "soul," not the body. Before showing the pavilion to her companion, Mme de T——— has presented herself as a sincere and sensitive woman, unlike the narrator's mistress, whom she criticizes for being coquettish, clever, artful, and never true. The language of sentiment dissimulates the purpose of the seduction: "I could not make sense of what I was hearing. Once again, we were heading down the great path of sentiment, and from this vantage point it was impossible to foresee where our steps would lead" (738). Sentiment plays the same role as chance: it serves to hide the physical reality of pleasure behind a veil that preserves decency.

The hero, of course, does not know that he is being manipulated by Mme de T———. But the narrator does not let us be duped by her stratagems: "It was a masterful maneuver. I felt that a blindfold had just been lifted from my eyes, and I didn't see the new one with which it was replaced. My lover appeared to be the falsest of all women, and I believed to have found a sensitive soul" (737). The irony of the text is deployed in the gap between the naiveté of the hero, persuaded that he holds the most sensitive of beings, and the intelligence of the narrator, now rid of his illusions, who knows that he was actually blindfolded by Mme de T——— in the very moment when she appeared to reveal the truth to him.

In an epigraph to the second edition Vivant Denon borrows a sentence from Saint Paul's letters to the Corinthians (2 Cor. 3.6): "The letter kills, the spirit vivifies." This epigraph is the key to reading *Point de lendemain.* Denon is warning his readers that to read the text at face value would be to kill it. The "letter" of the story is chance, the autonomy of things and of bodies, sentiment—all the masks that protect decency by erasing the visibility of design (*projet*). The "spirit" of the story is the irony that identifies this chance as a pure convention and a necessary sacrifice to the conventions of society. Not only should the insistence on chance and the vocabulary of sentiment not be taken at face value but the narrator's irony serves to reveal that they are but masks hiding the only truth, namely, pleasure.

In pleasure itself, however, there is also a decency. In the pavilion Mme de T———'s will again seems to intervene only to slow down and stop the desire that imposes itself as if in spite of her: "Mme de T——— was trying to move away from me but kept coming back all the more tender" (738). Resistance is the necessary veil of decency that must cover pleasure. The scene is articulated in four phases: passion, remorse, tenderness, and a total giving over of oneself to the other. Decency in pleasure consists in giving a sentimental meaning to the physical act because here again sentiment helps to remove anything that might be too voluntary, too determined, too animal in the physical act. Mme de T——— alternately plays the roles of the fearful woman who resists, the afflicted woman who seeks consolation in the very source of her affliction, and finally the lover who abandons herself romantically, while the spiritual or metaphorical vocabulary ("soul," "happiness," "idol," "love," "flame") prevails over that of the body ("caresses," "kisses," "pleasure"). Each phase, however, leads to the same conclusion: physical pleasure shared by the lovers. Unlike resistance, affliction, and tenderness, the very moment of pleasure remains in a discreet silence. The first time, it is described as a meeting of the souls: "Our souls met and multiplied" (738). The second time, the metaphor is somewhat more physical, employing a martial cliché: "Both parties hasten to obtain a second victory in order to secure their conquest" (738). The third time, after a long description of the harmonious accord between sensuality and nature, the moment of *jouissance* remains hidden behind a discrete and modest silence, expressed only by the elliptical suspension points between a denied future—Mme de T———'s intent—and an accomplished past—the fact: "One will not yield. . . . One has yielded" (739).[11] The fourth time, silence, which this time is designated as such and is even ironically said to be "long" by the narrator, again serves to describe elliptically the moment of pleasure: "'No, never. . . .' And after a long silence: 'But you do then love me a lot!'" (740).[12]

Physical pleasure is never articulated in words. Words express only feelings. But the text clearly shows what words serve to hide and where they ultimately lead: ellipsis points and silences are stronger than social and sentimental words. Through this silence in the text the body speaks and unmasks codes. The narrator, indeed, does not allow us to forget the reality hidden behind the veil of decency. He punctuates the description of the sublime amorous moment with these words: "I beg the reader to remember that I was twenty years old" (740). These twenty years are not the same naive and sentimental twenty years evoked at the very beginning of the story but rather the age of virile energy, when one can prove one's love four times over without weariness or decline. By evoking his age, the narrator emphasizes the verisimilitude and the realism of his story, and this ironic aside to the reader recalls that it is a matter of physical pleasure and not sentiment. The narrator looks for the reader's complicity against "that decent Mme de T———," that is, against the hypocritical code of decency that he has been deriding since the beginning of the story.

The first episode in the story, from the encounter at the opera to the scene in the pavilion, takes place under the sign of decency, but only to emphasize ironically the contrast between a crude reality (carnal desire, one-night affairs, repeated *jouissance*) and the appearance behind which this reality is hidden because of social hypocrisy. In this first episode the text shows that what we usually call reality is nothing but a hypocritical appearance that serves to hide our true reality, that of our body.

The Secret Room: Desire and Artifice

The ironical denunciation of the hypocrisy of the social code is even stronger in the second episode, as it is spoken by Mme de T——— herself, who radically changes both her tone and her discourse. Whereas in the first half she was concerned for her dignity and did not tolerate her lover's suspicions, now that the plan has been realized she unmasks her true colors: "'What a delicious night we've just spent,' she said, 'all because of the attraction of pleasure, our guide and our excuse!'" (740). Whereas Mme de T——— previously perfectly dissimulated the means of the manipulation, she now undoes her work by replacing sensitivity, sentiment, and refinement with the reduction of desire to a crude mechanism and a refusal of all dimensions beyond the physical, as if, now that her design has been realized, she simply no longer needs the hypocrisy of the code. In the tradition of *libertinage*, she gives the hero a lesson in materialist philosophy after the act of love. She teaches him that as long as the public knows nothing about it, their night of pleasure does not create any bond, any engagement, between them. She analyzes the pleasure of love and "reduces it to its simplest form" (740). This reduction enchants the narrator: inspired by Mme de T———, he feels "a strong disposition for the love of freedom," for which he excuses himself to the reader: "We are such *machines* (and I blush at the idea) that, instead of all the delicacy that tormented me before the scene which just took place, I found myself at least half to blame for the boldness of her principles; I found them sublime" (740).

After her bold lecture Mme de T——— awakens the hero's curiosity about a chamber her husband had built before their marriage "to strengthen his affections" and "to stimulate his soul" (741). The young man is dying to discover this place full of artificial erotic resources, which he thinks, becoming aware of his own fatigue, that he will no doubt need: "I must confess that I didn't feel all the fervor, all the devotion necessary for visiting this new temple—but I was very curious. It was no longer Mme de T——— whom I desired, it was the little room" (741).

Here again we find words and ideas recurrent in the other novels analyzed in this book. The spring that Mme de T——— now touches in the narrator is "curiosity," as Manon does, but in a less calculated way, in des Grieux and the Man of Quality in *Manon Lescaut*. Curiosity is obviously an important feeling at this stage since the narrator mentions it three times: "Prompted by a violent feeling of curiosity I promised to be only what she would want me to be" (740). "Thus she gradually aroused my curiosity about the little room" (741). "I was very curious" (741). Curiosity replaces desire; it also awakens sexual desire, but one linked to circumstances and not to the person who is the object of desire. "Curiosity," therefore, like "*machines*," reminds us of the mechanical conception of desire that we also find in *Thérèse philosophe* and in Crébillon's novels. The phrase "we are such *machines*" has attracted perhaps the most attention from Vivant Denon's critics, as it seems to reveal the libertine conception of desire in *Point de lendemain*. The chamber episode would prove that libertine desire is independent of the individual and activated by artificial means. Such would be the work of reduction brought about by *Point de lendemain*: the story would show that decency and sentiment are but masks concealing desire and that desire itself is but a mechanical artifice acting independently of people. Just as the doctor-philosopher La Mettrie argued in his 1747 treatise *L'Homme-machine*, *Point de lendemain* would ultimately prove that man is nothing but a machine.

In the little room, decency is done away with once and for all. The chamber is the space of indecency on two accounts: first, because it is there that the mechanism of desire is unveiled, and second, because bodies and pleasures are there exposed in the full light of day. Before actually taking the narrator to the little room, Mme de T—— first exhibits it to him through speech. The chamber is the contrary of the pavilion: the latter is encountered by chance, whereas the former is the determined object of a precise and avowed quest that sacralizes the place as an object of mystery. The site itself takes the place of the female body: when the lovers arrive "at the door of the apartment housing that vaunted chamber" (741), Mme de T—— offers him access to the room as if to the most intimate, secret part of herself. "'Remember,' she said gravely, 'you are supposed never to have seen, never even suspected, the sanctuary you're about to enter'" (742). The mechanical process of desire is not only revealed but also transformed parodically into a sacred ritual: "All this was like an initiation rite" (742).

The chamber is the ultimate space of artifice. In the heart of the chateau, hidden between a bedroom and several corridors, it artificially reproduces an English-style garden: a mixture of nature and human melancholy, with its latticed porticoes ornamented with flowers, its statue of Amor handing out crowns of flowers, its incense burners, its trophies, its canopy, its garlands, its intertwined ciphers, its plush carpet imitating grass, its dark grotto, and its picturesque charm. There is an echo of *La Nouvelle Héloïse* when the narrator enters the chamber and expresses his rapture: "I was astonished, delighted, I no longer knew what became of me, and I began in good faith to believe in magic. The door closed again, and I could no longer tell from whence I had entered. All I could see now was a seamless, bird's view of a grove of trees which seemed to stand and rest on nothing" (742). Saint Preux's terms upon discovering Julie's garden are remarkably similar: "Seeing no door, it seemed as if I had dropped from the clouds. . . . Being seized with astonishment, and transported at so unexpected a sight, I remained motionless for some time."[13] Both texts express the same rapture and the same magical impression. Denon's echo, however, is parodic. In *La Nouvelle Héloïse* Saint-Preux's initial impression of enchantment is soon replaced by a lesson explaining how the enchantment is fabricated at little expense, a lesson in which we can read the process of sublimation at stake in the novel. In *Point de lendemain* the enchantment born of artifice acts immediately and mechanically on the body: it leads right away to physical pleasure.

Mirrors cover the interior walls of the chamber and transform it into "a vast cage of reflective glass" (397). Objects are "so artistically painted" on the surface of these mirrors that it is no longer possible to distinguish the real thing from its reflection or bodies from their image. What until now was hidden behind the veils of chance, sentimental parlance, and a moonless night is revealed, exposed, reflected, and multiplied, making impossible any distinction between reality and images. Pleasure is now born of this exposition, of this *projet*: "Desires are reproduced through their images" (743). Pleasure is not annulled; on the contrary, it is amplified by its reflection in the chamber's mirrors.

One could also call indecent, in the moral more than in the physical sense of the word, the incessant references Mme de T―― makes to her friend the Comtesse. Following the pavilion scene, she first excuses herself for the negative remarks her sentimental hypocrisy led her to make about the Comtesse: "I am angry, truly angry about what I said to you about the Comtesse" (740). But then, at the moment they enter the chamber, she suddenly decides to name the Comtesse, as if this name would stop the hero from entering: "'But your Comtesse . . .' she said, stopping. I was about to reply when the doors opened: my answer was interrupted by admiration" (742). By reminding the narrator of the infidelity he is committing she prevents him from forming any illusions about the nature of his sentiment: the excitement produced by the place is suddenly stronger than all love and all links with the past. Finally, after the two lovers' last experience of *jouissance* in the artificial grotto built inside the chamber, the name of the Comtesse once again crosses Mme de T——'s lips: "Well then! Will you ever love the Comtesse as much as you love me?" (743). This last question, and the use of the verb *to love*, should not mislead us: Mme de T—— is not trying to take her friend's place by stealing her lover, nor is she saying that one night of pleasure is enough to create a true relationship; rather, she is saying that a moment of pleasure can be stronger than love. Mme de T—— keeps proving the same point: that social, sentimental, or moral reality has absolutely no power in the *moment* of pleasure. We have seen this law applied in all the novels analyzed in this book. The meaning of the verb *to love* is very clear: it only refers to sexual pleasure, which is not even linked to people anymore since the chamber, and not Mme de T——, is the object of the hero's desire.

If the story stopped here, one might conclude that it was only a utopia. It would say very little about the relationship between reality and pleasure. It would make us laugh at the expense of decency, shown to be only a hypocritical semblance, and reveal that the truth is played out elsewhere, that the truth is that of the body, of the mechanical being of human nature. But finally, in spite of all its irony, it would end up recognizing that decency, that is, social appearance, still must be respected. The style remains decent, and the narrator, after his intense night of pleasure, must slip out of the chamber at dawn so that Mme de T——'s reputation will not be compromised.

Tomorrow

But the story does not end here. *Point de lendemain* does describe the morning after, in three phases. The first is the moment when the young man finds himself alone in the garden at dawn. He has the feeling that he is awakening from a dream and "truth" is entering his mind again. In this state of mind he immediately asks himself a question: "I had nothing more pressing to do at that moment than ask myself if I was the lover of the woman I had just left, and I was quite surprised to discover that I didn't know how to answer" (744). The young man does not ask himself whether he made love with Mme de T——: the word "lover," in the eighteenth-century sense, refers to their relationship in the future, to their official status in the social reality. He wonders what effect this night of pleasure will have on his life. He tries to interpret it, to give a definite meaning to it. He wonders whether Mme de T—— had already broken up with the Marquis and took him either to punish or to replace the Marquis. These questions indicate that the young man seems to have already forgotten Mme de T——'s philosophy lesson regarding pleasure. This scene shows that the desire for meaning is a fundamental impulse. As soon as the young hero leaves Mme de T——, he immediately wonders about the meaning of the night, that is, about the consequences. Vivant Denon clearly acknowledges that every moment of pleasure has consequences in reality, even if only through the questions and doubts it generates in the protagonist's mind. Social, moral, and sentimental reality prevails over physical reality: we cannot live moments of pleasure entirely cut off from the rest of time and the rest of our existence since a single act immediately leads to the question of its meaning.

The young man does not have to find the answer to this question thanks to the arrival of the Marquis, Mme de T——'s official lover, who explains that this marvelous night was simply a comedy organized by Mme de T—— and the Marquis in order to fool the husband by directing his suspicions to the wrong lover. The Marquis asks the hero: "Did you play your part well? Did her husband find your arrival ridiculous? When is she sending you back? . . . Mme de T—— needed a squire, and you served as one for her, you entertained her on the way here; that was all she wanted" (744). The suspected young man will leave and the Marquis will stay and be happy with Mme de T—— in her husband's castle. Decency is safe. One could conclude that here again social reality prevails over physical reality. The night of pleasure is finally nothing but a veil preserving decency; a decent woman cannot openly introduce her lover in her husband's house. Mme de T—— uses the narrator to keep her love with the Marquis within the frame of decency.

Yet the narrator is not completely fooled since he keeps a certitude, that of physical pleasure. In spite of his surprise, the narrator knows that he too duped the Marquis, who ignores how his mistress and his friend spent the night together and brags about Mme de T——'s faithfulness to him: "I have molded her character to the point where there is perhaps no other woman in Paris whose faithfulness can be relied upon so completely" (745). "Excellent!" the narrator replies, and the reader cannot help laughing. One could say that sensual pleasure is the only reality that escapes the comedy. But the scene becomes even more ambiguous when the Marquis declares that the only flaw he sees in Mme de T—— is her physical insensibility: "Between you and me, I know of only one failing in her, which is that nature, though it gave her everything, refused her that divine flame which is the highest blessing. She inspires everything, causing all sorts of feelings, and yet she herself feels nothing. She's made of stone" (745). What are we to believe? Does Mme de T—— feign her frigidity to preserve the space of her pleasures? Or does she discover pleasure by chance, during that unexpected night? Or, finally, has she faked pleasure in order to better fool the narrator? The text makes us ask these questions but provides no answer; it leaves the choice of a response to us. Again, if the story ended here, the relation between pleasure and reality would not be clear, and one would not know which reality had triumphed over the other—that of physical pleasure or that of the social code?

The scene that brings together Mme de T—— and her two lovers is the true conclusion of the story, and the true "tomorrow," since this is the only scene that takes place after one of the night protagonists, Mme de T——, has slept and awakened. It is much awaited because the narrator introduces it with these words: "I nonetheless wanted to see Mme de T—— again: it was a pleasure [*une jouissance*] I couldn't deny myself" (746). The word *jouissance* is not without a sadistic connotation in this context and makes us expect a final scene of confrontation in which the young man will expose the manipulative Mme de T——, express his anger at being fooled, or at the very least take pleasure in her uneasiness, since it is not pleasant for anyone to learn of being duped. In *Les Liaisons dangereuses* the revelation of Mme de Merteuil's manipulations leads to the novel's catastrophic end: all the men who have been her lovers and her dupes—Valmont, Danceny, Prévan—want to take revenge on her, and the war and the loss of control that ensues result from Mme de Merteuil's excessive control. What is the result of Mme de T——'s manipulation in *Point de lendemain*?

The only feeling the narrator expresses in this final scene, paradoxically, is admiration: "We found ourselves all together [*en situation*]. M. de T——— had ridiculed and then dismissed me; my friend the Marquis was duping the husband and mocking me; I was paying him back in kind, all the while admiring Mme de T———, who was making fools of us all, without losing any of her dignity" (402). Not only does the narrator still admire Mme de T——— but what he admires in her is not her intelligence, her mastery of the game, or her talent as an actress but that she wages everything "without losing any of her dignity." What matters here is the link between the notions of the game and of dignity. The narrator admires Mme de T———'s dignity, which, as we learned in the first paragraph of the novel, is tied to decency. But is this decency, which the narrator never ceased to deride, from the moment of the encounter at the opera until the episode in the chamber, not definitively compromised by the elapsed night and the revelation of the comedy?

The notion of decency appeared twice just before. The Marquis used it first: "In all decency, we should begin with the husband" (400). Here "decency" has a purely social use: custom has it that the guest pays homage to the man of the house before addressing his wife. This use thus serves a comical end since it totally contradicts the reality of the situation—that of the body—since the two men who are preparing to respect decency by greeting the husband first are the same men who make a cuckold of him. We thus recognize here the decency derided by the narrator at the beginning of the story, a perfectly hypocritical social mask without any connection to the reality of human relationships.

The second use of the notion of decency is more significant, for it is the narrator who uses it in describing Mme de T———: "She spoke tenderly to him, and honestly and *decently* [*décemment*] to me" (401). In both versions of the text the word *decently* is italicized. In the eighteenth century italics were not used, as they are today, to draw the reader's attention to a word but to signal a quote; it seems that the narrator here is quoting himself and reminding the reader of his two previous uses of the word *decency* to characterize Mme de T——— at the beginning of the story. The two men—the official lover and the one-night lover, both deceived by Mme de T———, who used one of them to fool the other—find themselves at the head of her bed when she awakens. The hero knows why Mme de T—— is still asleep at such a late hour, and we cannot help but laugh at this statement by the Marquis, ridiculed and deceived: "Oh, everyone would agree that you are unrivaled in putting a woman to sleep" (746). This is the first moment that the narrator sees Mme de T—— after having learned that what he believed to be a night of such intense love was in fact only a premeditated comedy. He is curious to see how Mme de T—— will face this delicate situation, in which her secret is in the hands of a man who could potentially betray her. She addresses the tenderest of words to the Marquis; indeed, there could be no more natural reaction to the arrival of a lover whom one is happy to see. To the narrator, in contrast, she speaks "honestly and decently."

Her word "honestly" [*honnête*] must be understood in its seventeenth-century sense, as in the expression *honnête homme*, which designates the *gentilhomme* and not simply the honest man. Thus, "honestly" here does not have a moral implication but signifies, rather, "conforming to the norms of the good society." It indicates that Mme de T—— makes herself appear polite and courteous to the narrator, addressing him with the same words used by all good hostesses and all women who have received some gracious service. Does not her word "decently" have the same signification? As we saw at the beginning of the chapter, what is decent is also socially proper. Then why the redundancy? Why would Vivant Denon, whose style has "the precision of a scalpel,"[14] use two words to say the same thing? Should we interpret "decently" in a more modern sense, as the contrary of indecently? But clearly, in the presence of her lover the Marquis, Mme de T—— could not address the narrator with indecent allusions to the pleasures of the elapsed night. Why does the narrator specify that she spoke to him "decently"? If the word did not play an important role here, it would not be emphasized in italics.

In order to fully understand the word we must read it in context. Just before its appearance the narrator writes: "She laughed about it with me as much as was necessary to console me, and without lowering herself in my esteem" (747). Mme de T—— makes her laughter proportionate to the situation, to the states of mind of the two men at the head of her bed. She laughs with the Marquis out of politeness, but she moderates her laughter and puts a stop to the Marquis's laughter out of respect for the man she deceived: "'Come, Monsieur,' said Mme de T———, 'let's speak no more of it, and simply trust that I feel everything I should feel toward Monsieur'" (747). In the course of this brief scene decency is redefined: it is no longer only the mundane code, the hypocritical mask derided by the narrator; it now comes to designate a sense of the measure that allows one to accomplish exactly the gestures adequate to the situation at hand.

We now understand that it was thanks to her decency that Mme de T——— avoided the two pitfalls of the day after, the love that prolongs the moment of pleasure and the contempt that results from pleasure too easily given. She avoided contempt in the first part of the story by respecting the appearances of chance and of sentiment. She avoided love in the second part through her philosophy of pleasure and, above all, through the episode in the chamber. It is worth rereading Mme de T———'s speech when she first piques the hero's curiosity about the chamber. We understand retrospectively that each word is situational, that is, adapted to the situation at hand. Mme de T———'s affected cynicism is adapted to a determined end: to sever, without sadness, the romantic bond produced by the pavilion scene. Mme de T———'s chattering on about this and that, reported in direct discourse on the following page, serves the same end; all of her remarks are directed at making the narrator leave without causing him any suffering and without provoking any resentment by wounding the young man's pride. She insists that she succumbed so quickly that he could not possibly love her in return; she recalls the ill humor of her husband, which will have to be appeased by his leaving early in the morning after having so fully deceived him. The allusions to the chamber at this particular moment intervene only to sweeten the bitter truth that they must break off their relations: "'Do you remember how Monsieur looked this evening when he left us? . . .' She saw the impression these last words made on me, and immediately added: 'He was more lighthearted when he was so carefully arranging the little room I mentioned to you a short time ago'" (741). The chamber episode serves both to compensate the young man's necessary departure, discretely demanded by Mme de T———, and to undo the relation created between the protagonists in consummating their physical desires. Indeed, the hero's fatigue itself, which he insists upon, most likely plays a role in Mme de T———'s strategy, especially if we recall what Mme de Merteuil teaches us in *Les Liaisons dangereuses*, namely, that there is no better resource than fatigue from an excess of love to rid oneself of a tender and burdening lover.[15]

The chamber episode may well represent an excess, but this excess is in fact not excessive per se precisely because it serves a determined end: to give the hero everything so that he will no longer have anything to desire and hence will leave of his own accord. It is a measured, calculated excess. The excess Mme de T——— commits, which one might have interpreted as an act of indecency, is thus a decent act in the etymological sense of the word, already discussed above: it is an act that is proper or advisable in the present situation. The act is convenient or suitable not simply because it shows respect for social graces but because it is a skillful adaptation to a psychologically delicate situation. If the narrator admires Mme de T——— from the beginning of the story to its conclusion, it is precisely because she knows how to adapt herself remarkably well to all the nuances and complexities of the situation. If the narrator admires Mme de T——— at the end of the story, if *Point de lendemain* does not transform itself into a war as *Les Liaisons dangereuses* does, if this is a complete story and not simply an episode that should be integrated into a longer narrative, it is because of Mme de T———'s decency and the narrator's admiration for her: he senses all the subtleties of her behavior.[16]

Decency, at the end of the story, is not a purely social quality in the mundane sense of the word but, rather, a psychological and intersubjective one. It is a question not simply of following social graces but of displaying a perceptive acuity that allows one to measure one's actions and control their effects on the other, even when these actions are the most intimate and therefore the least social. Why does Mme de T——— remain so dignified? Because even while deceiving all the men around her she respects all of them by treating each according to his particular situation, that is, according to the social and intimate role he plays in relation to her. To her husband she gives the social appearance of respectability as well as the satisfaction of believing that he has chased away the lover, thus casting him in the role of the authoritarian and dignified husband. To her lover she offers tenderness and the happiness of believing himself to be her sole beloved, the only one capable of capturing her heart, and all the more assured of her fidelity in that he believes her to be frigid and thus uniquely susceptible to a sentimental attachment. To the narrator, finally, she gives her complicity, the pleasure of a night without consequence, and the acknowledgment of the power he holds over her, even though she had so fully manipulated him. "Good-bye, again. You are so charming. . . . Don't give the Countess cause to quarrel with me" (747). These final words of Mme de T———, recalling the existence of the Countess so perfidiously criticized by her and so perfectly forgotten by her lover, give an active role to the narrator: the absence of all consequences—such as a quarrel with the Countess—now depends only on him.[17]

In its social sense decency was only a hypocritical veil masking the truth, that is, a physical reality. At the end of the story, in its new use of the concept of decency, the text reconciles appearance and reality, social and physical reality. Redefined as the subtle adequation to a delicate situation, an intersubjective quality and a science of nuance, decency is reality itself, both moral and physical; there is no more contradiction between these two dimensions.

THE narrator's irony has shifted by the end of the story: it is no longer directed at Mme de T———'s mundane hypocrisy or the illusions of his own youth but, rather, at the reader's own expectation of a moral to the story: "I stepped into the carriage awaiting me. I looked hard for the moral of this whole adventure . . . and found none" (747). The three dots preceding the concluding words ironically evoke the three dots used in the story to designate elliptically the carnal act, which stylistic decency forbid him from naming. It derides the reader's desire to know the moral of the story as if this desire itself were voyeuristic.

The narrator's use of the word "moral" at the end is ambiguous. On the one hand, it echoes Mme de T———'s order to the narrator at the very outset—"Oh, no moralizing, I beg you!" (733)—and thus reminds the reader that moralizing is boring. But the word also refers to the meaning of the story, without moral connotation. In that sense there is no story without some sort of moral; it is obvious that the absence of a moral, and even more so the announced rejection of morals, does indeed represent a moral.

What is meant by this ironic allusion to the absence of moral on which the story ends?

It signifies that the very utterance of the moral (or of the *meaning* of the story) would itself be indecent. To draw the conclusion of the story would be to lack subtlety and levity. In the desire for meaning and interpretation there is a heaviness that would be indecent in a story about pleasure. It is this heaviness that the narrator shows when he first finds himself alone in the garden at dawn and wonders whether he is the lover of the woman he has just left. He needs to label the events that just took place; without labels, he does not know how to think about them. It is this heaviness that the official lover also shows when he proclaims proudly to have had some difficulty in capturing the heart of Mme de T—— and declares her only failing to be her frigidity. In comparison with Mme de T——, the two lovers of the story are equally ridiculous, the one who laughs secretly just as much as the one who wants to force the other to laugh: "Oh, what a fine adventure! But I fear you're not laughing about it enough for my taste. Don't you see just how comical your role is?" (400).

This speech by the Marquis is a direct echo of the famous scene in *L'École des femmes* in which Horace, the young lover, informs Arnolphe, the old fogy, of the trick the *ingénue* Agnès just played on him. Having discovered his pupil's deception and the failure of all his precautions, Arnolphe is not able to laugh as Horace encourages him to ("Vous n'en riez pas assez, à mon avis").[18] Thus, the end of *L'École des femmes* consecrates the triumph of love and youth. The end of *Point de lendemain*, however, does not lead to such a clear moral. It is much more subtle: there is neither a young lover nor an old fogy, nor is there an essence to the story. There are only *situations* in which decency, as a mark of humanity and a sense of negotiation, regulates the relations between beings and allows desire to be deployed without causing any harm. Whether proceeding by allusions or by light or skillful brushes of skin or of vanity, decency implies a subtlety that contrasts with the weightiness of sentiment, bodies, and meaning.

By its irony the text teaches us a lesson. It is this lesson that allows us to speak of an ethics of pleasure, in both senses of the word *ethics*, as a science of morality and an art of determining conduct. *Point de lendemain* does not simply enhance pleasure as a value at the expanse of any other reality, and it is therefore not a utopia. To be perfect, the moment of pleasure must not only be chosen but also constructed through a rigorous process that does not allow for error. The story teaches us a lesson in decency, and decency transforms pleasure into an art that goes beyond a merely mechanical conception of pleasure. The narrator's final admiration for Mme de T——— reveals another kind of decency, not the hypocritical veil covering the reality of that which decency forbids us from seeing laid bare but the perception of all the nuances of a situation, which allows one to adapt to it with subtlety and delicacy, and the understanding that we all exist only *en situation*, almost in the Sartrean sense of the word, that is, in the present moment and in relation to others.

Decency could also be given another name, *tact*. In French, tact is defined, first, as the "intuitive, spontaneous and delicate appreciation of what it is suitable to say, to do or to avoid in human relations" (*Petit Robert*). Tact, in that sense, is primarily a social quality and probably the main quality of a good *salonnière* in the eighteenth century. Tact, however, also signifies the sense of touch. *Point de lendemain* gives us a lesson in tact in all the senses of the word: the tactile quality of skins that have loved each other and given each other pleasure; the tact of Mme de T——— with regard to the susceptibilities of man, which must be treated with care; and finally the tact of the story's narration, which delivers its lesson with an ironic levity while seeming not to touch on any moral at all.

Conclusion

P LAYFULNESS, ambiguity, strategies of deception, and irony, all embodied by female characters, rather than a common theme or subject, bring together the works analyzed in this book. Each contains what the heroine of a 1788 pornographic novel, Nerciat's *Le Doctorat impromptu*, calls "a slap . . . to the sublime Platonism."[1] From Watteau to Vivant Denon, we notice a progression from an ambivalent acceptance of pleasure, to a cynical observation of the contradiction between noble feelings or principles and physical reality, to an unequivocal praise of the human qualities associated with pleasure. All these works, however, deliver essentially the same anti-idealist message, which runs counter to the Platonic and Cartesian tradition and constructs, against the true, a truth of appearances, surfaces, and simulacra.

In *Le Pélerinage à l'île de Cythère* the resistance to interpretation confronts the viewers with their own incapacity to escape the dichotomy that contrasts the superficial with the profound, the frivolous with the melancholic, the immanent with the transcendent. Watteau's work, which is at the origin of the new category *fête galante*, opens a space of ambiguity that will be explored throughout the eighteenth century in paintings and in novels. Watteau's modernity—the discrepancy in his work between word and image, thoroughly analyzed by Norman Bryson—is not only esthetic but also ethical: as the questions Watteau's paintings purposely inspire in the viewers remain unanswered, *Le Pélerinage à l'île de Cythère* and *Embarquement pour Cythère* teach them to accept ambiguity and the contradiction between interpretations.

In *Manon Lescaut* the masculine, moral, and noble framing of the narrative seems to repress pleasure: not only is Manon, the woman of pleasure, sent to America to preserve the son's honor and the father's name but she is accused by des Grieux of causing all his misfortunes. Yet *Manon Lescaut* reveals the inconsistency in keeping the privilege of sublime sentiments while yielding to curiosity and to the pleasure of displaying one's grief in a story, a pleasure of the imagination allegorized by Manon.

The title, preface, and plot of *Les Égarements du coeur et de l'esprit* lead readers to expect the young hero's deviations (*égarements*) to end: he should be, by the end of the story, "restored to himself," all the more since after meeting Hortense de Théville he discovers the distinction between the "true" sentiment she inspires in him and his superficial desire for a lady of the world, Mme de Lursay, who then comes to embody vanity. The novel, however, builds this moral and sentimental expectation only to deprive readers of the resolution: the story ends with Meilcour enjoying physical pleasure in Mme de Lursay's arms and sadly remembering his love for Hortense. The ironical ending of this "incomplete" novel indicates that no dialectical process can resolve the contradictions of the self in the "moment."

In *Thérèse philosophe* the heroine narrates her sexual adventures in order to show her readers how rational principles brought her happiness. Philosophy is enhanced as a tool of self-knowledge and self-control that allows women to defend themselves against potential abusers. But the novel reveals that enlightened philosophy has little power against the mechanical law of desire. The mimetic effect of voyeurism, described at length in the novel, not only creates funny scenes but also reveals the body's mechanical power. The novel, then, mocks the rational optimism of the Enlightenment as naïve by demonstrating that the power of the image, which is always associated with the feminine, is stronger than philosophy and reason. Thérèse embodies a reason that ends up acknowledging that reason, as *motivation*, is simply another name for desire. As *rational knowledge*, it can enlighten but not determine us.

In *La Religieuse* Suzanne's belief in a pure liberty, that of the mind freed from the interests of the body, transforms her into both an erotic bait and a tormentor. After establishing a clear distinction between the law and impartiality on the one hand and the body, nature, passion, partiality, and hysteria on the other hand, the novel changes the meaning of the word *law*: from a rule made of transparent words and established by men, it comes to mean the "animal functions" of human beings, their sexual instinct, which must be satisfied if they are not monsters. Suzanne, then, who desires nothing but liberty and who embodies an abstract conception of freedom, appears in the end less human than the Mother Superior of Sainte-Eutrope, who dies of madness and a frustrated desire for Suzanne. The novel thus reveals that liberty lies in accepting rather than denying the body's needs, or nature's partiality.

In *Point de lendemain* the narrator's irony attacks moral and social prejudices against pleasure. At the beginning the narrator mocks the "decent" Mme de T———: *decency* is an empty word, a mere veil that hides the "reality," the pleasure of the body. By the end, however, the narrator's irony is directed no longer at the *decent* Mme de T——— but at the reader, who is expecting "the moral of the story." The narrator's final and surprising admiration for Mme de T——— indicates that *Point de lendemain* should not be read as if it were just an episode of *Les Liaisons dangereuses*—a one-night affair that would have consequences if only the sequel were written. In *Point de lendemain* the absence of consequences is not a utopia but a reality, depending on a very important intersubjective quality, namely, decency. By the end of the story decency is redefined and the narrator's irony teaches readers a lesson in decency.

These works' pragmatic and anti-idealist message is sure to encounter resistance from the reader. Hence their ironic tone, which I emphasize in every chapter. Instead of affirming what they have to say, these works content themselves with letting the reader guess their message or even go so far as to set a trap and disappoint the reader's moral or sentimental expectations. This trap is evident in the conclusion of *Point de lendemain*, where the ellipsis in the last sentence addresses and mocks the reader: "I looked hard for the moral of this whole adventure . . . and found none."[2]

Their ironic address to the reader, or viewer, is a common element of all the works examined here. This irony appears most often in the breach between what the text makes its readers expect and what it ends up presenting to them, by denying them the meaning or the moral lesson for which they were rightly hoping. The text plays with its readers, as the painting plays with its viewers, and both create between them and their readers, or viewers, a dialogic exchange. Irony opens a space for ambiguous reception that is also a space for play, for resistance as well as dialogue. It permits these texts and paintings to transcend their immediate cultural context and to address us today. It is this irony that assures the works their modernity and makes them "classics."

Libertine irony is not Voltairian irony, a polemical irony that is used as an offensive weapon against the enemies of the "outside" and leads the combat of reason against the irrational.[3] Nor is it Baudelairean irony, the Romantic irony of the nineteenth century, in which the spirit attempts to establish a separate domain. It is, rather, an irony that affirms the impossibility of the autonomy of the spirit, an irony directed against the moral and metaphysical impulse, which is always privileged over that other dimension, denied and repressed: pleasure.

Irony affects the twentieth-century reader or viewer in much the same way it affected those of the eighteenth century, as if the resistance to finite conceptions of man were the same in the twentieth and eighteenth centuries and as if metaphysical aspirations were indeed atemporal. The works analyzed in this book mock and frustrate the reader's desire for morals and metaphysics. They show that this desire is ignorant of reality. They redefine reality, a reality that is both that of the body and that of the soul, a complex and subtle reality, full of unresolvable contradictions. Libertine painters and novelists contrast the metaphysical model of a dialectical process leading to the resolution of contradictions with a model that I characterize as one of alternation. This model proposes a self that is constituted by contradictions, so that superficiality is compatible with profound thoughts and ephemeral desires are compatible with lasting sentiments. Libertine novelists observe this psychological reality without making any moral comment.[4] But why are libertine works so anti-idealist? Why do they refuse to acknowledge that man's desire for transcendence and his willingness to sacrifice himself to greater causes such as Love, Liberty, or Reason are certainly his best, most noble instincts?

Libertine novelists do not reject the hierarchy of moral values. Their ambition is to remind us that we are not made of one piece and that man has a strong tendency to forget about the lower part of himself as soon as he is no longer in the "moment." Libertine novelists therefore try to establish a more proper balance. As the desire for transcendence has always been enhanced as the essence of humanity, and the pleasure instinct always criticized and repressed, libertine novelists, who are paradoxical moralists, show that "humanity" is as much in the body as it is in the soul.[5]

It is therefore in the name of reality that libertine works deride true and great sentiments. Their psychological model makes these works modern: their modernity consists in acknowledging the power of the image, of the surface of things. This power of the image limits rationality; one "moment" is enough to transgress suddenly one's established principles. This moment, in Crébillon's sense, can be caused by a pleasure of the senses or a pleasure of vanity. The strength of the moment often is not recognized. One often believes one's actions to be determined by purely abstracts motivations, when in fact one obeys simply the mechanical law of pleasure. This is the argument made by all the works analyzed in this book, with an evolution throughout the century: in *Manon Lescaut* the pleasure instinct is still criticized in spite of its real effect; in Crébillon's novels it is fully acknowledged; in *Point de lendemain* it is already more calculated.

These works, however, are not merely ironical and do not simply mock the metaphysical aspirations of their readers and viewers. There is another reason why they establish a psychological model that they consider more realistic: this psychological model allows them to teach readers tolerance. This is why I speak of an "ethics of pleasure." Pleasure has an ethical value. In that sense pleasure is on the side of reason. The acceptance of one's own pleasure or of the Other's pleasure as a fact of life appeals to a notion of common sense that favors tolerance and rejects any kind of extremism, any fanaticism, be it religious, rational, or sentimental.[6] Pleasure opposes reason only when reason claims to impose itself as a law and thus becomes extreme, fanatic, and, indeed, unreasonable.

These libertine works, then, show a use of reason that is in contrast to the idea that one hears more and more today concerning the Enlightenment and the reign of Reason. This idea is that of the tyranny of reason, which one holds responsible for all the evils of technocratic Western countries.[7] Without engaging in this political debate, this book aims to show that libertine works defined reason in a more subtle way than is usually recognized: reason, in the fiction of the Enlightenment, consists in adapting and proportioning thought, as well as acts, to a complex and contradictory reality, and not in adapting reality to a logical system of thought. Watteau's paintings; Prévost's, Crébillon's, and Diderot's novels; Denon's story; and *Thérèse philosophe* suggest that the old dichotomy between reason and the body, reason and sensation, reason and passion, reason and madness, is not valid. They seek to articulate a reason of the body, of passion, of sensation, and of madness. The ethics of pleasure shows that recognizing ironically the limits of one's own rationality is still the best use of reason.

NOTES

INTRODUCTION

1. On eroticism and eighteenth-century art, see Cryle, *Geometry in the Boudoir*; Posner, *Watteau: A Lady*; Sheriff, *Fragonard*; Sollers, *Les Surprises*; Stewart, *Engraven Desire*; and Wagner, *Erotica*.

2. *Libertinage* covers a long period of time and a wide range of works. The word *libertinage* comes from the Latin word *libertinus*, which, in the Roman republic referred to a specific social category, that of emancipated slaves, who did not yet have the rights of citizens. The concept of *libertinage* developed in the seventeenth century as a philosophical reaction against religious dogmas and refers to philosophers and writers such as Gassendi, Naudé, Théophile de Viau. In the eighteenth century the word *libertine* had a more worldly meaning, designating a "free" way of living, a transgression of moral and sentimental codes. In novels, from Richardson's *Clarissa* to Sade's *L'Histoire de Juliette*, the libertine character, or "rake," is usually the one who plots seduction and betrayal, for no other purpose than the pleasure of his performance. In the history of literature the category "libertine novels" designates works that represent seduction from the point of view of the libertine character, not of the victim (see Cazenobe, *Le Système*. Cazenobe coins the term *intentional libertinage* to designate the desire to control the process of seduction).

3. See Saint-Amand, *Séduire ou la passion des Lumières*.

4. Crébillon, *Les Égarements du coeur et de l'esprit*, 4.

5. On *roués* and *petit-maîtres*, or "dangerous men," see Michel Feher, "Libertinisms"; and idem, "A Woman's Liberties," introduction to *Dangerous Liaisons*, in *Libertine Reader*, 912–34.

6. Robert Darnton insists on the historicity of eroticism: what seemed erotic or comic in the eighteenth century does not seem so today (see his *Forbidden Bestsellers* and "Sex for Thought").

7. Several authors have shown the link between the seventeenth-century social concept of pleasure and literary texts or artistic works (see Brooks, *Novel of Wordliness*; Sheriff, *Fragonard*; and Vidal, *Watteau's Painted Conversations*). On the art of conversation, see Fumaroli, "La Conversation au XVIIe siècle."

8. Barthes, *Pleasure of the Text*, 53.

9. In his *Traité des sensations* Condillac argues that touch, and not sight, is the most important of the senses, the one that informs the others. Sight had always been considered the most spiritual sense in the tradition of Western metaphysics.

10. According to Lanson, the eighteenth century was a century of ideas, and not of literature: "One puts intelligence everywhere, and one imagines that it is enough for everything. Language, which is no longer used by artists, . . . becomes absolutely intellectual. It expresses nothing concrete or natural" (*Histoire de la littérature française*, 625, my translation. Where not otherwise noted, translations are my own). Lanson's acknowledgment that the eighteenth century was the century of reason contains an implicit criticism of reason: "Reason . . . becomes universal judge: no more domain of faith reserved, untouchable" (625). Lanson's view of the eighteenth century contains an ideology of literature. To be truly "literary," literature must be, in Lanson's view, full of feeling, that is, of spirituality (629). Lanson praises Rousseau over Voltaire: "I am . . . struck by what is excellent, deep and true in his work, and mostly by what it keeps lively and current, which interests our souls to the bottom. Voltaire touches us less deeply" (792).

11. Immanuel Kant, "Analytic of the Sublime," in *Critique of Judgement*, 110.

12. "We call sublime [that] which is absolutely great" (ibid., 106). "If we call anything not only great, but absolutely great in every point of view (great beyond all comparison), i.d. sublime, we soon see that it is not permissible to seek for an adequate standard of this outside itself, but merely in itself. . . . It follows hence that the sublime is not to be sought in the things of nature, but only in our ideas. . . . Because there is in our imagination a striving towards infinite progress, and in our Reason a claim for absolute totality, regarded as a real Idea, therefore this very inadequateness for that Idea is our faculty for estimating the magnitude of things of sense, excites in us the feeling of a supersensible faculty" (109). "In the immensity of nature, and in the inadequacy of our faculties for adopting a standard proportionate to the esthetical estimation of the magnitude of its realm, we find our own limitation; although at the same time in our rational faculty we find a different, non-sensuous standard, which has that infinity itself under it as a unit, and in comparison with which everything in nature is small. Thus in our mind we find a superiority to nature even in its immensity" (125).

13. Casanova, *Histoire de ma vie*, 1:618, my translation.

14. See Kavanagh, *Esthetics*. Kavanagh starts his book by arguing "for the importance to Enlightenment culture, to its tensions, contradictions, and achieve-

ments, of a new sense of existence within a present freed from the weight of past and future" (1).

15. On the concept of energy and its role in the literature, philosophy, and science of the French Enlightenment, see Delon, *L'Idée d'énergie*.

16. On the observance of reality and the absence of moral judgments in eighteenth-century novels, see Bennington, *Sententiousness and the Novel*. Bennington focuses on the social rather than the physical aspect of reality.

17. *Histoire de Dom Bougre*, 137.

18. Marivaux, *Up from the Country*, 42.

19. See Showalter, *Evolution of the French Novel*.

20. See May, *Le Dilemme du roman au XVIIIe siècle*.

21. See Diderot, *Sur les femmes*; Marivaux, *Oeuvres de jeunesse*; and idem, "Lettre sur les habitants de Paris," in *Journaux et Oeuvres diverses*, 28. In his preface to *Les Aventures de *** ou les effets surprenants de la sympathie* Marivaux portrays the lady to whom the fictive author of the *Aventures* addresses his novel. This portrayal allows him to sketch the profile of his ideal reader: "He wrote these same adventures for this lady he loved. She had refined taste; . . . she was born, like all the fair sex, with this inner feeling which is almost always as noble as it is tender, and which alone judges sanely whether movements given to the heart are true or false." The same weakness that traditionally depreciates women as readers and literary judges, that is, their lack of education, now becomes their main quality as readers: for Marivaux, women are good judges by reason of their instinctive "inner feeling," which is "independent from the sterile laws of art." Women are thus considered the best literary critics, whose true criteria of value or pleasure are the very proof of the pedants' bad judgment: "The secret pleasure they will have reading will be the truest proof of our scholars' little knowledge and bad taste" ("Avis de l'auteur des *Aventures de ****," 5; see also Cusset, "L'Adresse au lecteur").

22. See Démoris, *Le Roman à la première personne*; and Russo, *First-Person Narratives*.

23. Nerciat, *Le Diable au corps*, 98. An 1800 pornographic novel, *L'Enfant du bordel*, starts with this strong statement: "The magnate's as the cobbler's son are the result of a kick with the ass, and some people who are on a throne were born from the lackeys who serve them" (19).

24. This "attraction of the contrary" is Rex's thesis (see Rex, *Attraction of the Contrary*). Pleasure also can lead to social promotion (see Huet, *Le Héros*).

25. Two contemporary critics, Anne Deneys-Tuney in France and Thomas Kavanagh in the United States, insist on the role of the unforeseen, or the incalculable, which one calls the body and the other calls chance (see Deneys-Tuney, *Ecritures du corps*; and Kavanagh, *Enlightenment*).

26. Prévost, *Manon Lescaut*, trans. Tancock, 4.

27. See Lenglet-Dufresnoy, *De l'usage des romans*; and Diderot, *Eloge de Richardson*:

"By a novel we meant until today a tissue of fanciful and frivolous events, whose reading was dangerous for taste and morals. I would like us to find another name for Richardson's works, which elevate the mind, which touch the soul, which breath everywhere love of the good, and which are also called novels" (192).

28. On the link between the rise of the novel and subjectivity, see Benrekassa, *Fables de la personne*.

29. A short pamphlet by Boudier de Villemert summarizing this claim specific to the eighteenth century is polemically entitled *Apologie de la frivolité* (In defense of frivolity).

30. Nietszche, *Human, All Too Human*, 94.

31. See Marivaux, *Up from the Country*, 131.

32. On *Les Liaisons dangereuses* and the relationship between libertinage and love, see Cusset, *Libertinage and Modernity*, introduction.

33. On Restif, See Porter, *Restif's Novels*.

34. See Miller, *French Dressing*. On "feminine writing" and feminine authorship, see DeJean, *Tender Geographies*; Didier, *L'Écriture-femme*; and Trousson, *Les Romancières du grand siècle*.

1. 1717: Cythère, or Ambiguity

1. His friend and biographer Caylus tells us that Watteau was a brilliant, talented copyist with a good sense of humor, who one day dazzled his boss by perfectly reproducing a painting of an old woman reading by the Flemish painter Gerard Dou—a painting now at the Hermitage in Saint Petersburg—without even having the original before his eyes (see Caylus, *Life of Antoine Watteau*).

2. See Ségolène Bergeon and Lola Faillant-Dumas, "The Restoration of the *Pilgrimage to the Island of Cythera*," in Morgan Grasselli and Rosenberg, *Watteau, 1684–1721*, 460–64.

3. "That vivacity . . . may be inspired by an eager need to transfer at once to the canvas some effect conceived in the imagination. It was a need that seized him at times, but it was less compelling than his pleasure in drawing. The exercice of drawing had infinite charms for him and although sometimes the figure on which he happened to be at work was not a study undertaken with any particular purpose in view, he had the greatest imaginable difficulty in tearing himself away from it" (Caylus, *Life of Antoine Watteau*, 25).

4. I was quite pleased to see that my analysis of Watteau's *Le Pélerinage* was very similar to Kavanagh's reading of Watteau in *The Esthetics of the Moment* when we had not read each other. I completed this chapter on Watteau in 1995, and Kavanagh's book was published in 1996, when I was out of the country. My first article on Watteau also came out in 1996. This similarity of interpretations seems to confirm

the validity of our readings, unless it simply means that we both underwent the same influence. Bryson's *Word and Image*, however, a major inspiration for me in this chapter, is not quoted by Thomas Kavanagh.

5. See Bryson, *Word and Image*, 58–88.

6. Watteau's representation of Cythera has cultural, social, and theatrical origins, as several critics have recently shown. Watteau probably knew quite well many short plays—called *parades*—shown at fairs like the fair at Saint-Germain, which staged pilgrimages to Cythera and became increasingly popular after the exile of the Italian Comedians in 1697. It is probable that these plays, written by Fuzelier, Charpentier, and Letellier, influenced Watteau by adding a satirical and comic dimension to the courtly myth of Cythera. Watteau's representation of Cythera, then, cannot be dissociated from the sense of theatricality and foolery that was quite strong among both the lower classes and aristocrats in the early eighteenth century. Cythera is also reminiscent of leisure, practiced as an art by early eighteenth-century aristocrats, who used gardens as theatrical settings where they could play and converse without paying any real attention to nature (see Démoris, "Les Fêtes galantes"; François Moureau, "Watteau in His Time," in Morgan Grasselli and Rosenberg, *Watteau, 1684–1721*; and Tomlinson, *La Fête galante*).

7. Cythera is an island, and Elysium a garden, but I am using the word *garden* in the eighteenth-century sense of a "place artistically planted either for our needs or for our pleasures" (Diderot and d'Alembert, *Encyclopédie*, s.v. "jardin"). Watteau represents an urban garden, not a wild island, as Horace Walpole noticed in 1771: "Watteau's trees are copied from those of the Tuileries and villas near Paris; a strange scene to study nature in!" (Rosenberg, *Vies anciennes*, 102). On the other hand, Elysium is first described by Saint Preux as an enchanted island. Thus, Cythera and Elysium are both at the same time island and garden.

8. On the notion of allegory about Julie's garden, see Paul de Man, "The Rhetoric of Temporality," in De Man, *Blindness and Insight*, 187–228.

9. *Le Pélerinage à l'île de Cythère* is at the origin of the category of the *fête galante* and inspired many followers. Saint Preux's description of Elysium in *La Nouvelle Héloïse* reflects a new relation to nature that was often theorized in treatises on gardens in the last third of the 18th century, such as Jean-Marie Morel's *Théorie des jardins* (1776), Claude-Henri Watelet's *Essai sur les jardins* (1774), and Girardin's well-known *Promenade ou itinéraire des jardins d'Ermenonville* (1788), often confused with Rousseau's own views on gardens.

Julie, ou la nouvelle Héloïse not only inspired a new fashion in gardens but also transformed sensibilities in the last third of the eighteenth century. This novel had a huge cultural impact on late-eighteenth-century society (see Labrosse, *Lire au XVIIIe siècle*).

10. Derrida, after Lévi-Strauss, uses Rousseau's work to ground his analysis of the distinction between written and spoken word and between nature and culture (see Derrida, *De la grammatologie*).

11. See Crow, "Codes of Silence" and *Painters and Public Life*.

12. See Lamblin, *Peinture et temps*.

13. See Barthes, *L'Obvie et l'obtus*; Diderot, *Selections: Diderot on Art*, vol. 2; and Kavanagh, *Esthetics of the Moment*.

14. Two recent studies propose to go beyond the traditional opposition between word and image (see Bal, *Reading Rembrandt*; and Miller, *Illustration*).

15. See Rousseau, *Julie, ou la nouvelle Héloïse*, 2:132. Page references, hereafter given in the text, are to William Kenrick's translation, *Eloisa, or a Series of Original Letters*, in 2 volumes. The letter on Elysium, letter 130, is in vol. 2, pp. 131–63. When Kenrick's translation is not close enough to the French text for the purpose of my analysis, I provide my own translation and do not give page numbers. A new translation of Rousseau's novel was published after I completed this chapter: *Julie, or the New Heloïse*, trans. Stewart and Vaché.

16. We also often find the verb *to form* (*former*) in Saint Preux's description. The frequent use of this verb shows that the mental pleasure of understanding rational cause by analyzing confused sensation soon replaces the sensual pleasure of seeing a beautiful and magic place: "Then it was I first discovered, not without astonishment, that this verdant and bushy umbrage, which had deceived me so much at a distance, *was formed* by these luxuriant and creeping plants" (136, my emphasis); "The same streams running at proper distances . . . *form* a kind of artificial springs" (138, my emphasis).

17. Arabesques play an important role in Watteau's paintings. Thomas Crow reminds us that Watteau was a student of Claude Audran III, *concierge* at the Luxembourg Palace and a master in arabesques and ornamental forms, around 1707 (see Crow, *Painters and Public Life*, 59).

18. "Ce qui les constitue en *parerga*, ce n'est pas simplement leur extériorité de surplus, c'est le lien structurel interne qui les rive au manque à l'intérieur même de l'*ergon*. Et ce manque serait constitutif de l'unité même de l'*ergon*" (Derrida, *Vérité en peinture*, 69).

19. Posner, *Antoine Watteau*, 192.

20. On Watteau's models, see Posner, *Antoine Watteau*.

21. Mary Vidal, for instance, although her close reading is very precise, does not mention this element in her discussion of the painting because she focuses on social relationships (see Vidal, *Watteau's Painted Conversations*).

22. On this movement of reaction against rococo painting and theatricality, see Fried, *Absorption and Theatricality*.

23. From Théophile Gautier to Théodore de Banville the same reversal occurs: Watteau's paintings express melancholy because they represent a dream the viewer-

poet cannot reach: "Je m'en allais l'âme triste et ravie;—En regardant j'avais compris cela:—Que j'étais prêt du rêve de ma vie,—que mon bonheur était enfermé là," Gautier writes in his poem "Watteau" in 1835. Verlaine writes in 1867: "Ils n'ont pas l'air de croire à leur bonheur—Et leur chanson se mêle au clair de lune—Au calme clair de lune de Watteau" (see Posner, "Watteau mélancolique"; see also Ireland, "Aspects of Cythera," and Jones, "Vues sur Cythère"). As Philippe Sollers observes in his novel *La Fête à Venise*, there is no *clair de lune* in Watteau's paintings.

24. Levey, "The Real Theme," 185.

25. See Le Coat, "Le Pélerinage à l'île de Cythère."

26. On the playfulness of putti in eighteenth-century paintings, see Stewart, "Diana, and the Voyeurs" and "Decency and Indecency" (271–333) in *Engraven Desire*, 134–73 and 271–333, respectively.

27. This is a very erotic posture. In *Thérèse philosophe* (1748) the young heroine discovers sexual pleasure by moving instinctively and suddenly embracing her bedpost: the rubbing of her intimate parts against the bedpost causes her first orgasm. The putto's posture in Watteau's painting suggests such a rubbing and the pleasure that can result from it.

28. According to Marin, "The pleasure principle is thus—at minimal cost—subjected to the reality principle and the utopia disappears in the economics of a well-conceived project, in the time of a dialogue. Unless it is the reverse, and this might be the sense of the enigma, that the real and its calculations, work and its pains, the time of waiting and realization are abolished, or rather integrated, without effort nor obstacle, in pleasure" ("Le Jardin de Julie," 74, my translation).

29. It should also be noted that an image of Elysium was not among the twelve prints Rousseau ordered from the engraver Gravelot to illustrate his novel and visually commemorate important scenes from *La Nouvelle Héloïse*. Thus, Julie's garden exists only through the narrative, in Saint Preux's description of the garden and mostly in the effect the symbolic meaning of the garden has on him (Labrosse, "Sur les estampes de *La nouvelle Héloïse*").

30. This is why, after asking for a key to the garden, Saint Preux expresses his disappointment at being given Julie's instead of Fanchon's or M. de Wolmar's key: Julie's trustful gift of this symbolic key tends to de-eroticize her body, as André Blanc has argued; her ingenuousness does not fit the desire of Saint Preux, who at that very moment is looking for imaginary traces of their forbidden love (see Blanc, "Le Jardin de Julie").

31. Kant, *Critique of Judgement*, 110.

32. One could object, however, that Julie's and Saint Preux's internal revolutions are immediate: both take place in one moment. How can we say, then, that the spiritual revolution described by Rousseau contradicts the power of the moment, that is, the instinctive satisfaction of the senses? First, we need to remember that words, and not a visual or tactile sensation, are at the origin of the sudden revolu-

tion. The words uttered by the priest and by M. de Wolmar contradict sensual pleasure. Second, although the revolution takes place in one moment, its effect is to last forever, through an effort that needs to be renewed continually.

33. See McDonald, *Dialogue of Writing*; and Stewart, *Half-Told Tales*.

34. Markovits, "Rousseau et l'éthique de Clarens," 329.

35. Starobinski stresses the importance of time: "In order to reconcile irreconcilabilities, he had to invent a dialectic progress, go through intermediary states, have recourse to an effort of surpassing oneself, set in motion an evolution [*un devenir*]. This explains the main role that Rousseau gives to time in *La Nouvelle Héloïse*" (*Jean-Jacques Rousseau*, 110, my translation).

36. "As Rousseau contends in *La Nouvelle Héloïse*, a novel that in so many ways announces the nineteenth-century tradition, to understand his characters one must know them both young and old, and know them through the process of aging and change that lies in between, a process worked out over a stretch of pages" Brooks, *Reading for the Plot*, 21).

37. Denon writes: "The aspect of landscape, the voluptuousness of nature, the subject which seems to contain only grace and lightness, everything is treated with a plenitude of ideas which gives the depth and the philosophy of a Poussin composition to it" (Rosenberg, *Vies anciennes*, 126, my translation).

2. 1731: Manon, or Pleasure

1. Prévost, *Manon Lescaut*, trans. Tancock, 3. Hereafter page references are given in the text.

2. Prévost's agitated and wandering life was also marked by the tension between two contradictory desires, the desire to freely follow his pleasure and the desire to limit his freedom by belonging to the old regime's most rigorous institution, the monastery. While writing *Mémoires d'un homme de qualité*, Prévost himself experienced a violent crisis, as autobiographical fragments in *Le Pour et contre* indicate: "But I recovered some feeling, and recognized that this vivid heart was still burning under the ash. The loss of my freedom distressed me and made me cry. It was too late. For five or six years I looked for comfort in the charms of study. My books were my faithful friends; but they were dead for me. Eventually I took advantage of a small dissatisfaction, and went away" (quoted in Deloffre and Picard, "Genèse de *Manon Lescaut*," 40). To describe his life in the convent, Prévost always uses the same image: the image of death, of the grave in which he is buried alive. Books, whether written or read by Prévost, are faithful friends, but they are on the side of death; on the other side there is the "burning heart." Yet it was Prévost himself who chose to become a monk in 1721, after a brief time in the army. This tension between life and pleasure on one side and retirement to a monastery and renunciation of pleasure on the other characterizes Prévost's life as well as his

fiction. For more details on Prévost's life, see Deloffre and Picard, "Genèse de *Manon Lescaut*"; Harrisse, *L'Abbé Prévost* and *La Vie monastique*; and Sgard, *L'Abbe Prévost* and *Prévost romancier*.

3. See Jean Sgard, "Manon et les filles de joie," in *Vingt études sur Prévost d'Exiles*.

4. See Nancy Miller, "1735: The Gender of the Memoir-Novel," in *French Dressing*, 86.

5. See Thomas Kavanagh, "Chance, Reading, and the Tragedy of Experience: Prévost's *Manon Lescaut*," in *Enlightenment*, 156.

6. See Fort, "Manon's Suppressed Voice"; Lotringer, "Manon l'écho"; Nancy Miller, "Love for a Harlot: *Manon Lescaut*," in *The Heroine's Text*; Proust, "Le Corps de Manon"; and Segal, *The Unintended Reader*.

7. See Miller, *The Heroine's Text*, 74.

8. On the art of pleasing, see Dens, *L'Honnête Homme*; and Magendie, *La Politesse mondaine*. Many treatises about the art of pleasing were published in the seventeenth century: Du Souhait's *Le Parfait Gentilhomme* (1600), Nervèze's *Le Guide des courtisans* (1606), Nicolas Pasquier's *Le Gentilhomme* (1611), Eustache de Refuge's *Le Traité de la cour* (1616), Guez de Balzac's *Aristippe ou la cour* (1618), Nicolas Faret's *L'Honnête Homme, ou l'art de plaire à la cour* (1630). As Peter Brooks argues in *The Novel of Wordliness*, in the second half of the century the focus shifted from the court to the city and to aristocratic salons. This new focus is evident in Chevalier de Méré's *Conversations* (1669), Chaslème's *L'Homme de qualité ou les moyens de vivre en homme de bien et en homme du monde* (1672), Madeleine de Scudery's *Les Conversations sur divers sujets*, Goussault's *Le Portrait de l'honnête homme* (1689), Jean-Baptiste Morvan de Bellegarde's *Les Réflexions sur ce qui peut plaire ou déplaire dans le commerce du monde* (1688), and Pierre Ortigue de Vaumorière's *L'Art de plaire dans la conversation* (1688).

9. Robert Chasles, "Histoire de Monsieur Des Frans et de Silvie," in *Les Illustres Françaises*, 354.

10. Ibid., 393.

11. In his translation of the novel Tancock never translates the French word *transport* in the same way twice; thus, he loses this important concept. I therefore supplement Tancock's translation by adding in brackets the literal translation with the English word *transport*.

12. See Ross, "Narrative of Fascination," 204.

13. Tiberge uses the old meaning of the word *libertine*: "heretic, not respectful of Christian dogma." Des Grieux uses the word in a more modern sense when he apologizes to the father superior in Saint-Lazare for his behavior and defends himself against the accusation that he is a libertine who could be amended by punishment and prison.

14. Listening to a story gives pleasure, as the only use of the word *pleasure* in the last part of the novel reveals: "I told him part of our story, which he heard with pleasure" [*Je lui racontai une partie de mon histoire, qu'il entendit avec plaisir*] (192), des

Grieux says about the Governor, who then causes his misfortune. On the pleasure of telling stories, see Etienne Joyeux, "Les Récits de des Grieux."

15. Montesquieu, *Pensées*, 1253, pensée 940.

3. 1736–1738: Mme de Lursay, or Vanity

1. Crébillon, *Les Égarements du coeur et de l'esprit*, 17. Page references, hereafter given in the text, are to Barbara Bray's translation, *The Wayward Head and Heart*.

2. Sgard, "La notion d'égarement chez Crébillon," 240, my translation.

3. *Dictionnaire de Trévoux*, 1771, s.v. "égarement," quoted in ibid., 243.

4. In Prévost's *Manon Lescaut*, for instance, published in 1731, five years before *Les Égarements*, we find the word *égarement* at the end of des Grieux's narrative, when he mentions his father's death and expresses his guilt: "J'ai appris, par la réponse de mon frère aîné, la triste nouvelle de la mort de mon père, à laquelle je tremble, avec trop de raison, que mes *égarements* n'aient contribué" (204, my emphasis).

5. See Semiek, *La Recherche morale et esthétique*.

6. Sgard, "La notion d'égarement chez Crébillon," 242.

7. Raymond Trousson, introduction to *Les Égarements*, in *Romans libertins*, 9.

8. Kavanagh, "The Moment's Notice: Crébillon's Game of Libertinage," in *Enlightenment*, 219.

9. This is, for instance, Peter Brooks's interpretation in "Crébillon, Duclos, and the Experience of Wordliness," in *Novel of Wordliness*, 11–43; it is also Foucault's interpretation in "Un si cruel savoir."

10. Stefen Frears's film *Dangerous Liaisons* begins with alternating scenes in which Valmont and Merteuil are seen at their toilette, preparing themselves for the libertine game.

11. Anne Giard observes that the word *world* (*monde*) has a double meaning in Crébillon's novels: it means both the social space that Meilcour enters by virtue of his age and social rank and a mental space, a set of rules he has to learn in order to behave properly in this social world (see "Le Monde" and *Savoir et récit*).

12. Brooks writes: "The narrative structure of the novel closely controls our reactions as readers. Not only does the narrative tone preclude any provincialism, sentimentality, or naive moralism on our part, the structural distance between Meilcour-as-narrator and Meilcour-as-protagonist defines the distance at which me must hold characters and action" (*Novel of Wordliness*, 32).

13. "In order to clarify the situation the sooner, he set out to make a display of his charms. He had a good leg: he made the most of it. He laughed as often as he could to show his teeth, and assumed the bold postures that set his figure off to best advantage and demonstrated its graces most amply" (93).

14. On moment, movement, and desire, see Kavanagh, *Enlightenment* and *Esthet-*

ics; Mauzi, *L'Idée du bonheur*; Poulet, *Etudes sur le temps humain*; and Versini, *Laclos et la tradition*.

15. In Crébillon's novel, as in other libertine novels, the word *occasion* is synonymous with *moment*. Etymologically, *occasion*, from the Latin word *occasus*, means "fall." The word *occasion*, which has lost the strength of its original meaning to come to mean simply "circumstance" or "opportunity" in the twentieth century, was already devoid of moral connotation in libertine novels, which give a concrete and physical value to the concept: "Freedom, opportunity [*occasion*], solitude, the walk and groves, everything is against her," La Morlière writes in *Angola, histoire indienne*, a 1746 novel in which Crébillon's influence appears through the repeated use of the word *occasion*. In the eighteenth-century libertine vocabulary the word *occasion* had a specific meaning that made readers expect an erotic scene. (Trousson, *Romans libertins*).

16. Crébillon, *La Nuit et le moment*. See also idem, *L'Ecumoire*, 230–31, and *Le Sopha*, 84–86.

17. Crébillon, *Le Hasard du coin du feu*, 169, my translation.

18. The libertine notion of the moment, or the occasion, may remind us of the Greek concept *kairos* (meaning "opportunity" or "decisive instant"), represented in Greek mythology as a young man with wings. Humanists in the Renaissance linked the concept *kairos*, which Romans feminized as *occasio*, with a contradictory concept, that of *metanoia* (*poenitentia* in Latin), that is, regret, or yearning after a missed opportunity or fleeing instant; this sad feeling thus doubles the moment and inscribes it in a duration. Such a feeling is never found in eighteenth-century libertine texts, in which the moment is experienced as an autonomous unit that obeys no law but the law of the body and cannot be negated by a contradictory counterpart. Libertine novels thus reveal a concept of time that is not humanist (see Ripa, *Iconologia*; and Erwin Panofsky, "Father Time," in *Studies in Iconology*).

19. *Webster's New Twentieth-Century Dictionary*, 2d ed., s.v. "moment." For the eighteenth-century definition, see Diderot and d'Alembert's *Encyclopédie*:

> *Moment* ou *momentum*, en Méchanique, signifie quelquefois la même chose qu'*impetus*, ou la quantité du mouvement d'un mobile. Voyez MOUVEMENT. Dans la comparaison des mouvements des corps, la raison de leurs moments est toujours composée de celles de la quantité de matière, et de la vitesse du mobile, de façon que le *moment* d'un corps en mouvement peut être regardé comme le produit fait de sa quantité de matière et de vitesse. . . . Moment, s'emploie plus proprement et plus particulièrement dans la Statique, pour désigner le produit d'une puissance par le bras du levier auquel elle est attachée, ou, ce qui est la même chose,

par la distance de sa direction au point d'appui; une puissance a
d'autant plus d'avantage, toutes choses d'ailleurs égales, et son
moment est d'autant plus grand, qu'elle agit par un bras de levier
plus long. Voyez LEVIER, BALANCE et MÉCANIQUE.

20. Wald Lasowski, *Libertines*, 27.

21. So Mme de Lursay may be considered the only happy character at the end
of the novel, the only winner. This is Jean Dagen's interpretation, in *Introduction à la
sophistique amoureuse*, 65.

22. Foucault: "Un si cruel savoir," 609, my translation.

23. Kavanagh, *Enlightenment*, 224.

24. Prévost, *Manon Lescaut*, trans. Tancock, 111.

25. Sgard, "La notion d'égarement chez Crébillon," 244.

26. Bernadette Fort also suggests that Crébillon chose the Regency as a temporal setting for his story because it was a time when traditional values collapsed
after being maintained during the long reign of Louis XIV. The transformation of
customs and morals that took place at that time probably fascinated a skeptic, a
relativist, and a psychologist interested in moral dilemmas such as Crébillon (see
Fort, *Le Language de l'ambiguïté*, 10).

27. Brooks, *Reading for the Plot*, 52.

28. On irony in Crébillon's work, see Géraud, *La Lettre et l'esprit*.

4. 1748: Thérèse, or Reason

1. *Thérèse philosophe*, in *Oeuvres anonymes du XVIIIe siècle* 3:9; the English translation
is from *Forbidden Bestsellers*, trans. Robert Darnton, 249. Hereafter page references
are given in the text. Darnton translated the novel only partly. When I use
Darnton's translation I give the page in the French version followed by the page in
Darnton's edition. Sometimes I change one or two words in Darnton's translation
to be closer to the French text. For instance, Darnton uses the English word *member*
even when the French text reads *trait* or *dard*.

The novel's author was believed to be the Marquis Boyer d'Argens or even
Diderot, but there is no certainty concerning the authorship (see Darnton, *Forbidden Bestsellers*; Roger, "Au bonheur des dames sensées"; and Trousson, *Romans libertins*).

2. "I was more than thirty years old before I looked at any of those dangerous
books which a beautiful lady of the world finds inconvenient, because, she says,
they must be read with a single hand" (Rousseau, *Les Confessions*, 39, my translation).

3. See Darnton, *Forbidden Bestsellers*; and Hunt, *Invention of Pornography*, 9–45.

4. Darnton, *Forbidden Bestsellers*, 108–9.

5. Ibid., 107, 113.

6. Hunt, *Invention of Pornography*, 44.

7. Brooks, *Body Work*, 96.

8. See Kelly, *Telling Glances*. Kelly writes about Diderot's *La Religieuse*: "The text is itself a scenario of seduction viewed by a voyeur: the male writer-spectator observes female seductions and the origin of sexuality in such a way as to condemn and thereby master female sexuality, subjectivity, and writing" (32).

9. See Mulvey, *Visual and Other Pleasures*: "In a world ordered by sexual imbalance, pleasure in looking has been split between active—male and passive—female. The determining male gaze projects its phantasy on to the female figure which is styled accordingly" (19).

10. Many eighteenth-century pornographic novels involve almost exclusively monks and nuns and attract readers with their revealing titles: *Le Portier des Chartreux* (1741), *Les Quarante Manières de foutre dédiées au clergé de France* (1790), *Le Triomphe des religieuses ou les nonnes babillardes* (1748), *Lettres galantes et philosophiques de deux nonnes* (1797). The first scene that Saturnin spies on in *Le Portier des Chartreux* involves his alleged mother and Father Polycarpe. He later learns that his own father is a monk. In the convent to which his father takes him monks are far from renouncing carnal pleasure: they keep a number of available women in a place called "la piscine." Sadean novels are unsurprisingly replete with religious characters, who are among the most accomplished libertines: the cruel monks of Sainte-Marie des Bois in *La Nouvelle Justine*, the Carmelite Claude, the Cardinal de Bernis, and Pope Pius VI in *L'Histoire de Juliette*. In pornographic novels the words *monk* and *priest* become synonymous with *libertine*, and *nun* with *lesbian*. As in Diderot's *La Religieuse*, nuns in erotic novels give pleasure to each other, most often with the help of dildos, which are more common than crosses inside convents. The monk's sexual prowess is an eighteenth-century legend, as proved by the expression "to get hard like a Carmelite" [*bander comme un Carme*], which can be found in almost all eighteenth-century pornographic texts.

11. On this scandal see Darnton, *Forbidden Bestsellers*; Roger, "Au bonheur des dames sensées"; and Trousson, *Romans libertins*.

12. This physiological argument against religion is common in the eighteenth century. The article "Femme" in the *Encyclopédie*, for example, written by Desmahis, who is not as extreme as Diderot on this point, mentions an age of devotion in women, the age when their physical appearance no longer allows them to be charming and the discourse of virtue therefore replaces that of seduction.

13. "Cachez ce sein que je ne saurais voir." Wilbur translates this as "Cover that bosom, girl. The flesh is weak" (Molière, *Tartuffe*, 389).

14. On the pedagogical model of the eighteenth-century pornographic novel,

see Peter Cryle, "Toward the Learner-Centered Boudoir" in *Geometry in the Boudoir*, 71–91.

15. *Histoire de Dom Bougre, portier des Chartreux* is also one of the key eighteenth-century pornographic texts and was a bestseller in its day. On *Le Portier des Chartreux*, see Walter Rex, "Three Literary Approaches to the Art of Love," in *Attraction of the Contrary*, 30–38.

Le Portier des Chartreux and *Thérèse philosophe* are the texts the most often quoted in other eighteenth-century pornographic novels. *Le Portier des Chartreux* is quoted in *Thérèse philosophe* and Sade's *L'Histoire de Juliette*, and *Thérèse philosophe* is quoted in Restif's *Monsieur Nicolas* and Nerciat's *Felicia ou mes fredaines*, the anonymous *Lucette ou les Progrès du libertinage*, Sade's *L'Histoire de Juliette*, and Restif's *Monsieur Nicolas* (see Delon, "La Réflexivité du roman libertin").

16. One speaks, in French, of a *promesse de Gascon*. Gascons, from the French region Gascogne, are supposed to make promises they cannot hold. I do not know the origin of this legend.

17. See Delon, *L'Idée d'énergie*.

18. The materialist philosopher and physician Julien Orfray de La Mettrie, born in Saint-Malo in 1709, published in 1745 *Histoire naturelle de l'âme*, later entitled *Traité de l'âme*, a materialist treaty based on medical observation that was condemned to be burned by the Paris Parliament on 9 July 1746. La Mettrie had to flee to Leyde, where he published *L'Homme machine* in 1747. This essay provoked an even greater scandal, and La Mettrie found asylum at the court of Fréderic II in Berlin, where he died of indigestion on 11 November 1751.

19. On the use of Sappho's myth in literature, see DeJean, *Fictions of Sappho*.

20. Sade, *Histoire de Juliette*, *Oeuvres* 8:443.

21. "Durand had never been able to enjoy ordinary pleasures: she was obstructed, but . . . her clitoris, as long as a finger, inspired in her the most ardent taste for women. She fucked and sodomized them" (ibid., 9:431).

22. See Frappier-Mazur, *Sade ou l'écriture de l'orgie*.

23. La Durand, in love with Juliette, prostitutes her to men and builds a brothel with secret cabinets from which they can watch men's passions (see Cusset, "La Passion selon Juliette").

24. Sapphism has a very important place in either the frame, the resolution, or the central episode of most erotic novels. Sapphism signifies not only a sexual relationship between two women but also female friendship and the playful link between women that allows them to laugh at everything. The voyeuristic construction of erotic novels in which a woman tells or writes her adventures to another woman leads to the derision of male desire. If Nerciat's *Le Doctorat impromptu* recounts how Erosie's "anti-masculine system" ends, Erosie writes her story for another woman, Juliette, who was her intimate friend in the convent. In *Lettres galantes et philosophiques de deux nonnes* the narrators are also women who write

to each other. Mirabeau's *L'Education de Laure* is also a female narrative; the story of a daughter "educated" by her libertine father, it ends with the homosexual love of Laure and Eugénie. Laure takes Eugénie's virginity and tells her, "If you feel happy using it (the dildo), our tender friendship will be everything for us" (442). In *La Philosophie dans le boudoir* a woman, Mme de Saint-Ange, directs all operations and takes charge of Eugénie's education. *Dom Bougre*, whose narrator is a man, contains Suzon's narrative, which in turn contains Monique's narrative. Monique, speaking to Suzon, recounts scenes of sapphic love in which complex dildos are used: "This is what I thought up so we could do without men" (332). The heroine of *La Cauchoise* recounts her romance with Sister Prudence, a nun who was clever enough to have "a tinman among her friends make a dildo for her, which had two penis heads on the end, with a spring in the middle which would drop milk that had been put inside into the two wombs at the same time" (411). The dildo filled with milk makes the illusion perfect: "We will have the same pleasure as if we were man and woman."

25. This is an echo of an eighteenth-century topos: that women have a much greater capacity for sexual enjoyment than men. In Nerciat's *Le Diable au corps* the abbé exclaims, "Women! first they rebel against anything fun which is proposed to them; but, once they appreciate it—it is the devil! they would go, then, a hundred times further than us" (79).

26. Darnton, *Forbidden Bestsellers*, 112.

27. *Lettres galantes et philosophiques de deux nonnes* (1797), in *Oeuvres anonymes du XVIIIe siècle* 3:273.

28. In *Dom Bougre*, when Toinette and Polycarpe catch Saturnin and Suzon watching them, the reversal of the situation also reveals a reversal in the power relation. Saturnin, who dominated the scene before from his position as a voyeur, is forced to hide under the bed, fearing Toinette's punishment, until he is finally caught: "I saw that she held out her arm to catch me, I crawled backwards, but she seized me. By which part? By the cock. I had no way left to defend myself, I came forth as soon as I could, she drew me toward herself, for she had not lost her grip" (101). The male member becomes the "grip" the woman takes to affirm her power.

5. 1760: SUZANNE, OR LIBERTY

1. This excitement is evident in Diderot's reaction upon learning that Croismare had answered the letter of the fictitious Suzanne: "The Marquis answered! Is it true? Is his heart really mad? Is his mind really in the air? Isn't someone tricking me?" (Diderot to Mme d'Epinay, February 1760. See *La Religieuse*, 210–30; the *préface-annexe* is not translated).

2. *La Religieuse*, 213–14; hereafter, unless otherwise noted, page references are to Tancock's translation.

3. See May, *La Religieuse de Diderot*; and Mauzi, "Humour et colère dans *La religieuse*."

4. On the "seduction" operated by the text, see David Marshall, "La Religieuse: Sympathy and Seduction," in *Surprising Effects*. On the relation between the *préface-annexe*, the reader, and the novel, see Caplan, *Framed Narratives*; and De la Carrera, "Epistolary Triangles."

La Religieuse and particularly the *préface-annexe* contain a metadiscourse on fiction. For instance, we know that Diderot himself added the following anecdote to the manuscript of the preface before it was published in the *Correspondance littéraire* in 1770: "One of our mutual friends visited him and found him yielding to grief, his face covered with tears. 'What happened to you?' M. d'Alainville said. 'You are in such a state!' 'What happened to me?' M. Diderot answered; 'I am grieved by a tale I am telling myself.'"

5. Suzanne receives a letter that her mother says she sent one day before writing it (54); she recommends her friend Ursule to the Marquis's pity as if she were still alive (68), whereas Ursule dies in the novel (116). Suzanne does not age with time. At the beginning of the novel Suzanne is sixteen and a half years old. If we take into consideration all the notations of time in the novel, we see that her narrative covers approximately six or seven years, so that she should be at least twenty-two years old when she writes her memoirs and engages in the epistolary exchange with the Marquis, but Diderot decides that she is seventeen and even erases the age "nineteen" he wrote at first. "One might find her a little young, because I think that she is scarcely seventeen years old; but if she lacks the experience of age, the experience of unhappiness makes up for it," Madame Madin writes to the Marquis on 16 February 1760 (227). His heroine's eternal youth serves to seduce the Marquis de Croismare and proves that the pleasure given by fiction makes the heroine more convincing than a rational calculation.

6. See Mylne, *Eighteenth-Century French Novel*; and Stewart, *Imitation and Illusion*.

7. See Rex, "Secrets from Suzanne: The Tangled Motives in *La Religieuse*," in *Attraction of the Contrary*, 125–35. "It was this shock of recognition that brought on the energetic decision to do anything in the world rather than suffer the same fate" (129). See also Stewart, *Half-Told Tales*, 83–113.

8. Diderot, *Sur les femmes*, 952. A. L. Thomas, an academician born in Clermont-Ferrand in 1732, in March 1772 published an essay entitled *Essai sur le caractère, les moeurs et l'esprit des femmes dans les différents siècles*; he was reputed to be a virgin (see Badinter, *Qu'est-ce qu'une femme?* 9–34).

9. See Jullien, "Locus hystericus."

10. See Mauzi, "Humour et colère dans *La Religieuse*."

11. Diderot, *Oeuvres*, 979, my translation.

12. On the monster and the key role it played in eighteenth-century thought and imagination, see Huet, *Monstrous Imagination*.

13. On the role of the reader as voyeur, see Dorothy Kelly, "The Primal Scene of Seduction, Voyeurism, and *La religieuse*," in *Telling Glances*, 12–33.

14. See Jacques Proust, "Cantate de l'innocent," in *L'Objet et le texte*, an essay in which he stresses the ambivalence of a heroine who seems to appeal to her address-ee's reason and sense of justice when she in fact provokes his desire: "[The] voice [of reason] is not powerful enough to completely suppress the discourse it is supposed to transcend. . . . It is still the proteiform and anarchical discourse of desire: Suzanne flirts with the Marquis at the same time that she strives to appear innocent and pure" (156). See also Kempf, *Diderot et le roman*.

15. In many of Crébillon's novels and tales as well as other libertine novels the verb *to prove* specifically means a sexual act: "She answers him only by proving to him that she loves him" (*La Nuit et le moment*, 128). "After a long fight, Célie is forced, not to recognize, but to prove that she is defeated" (*Le Hasard du coin du feu*, 202). The verb can also be found on pp. 88, 98, 99, 197, and 215.

16. If Diderot presents homosexuality as a perversion of natural sexuality, whose aim should be procreation, in *Supplément au voyage de Bougainville*, he talks very naturally about sapphic love in his letters to Sophie Volland, whom he suspected of cheating on him with his sister, who was fond of nuns and other women. Diderot clearly expresses his jealousy in a letter of 15 September 1760, when he had finished writing of *La Religieuse*: "Are you forgetting me in tumultuous feasts and your sister's arms? Madame, take care of your health and don't forget that pleasure too makes you tired" (*Lettres à Sophie Volland*, 115). We should also remember that the physician Bordeu, in *Rêve de d'Alembert*, recognizes as natural everything that exists in nature.

17. The very way Suzanne eventually learns the language of the senses, which she had previously refused to acknowledge, is meaningful: her body remains safe. She learns from behind a wall, when she hears the Mother Superior speak to the confessor. This "unveiled" truth is kept at a safe distance by language, the wall that separates and hides the bodies, and the context of religious confession. Further-more, Suzanne's violation of the law (breaking the secrecy of confession) is imme-diately redeemed by her address to the Marquis de Croismare, who then plays the role of confessor and protects the heroine from the threat of the body. From beginning to end, Suzanne uses the law in order to fight the arbitrary nature of passion and the principle of pleasure, which drive all the other women.

18. See Pontalis and Laplanche, *Fantasme originaire*.

19. Diderot, *Sur les femmes*, 952.

6. 1777: MME DE T——, OR DECENCY

1. Denon, *Point de lendemain*, 732. Pages references, hereafter given in the text, are to Lydia Davis's translation, *No Tomorrow*.

2. Denon's story was published by Desjonquères with an introduction by René Démoris (1987), in *Romans libertins*, edited by Raymond Trousson (1993), and in Collection Folio with an introduction by Michel Delon (1995).

3. Philippe Sollers is the only author to vigorously refute this interpretation. In his chapter on *Point de lendemain* Sollers decides to call the narrator of the story, whose name we do not know, "Vivant," and he emphasizes the following words appearing in Dorat's foreword: "The core of it, furthermore, is true" (*Le Cavalier*, 81). Sollers's theory of pleasure is provocative; he uses it to oppose himself to all of those who are afraid of freedom and to deride the humanists. He affirms that pleasure is a reality but does not tell us in what way. There is an elitism of pleasure in Sollers's work: pleasure is "a matter of predestination, of grace, and of gratuitousness."

4. Delon, introduction to *Point de lendemain*, 7–8. This reduction was previously discussed in Coulet, *Le Roman jusqu'à la révolution*, 450.

5. Trousson, introduction to *Point de lendemain*, in *Romans libertins*, 1298.

6. Kundera, *La Lenteur*, 142.

7. Kavanagh, in *Enlightenment*, 186.

8. The narrator ironically emphasizes Mme de T——'s "principles of decency" by qualifying them with "scrupulously." In the 1777 version, in which the narrator opens the story by introducing himself as a twenty-five-year-old libertine thirsty for conquest and vengeance, and not as the naive and duped twenty-year-old young man he will become in the 1812 version, we find the same insistence on Mme de T——'s decency and the same ironic emphasis at the end of the first paragraph: "She . . . threatened to love me madly, without any compromise of her dignity or her taste for decencies; for, as we shall see, she was scrupulously attached to these" (73). In 1777 the plural form of *decency* indicates a simple taste, similar to a taste for a culinary delicacy; by 1812 it has become a principle.

9. For Kavanagh, this contact is truly a matter of chance. He distinguishes between, on the one hand, the plan organized by Mme de T—— (to bring along the narrator in order to deceive her husband) and, on the other, the sexual affair, which Mme de T—— had not planned and which occurred only as a result of the intervention of the chance of the moment, a moment cut off from the rest of time and from reality. According to Kavanagh, it is this moment that represents the utopia, or the dream of a pleasure without any consequence: "It was by design that Mme de T—— chose a companion for the evening. But it was by chance that her specific choice of the narrator led to the movement of desire and pleasure initiating another story, unwriteable by the narrator, of how that chance event will go on to affect her relation to her lover, the Marquis" (*Enlightenment*, 195).

In contrast to Kavanagh, I do not attribute the first physical contact between the protagonists to the pure intervention of chance. Three things, it seems to me, discredit the thesis of chance: (1) the piece of information the narrator gives us in the story's first paragraph concerning Mme de T——'s designs on him; (2) the fact that chance (this first moment of chance, as well as all the others that will follow) always serves a function precisely determined within the framework of the seduction process; and (3) the unmistakable element of irony in the narrator's insistence on the role of chance in the first part of the story.

10. This is the problem Célie faces in Crébillon's *Le Hasard du coin du feu*. Seducing the Marquis is quite a difficult task within the limits of decency, when the Marquis refuses to utter the love avowal she seeks from him and in addition tells her very clearly that although he takes advantage of the "moment," he would nonetheless certainly despise a woman who showed her sensual desire for him. Finally Célie, under the pretext that she is cold, uncovers her leg to expose it to the fire. Crébillon writes ironically that we cannot judge her intention since it is impossible for us to know exactly by which degree of cold another person is affected.

11. Lydia Davis here translates, "They will never yield. . . . They surrender," when the French text reads, "On ne cèdera point . . . on a cédé." Ironically, "on" designates Mme de T——, not the narrator, who does not need to "yield" since he is the seducer in this situation. The repetition of the verb, *céder*, is important, as is the use of the future and of the past tense, to show the contradiction between "decent" intentions and physical facts.

12. Here again I have changed Davis's translation, for I do not think that her translation—"you do know how to love me!"—respects the spirit of the text, which reads in French, "Tu m'aimes donc bien!" The meaning is obviously sexual, but the expression is not. The verb *to know* in Davis's translation insists on the technical aspects of sex, whereas Mme de T—— does not.

13. Rousseau, *Julie, ou la nouvelle Héloïse*, 132–33.

14. Delon, introduction to *Point de lendemain*, 7.

15. When the Marquise de Merteuil decides to leave Belleroche, she uses love and sensual exhaustion as a stratagem since neither coldness, caprices, nor squabbles seem to discourage him: "Once there, I shall so overburden him with love and caresses, we shall live so exclusively for each other, that I am certain he will long even more than I for the end of this expedition which he regards in prospect as so great a happiness" (Laclos, *Dangerous Liaisons*, letter 113, 1152).

16. This is why we cannot equate *Point de lendemain*'s narrator with Belleroche in *Les Liaisons dangereuses* nor say that *Point de lendemain* is simply the male version of the episode in which Mme de Merteuil dismisses her lover. There is an important difference between Belleroche and *Point de lendemain*'s narrator: Belleroche, whom we see only through Mme de Merteuil's eyes, is presented as someone quite stupid and tender; he never learns that he has been manipulated by Mme de Merteuil. In *Les Liaisons dangereuses* power, control, and manipulation are all on one side; it is a story of control and not of balance.

17. Should we say that the narrator, if we assume that he is Vivant Denon,

takes revenge on Mme de T—— by writing and publishing the story and thus contradicting her lesson of discretion? But the story was published anonymously in 1777 and 1778, and it contains no proper names; it was only in 1812, thirty-five years later, that Vivant Denon published the story under his name.

18. "'Horace: As for my jealous rival, isn't the role he's played in this affair extremely droll? Well?' Arnolphe: 'Yes, quite droll.' Horace: 'Well, laugh, if that's the case!' (*Arnolphe gives a forced laugh.*) 'My, what a fool! He fortifies his place against me, using bricks for cannon balls, as if he feared that I might storm the walls; . . . and then he's hoodwinked by the girl he meant to keep forever meek and innocent! . . . The whole thing's been so comical that I find that I'm convulsed whenever it comes to mind. You haven't laughed as much as I thought you would.' Arnolphe: (*with a forced laugh*) 'I beg your pardon: I've done the best I could'" (Molière, *School for Wives*, 85).

CONCLUSION

1. "Where can we be misled by the transport of these senses that are so much scorned in the peaceful calculations of modest philosophy and that we have the presumption to believe our reason can control! Ah! Juliette, what a slap you will see me give to the sublime Platonism!" (Nerciat, *Le Doctorat impromptu*, 68).

2. Denon, *No Tomorrow*, 747.

3. On Voltaire's irony, see Barthes, "Le Dernier des écrivains heureux," 9–17; Cusset, "Voltaire"; and Jean Starobinski, "Le Fusil à deux coups de Voltaire," in *Le Remède dans le mal*.

4. In *La Lenteur* Kundera observes that psychological analysis is probably the strongest element of eighteenth-century libertine novels. On the amoral, pragmatic attitude of libertine novelists, see Bennington, *Sententiousness and the Novel*.

5. This is what Montesquieu does in *Les Lettres persanes* when he has one of the eunuchs write that the operation to which he was forcefully submitted when he was still a child deprived him of his "humanity." In this context the word *humanity* refers only to the male member, not even to desire, as the eunuch's argument is precisely that he still feels desire but has lost the means to satisfy and appease it (letter 42).

6. On the critique of fanaticism in the eighteenth century, see Voltaire, *Dictionnaire philosophique*, s.v. "fanatisme."

7. See Adorno and Horkheimer, *Dialectic of Enlightenment*; and Saul, *Voltaire's Bastards*.

BIBLIOGRAPHY

Adorno, Theodor W., and Max Horkheimer. *Dialectic of Enlightenment.* Trans. John Cumming. New York: Continuum, 1972.

Badinter, Elisabeth. *Qu'est-ce qu'une femme?* Paris: POL, 1989.

Bal, Mieke. *"Reading Rembrandt": Beyond the Word-Image Opposition.* Cambridge: Cambridge Univ. Press, 1991.

Barthes, Roland. "Le Dernier des écrivains heureux." Preface to *Romans et contes,* by Voltaire. Paris: Gallimard, 1972.

———. *L'Obvie et l'obtus: Essais critiques 3.* Paris: Seuil, 1982.

———. *Le Plaisir du texte.* Paris: Seuil, 1973. Trans. Richard Miller under the title *The Pleasure of the Text* (New York: Hill & Wang, 1975).

Benichou, Paul. *Morales du grand siècle.* Paris: Gallimard, 1948.

Bennington, Geoffrey. *Sententiousness and the Novel: Laying Down the Law in Eighteenth-Century French Fiction.* Cambridge: Cambridge Univ. Press, 1985.

Benrekassa, Georges. *Fables de la personne: Pour une histoire de la subjectivité.* Paris: PUF, 1985.

Blanc, André. "Le Jardin de Julie." *Dix-huitième Siècle* 14 (1982): 357–76.

Boudier de Villemert, Pierre-Joseph. *Apologie de la frivolité: Lettre à un Anglois.* Paris: Prault père, 1750.

Brooks, Peter. *Body Work: Objects of Desire in Modern Narrative.* Cambridge: Harvard Univ. Press, 1993.

———. *The Novel of Wordliness.* Princeton: Princeton Univ. Press, 1969.

———. *Reading for the Plot: Design and Intention in Narrative.* New York: Vintage, 1985.

Bryson, Norman. *Word and Image: French Painting of the Ancien Regime.* 1981. Reprint, Cambridge: Cambridge Univ. Press, 1989.

Caplan, Jay. *Framed Narratives: Diderot's Genealogy of the Beholder.* Minneapolis: Univ. of Minnesota Press, 1985.

Casanova, Giovanni Giacomo. *Histoire de ma vie: suivie de textes inédits.* Ed. Francis Lacassin. 3 vols. Paris: Laffont, Collection Bouquins, 1993.

Caylus, Anne-Claude-Philippe, comte de. *The Life of Antoine Watteau.* In *French Eighteenth-Century Painters,* by Edmond de Goncourt and Jules de Goncourt, trans. Robin Ironside, 10–29. Ithaca: Cornell Univ. Press, 1981.

Cazenobe, Colette. *Le Système du libertinage.* Oxford: Voltaire Foundation, 1991.

Chasles, Robert. *Les Illustres Françaises.* Paris: Belles-Lettres, 1959.

Chouillet, Jacques. "Manon en Amérique." *French American Review* 6 (1982): 189–95.

Condillac, Étienne Bonnot de. "Extrait raisonné du *Traité des sensations.*" In *Traité des sensations.* 1798. Reprint, Paris: Fayard, 1984.

Coulet, Henri. *Le Roman jusqu'à la révolution.* 2 vols. Paris: Armand Colin, 1967.

Crébillon, Claude Prosper Jolyot de. *L'Écumoire, ou Tanzai et Néadarné.* 1756. Paris: Nizet, 1976.

———. *Les Égarements du coeur et de l'esprit.* Ed. René Etiemble. Paris: Gallimard, 1977. Trans. Barbara Bray under the title *The Wayward Head and Heart* (Westport, Conn.: Greenwood Press, 1963).

———. *La Nuit et le moment. Le Hasard du coin du feu.* Ed. Jean Dagen. Paris: Garnier Flammarion, 1997.

———. *Le Sopha.* 1742. Reprint, Paris: U.G.E., 1966.

Crow, Thomas. "Codes of Silence: Historical Interpretation and the Art of Watteau." *Representations* 12 (1985): 2–14.

———. Introduction to *Selections: Diderot on Art,* trans. John Goodman. 2 vols. New Haven: Yale Univ. Press, 1995.

———. *Painters and Public Life in Eighteenth-Century Paris.* 1985. Reprint, New Haven: Yale Univ. Press, 1988.

Cryle, Peter. *Geometry in the Boudoir: Configurations of French Erotic Narrative.* Ithaca: Cornell Univ. Press, 1994.

Cusset, Catherine. "L'Adresse au lecteur dans les préfaces de Marivaux." In *Marivaux et les Lumières: L'Éthique d'un romancier,* 129–36. Aix-en-Provence: Université de Provence, 1996.

———. "Cythère et l'Elysée: Jardins et plaisir de Watteau à Rousseau." *Dalhousie French Studies* 29 (1994): 65–84.

———. "La Jambe de la vérité." *Dix-huitième Siècle* 24 (1992): 383–96.

———. "A Lesson of Decency: Pleasure and Reality in Vivant Denon's *Point de lendemain.*" In *The Libertine Reader: Eroticism and Enlightenment in Eighteenth-Century France,* ed. Michel Feher, 722–31. New York: Zone, 1998.

———. "La Passion selon Juliette." *L'Infini* 31 (1990): 17–26.

———. *Les Romanciers du plaisir.* Paris: Champion, 1998.

———. "Sade: Critique of Pure Fiction." In *The Divine Sade,* ed. Deepak Narang Sawhney, special issue of *PLI—Warwick Journal of Philosophy* 5 (1994): 115–31.

———. "The Suspended Ending or Crébillon's Irony." In *The Libertine Reader: Eroticism and Enlightenment in Eighteenth-Century France,* ed. Michel Feher, 750–65. New York: Zone, 1998.

————. "Voltaire: Le Ridicule, arme mortelle?" *L'Infini* 25 (1989): 57–60.

————. "Watteau: The Aesthetics of Pleasure." In *Icons—Text—Iconotext: Essays on Ekphrasis and Intermediality*, ed. Peter Wagner, 121–35. Berlin: Walter de Gruyter, 1996.

————, ed. *Libertinage and Modernity*. Special issue of *Yale French Studies* 94 (1998).

Dagen, Jean. *Introduction à la sophistique amoureuse dans Les Égarements du coeur et de l'esprit de Crébillon fils*. Paris: Champion, 1995.

Darnton, Robert. *The Forbidden Bestsellers of Pre-Revolutionary France*. New York: W. W. Norton, 1995.

————. "Sex for Thought." *New York Book Review*, 27 December 1994.

DeJean, Joan. *Fictions of Sappho*. Chicago: Univ. of Chicago Press, 1989.

————. *Tender Geographies: Women and the Origins of the Novel in France*. New York: Columbia Univ. Press, 1991.

De la Carrera, Rosalina. "Epistolary Triangles: The Preface-Annexe of *La Religieuse* Reexamined." In *Success in Circuit Lies: Diderot's Communicational Practice*, 263–80. Stanford: Stanford Univ. Press, 1997.

Deloffre, Frédéric, and Raymond Picard. "Genèse de *Manon Lescaut*." In *Manon Lescaut*, by abbé Prévost, ed. Frédéric Deloffre and Raymond Picard. 2nd ed. Paris: Garnier, 1990.

Delon, Michel. *L'Idée d'énergie au siècle des Lumières*. Paris: PUF, 1988.

————. Introduction to *Point de lendemain de Vivant Denon suivi de La petite maison de Jean-François Bastide*. Ed. Michel Delon. Paris: Gallimard, 1995.

————. "La Réflexivité du roman libertin." In *Offene Gefüge-Literatursystem und Lebenswirklichkeit*, ed. Henning Kraus, 75–89. Tübingen: Gunter Narr Verlag, 1994.

De Man, Paul. *Blindness and Insight*. Minneapolis. Univ. of Minnesota Press, 1983.

Démoris, René. "Les Fêtes galantes chez Watteau et dans le roman contemporain." *Dix-huitième Siècle* 3 (1971): 337–57.

————. Introduction to *Point de lendemain*. Paris: Desjonquères, 1987.

————. *Le Roman à la première personne du classicisme aux Lumières*. Paris: Armand Colin, 1975.

————. *Le Silence de Manon*. Paris: PUF, 1995.

Deneys-Tuney, Anne. *Ecritures du corps de Descartes à Laclos*. Paris: PUF, 1992.

Denon, Vivant. *Point de lendemain*. In *Romanciers du XVIIIe siècle*, ed. René Etiemble, 2:385–402. Paris: Gallimard, Bibliothèque de la Pléiade, 1965. Trans. Lydia Davis under the title *No Tomorrow*, intro. Catherine Cusset, in *The Libertine Reader: Eroticism and Enlightenment in Eighteenth-Century France*, ed. Michel Feher (New York: Zone, 1997), 721–47.

Dens, Jean-Pierre. *L'Honnête Homme et la critique du goût: Esthétique et société au XVIIe siècle*. Lexington, Ky.: French Forum, 1981.

Derrida, Jacques. *De la grammatalogie*. Paris: Minuit, 1967.

————. *La Vérité en peinture*. Paris: Flammarion, 1978.

Diderot, Denis. *Eloge de Richardson*. In *Oeuvres complètes*, ed. Jean Varloot, vol. 13, *Arts et lettres (1739–1766)*. Paris: Hermann, 1980.

————. *Lettres à Sophie Volland*. Ed. Jean Varloot. Paris: Gallimard, 1984.

————. *La Religieuse*. Ed. Jacques Chouillet and Anne-Marie Chouillet. Paris: Librairie Générale Française, 1983. Trans. Leonard Tancock under the title *The Nun* (London: Penguin, 1974).

————. *Selections: Diderot on Art*. Trans. John Goodman. Intro. Thomas Crow. 2 vols. New Haven: Yale Univ. Press, 1995.

————. *Sur les femmes; Supplément au voyage de Bougainville*. In *Oeuvres*, ed. André Billy. Paris: Gallimard, 1951.

Diderot, Denis, and Jean Le Rond d'Alembert. *Encyclopédie, ou Dictionnaire raisonné des arts, des sciences, et des métiers*. 17 vols. Paris: Briasson, 1751–65.

Didier, Béatrice. *L'Écriture-femme*. Paris: PUF, 1981.

Dieckmann, Herbert. "The Preface-Annexe of *La Religieuse*." *Diderot Studies* 2 (1953): 21–47.

Feher, Michel. "Libertinisms." Introduction to *The Libertine Reader: Eroticism and Enlightenment in Eighteenth-Century France*, ed. Michel Feher. New York: Zone, 1997.

Fort, Bernadette. *Le Langage de l'ambiguïté dans l'oeuvre de Crébillon*. Paris: Editions Klincksieck, 1978.

————. "Manon's Suppressed Voice: The Uses of Reported Speech." *Romanic Review* 76 (1985): 172–91.

Foucault, Michel. "Un Si Cruel Savoir." *Critique* 18 (1962): 605–7.

Frappier-Mazur, Lucienne. *Sade ou l'écriture de l'orgie*. Paris: Nathan, 1991.

Fried, Michael. *Absorption and Theatricality: Painting and Beholder in the Age of Diderot*. Berkeley: Univ. of California Press, 1980.

Fumaroli, Marc. "La Conversation au XVIIe siècle: Le Témoignage de Fortin de la Hoguette." In *L'Esprit et la lettre: Mélanges offerts à Jules Brody*, ed. Louis Van Delft, 92–106. Tubingen: Gunter Narr Verlag, 1991.

Furetière. *Dictionnaire universel*. La Haye: A. et R. Leers, 1690.

Géraud, Violaine. *La Lettre et l'esprit de Crébillon fils*. Paris: SEDES, 1995.

Giard, Anne. "Le *Monde* dans *Les égarements*." *Stanford French Review* 9 (1985): 33–46.

————. *Savoir et récit chez Crébillon*. Paris: Champion; Genève: Slatkine, 1986.

Girardin, Emile. *Promenade ou itinéraire des jardins d'Ermenonville*. Paris: Mérigot père, 1788.

Goncourt, Jules, and Edmond Goncourt. *French Eighteenth-Century Painters*. Trans. Robin Ironside. Ithaca: Cornell Univ. Press, 1981.

Goulemot, Jean-Marie. *Ces livres qu'on ne lit que d'une main: Lecture et lecteurs du livre pornographique au XVIIIe siècle*. Rev. ed. Paris: Minerva, 1994.

Harrisse, Henry. *L'Abbé Prévost: Histoire de sa vie et de ses oeuvres d'après des documents nouveaux*. Paris: Calmann-Lévy, 1896.

―――. *La Vie monastique de l'abbé Prévost*. Paris: Leclerc, 1903.

Histoire de Dom Bougre, portier des Chartreux. In *Oeuvres anonymes du XVIIIe siècle*, vol. 1, *L'Enfer de la Bibliothèque nationale*, vol. 3. Paris: Fayard, 1985.

Huet, Marie-Hélène. *Le Héros et son double: Essai sur le roman d'ascension sociale au XVIIIe siècle*. Paris: Corti, 1975.

―――. *Monstrous Imagination*. Cambridge: Harvard Univ. Press, 1993.

Hunt, Lynn, ed. *The Invention of Pornography: Obscenity and the Origin of Modernity, 1500–1800*. New York: Zone, 1993.

Ireland, K. R. "Aspects of Cythera: Neo-Rococo at the Turn of the Century." *Modern Language Review* 70 (1975): 721–30.

Jones, Shirley. "Vues sur Cythère . . . Watteau et la critique romantique du XIXe siècle." *Revue des Sciences Humaines* 157 (1975): 5–21.

Joyeux, Etienne. "Les Récits de des Grieux." *French Studies of Southern Africa* 9 (1980): 2–18.

Jullien, Dominique. "Locus hystericus: L'Image du couvent dans *La religieuse* de Diderot." *French Forum* 15 (May 1990): 133–49.

Kant, Immanuel. *Critique of Judgement*. Trans. J. H. Bernard. London: Macmillan, 1931.

Kavanagh, Thomas. *Enlightenment and the Shadows of Chance: The Novel and the Culture of Gambling in Eighteenth-Century France*. Baltimore: Johns Hopkins Univ. Press, 1993.

―――. *Esthetics of the Moment: Literature and Art in the French Enlightenment*. Philadelphia: Univ. of Pennsylvania Press, 1996.

Kelly, Dorothy. *Telling Glances: Voyeurism in the French Novel*. New Brunswick, N.J.: Rutgers Univ. Press, 1992.

Kempf, Roger. *Diderot et le roman, ou le démon de la présence*. Paris: Seuil, 1964.

Kundera, Milan. *La Lenteur*. Paris: Gallimard, 1995.

Labrosse, Claude. *Lire au XVIIIe siècle: La Nouvelle Héloïse et ses lecteurs*. Lyon: Presses Universitaires de Lyon, 1985.

―――. "Sur les estampes de *La nouvelle Héloïse* dessinées par Gravelot." In *L'Illustration du livre et de la littérature au XVIIIe siècle en France et en Pologne, Cahiers de Varsovie* 9 (1982): 85–103.

Laclos, Choderlos de. *Les Liaisons dangereuses*, ed. Joël Papadopoulos with a preface by André Malraux (Paris: Gallimard, 1972). *Dangerous Liaisons*. Trans. P. W. K. Stone, intro. Michel Feher, in *The Libertine Reader: Eroticism and Enlightenment in Eighteenth-Century France*, ed. Michel Feher. New York: Zone, 1997.

Lamblin, Bernard. *Peinture et temps*. Paris: Klincsieck, 1983.

La Mettrie, Julien Orfray de. *L'Homme machine*. Leyden: E. Luzac fils, 1747.

———. *Traité de l'âme*. Paris: David, 1745.

Lanson, Gustave. *Histoire de la littérature française*. Reprint of 1920 ed., Paris: Hachette, 1971.

Le Coat, Gérard. "Le Pélerinage à l'île de Cythère: Un Sujet 'aussi galant qu'allégorique.'" *Revue d'art canadienne* 2 (1975): 9–23.

L'Enfant du bordel (1800). Ed. Michel Delon. Paris: Zulma 1992.

Lenglet-Dufresnoy, Nicolas. *De l'usage des romans, où l'on fait voir leur utilité et leurs différences*. 1734. Reprint, Genève: Slatkine, 1970.

Lettres galante et philosophiques de deux nonnes (1797). *Oeuvres anonymes du XVIIIe siècle*, vol. 3, *L'Enfer de la Bibliothèque nationale*, vol. 5. Paris: Fayard, 1986.

Levey, Michael. "The Real Theme of Watteau's Embarkation for Cythera." *Burlington Magazine* 103 (1961): 180–85.

Lewinter, Roger. *Diderot ou les mots de l'absence: Essai sur la forme de l'oeuvre*. Paris: Editions Champ Libre, 1970.

———. "Introduction à *La religieuse*." In *Oeuvres complètes de Diderot*, ed. Roger Lewinter, vol. 4. Paris: Club Français du Livre, 1970.

Lotringer, Sylvère. "Manon l'écho." *Romanic Review* 63 (1972): 92–110.

Magendie, Maurice. *La Politesse mondaine et les théories de l'honnêteté en France au XVIIe siècle, de 1600 à 1660*. 1925. Reprint, Genève: Slatkine, 1970.

Marin, Louis. "Le Jardin de Julie." In *Lectures traversières*, 63–87. Paris: Albin Michel, 1992.

Marivaux, Pierre. *Journaux et oeuvres diverses*. Ed. Frédéric Deloffre and Michel Gilot. Paris: Classiques Garnier, 1968.

———. *Les Aventures de *** ou les effets surprenants de la sympathie*. In *Oeuvres de jeunesse*, ed. Frédéric Deloffre. Paris: Gallimard, Bibliothèque de la Pléiade, 1972.

———. *Oeuvres romanesques*. Ed. Frédéric Deloffre. Paris: Gallimard, 1972.

———. *Le Paysan parvenu*. Ed. Michel Gilot. Paris: Garnier Flammarion, 1965. Trans. Leonard Tancock under the title *Up from the Country* (New York: Penguin, 1980).

Markovits, Francine. "Rousseau et l'éthique de Clarens: Une Économie des relations humaines." *Stanford French Review* 15 (1991): 323–48.

Marshall, David. *The Surprising Effects of Sympathy: Marivaux, Diderot, Rousseau, and Mary Shelley*. Chicago: Univ. of Chicago Press, 1988.

Mauzi, Robert. "Humour et colère dans *La religieuse*." Introduction to *Oeuvres complètes de Diderot*, ed. Roger Lewinter, vol. 4. Paris: Club Français du Livre, 1970.

———. *L'Idée du bonheur dans la littérature et la pensée française au XVIIIe siècle*. 1960. Reprint, Genève: Slatkine, 1979.

May, Georges. *Le Dilemme du roman au XVIIIe siècle: Etude sur les rapports du roman et de la critique (1715–1761)*. New Haven: Yale Univ. Press; Paris: PUF, 1963.

———. *La Religieuse de Diderot*. Paris: PUF, 1954.

McDonald, Christie. *The Dialogue of Writing: Essays in Eighteenth-Century French Literature.* Waterloo, Ont.: W. Laurier Univ. Press, 1984.

Miller, J. Hillis. *Illustration.* Cambridge: Harvard Univ. Press, 1992.

Miller, Nancy K. *French Dressing: Women, Men, and Ancien Regime Fiction.* New York: Routledge, 1995.

―――. *The Heroine's Text: Readings in the French and English Novel, 1722–1782.* New York: Columbia Univ. Press, 1980.

Molière. *The School for Wives.* In *Four Plays,* trans. Richard Wilbur. New York: Harcourt Brace Jovanovich, 1978.

―――. *Tartuffe.* In *Four Plays,* trans. Richard Wilbur. New York: Harcourt Brace Jovanovich, 1978.

Montesquieu. *Les Lettres persanes.* In *Oeuvres complètes,* ed. Roger Caillois, vol. 1. Paris: Gallimard, Bibliothèque de la Pléiade, 1946.

―――. *Pensées.* In *Oeuvres complètes,* ed. Roger Caillois, vol. I. Paris: Gallimard, Bibliothèque de la Pléiade, 1946.

Morel, Jean-Marie. *Théorie des Jardins.* Paris: Pissot, 1776.

Morgan Grasselli, Margaret, and Pierre Rosenberg, eds. *Watteau, 1684–1721.* Paris: Editions de la Réunion des musées nationaux, 1984. Published in English under the same title by the National Gallery of Art, Washington, D.C., 1984.

Moureau, François. "Watteau in His Time." Trans. Robert Berry. In *Watteau, 1684–1721,* ed. Margaret Morgan Grasselli and Pierre Rosenberg, 469–506. Paris: Editions de la Réunion des musées nationaux, 1984.

Mulvey, Laura. *Visual and Other Pleasures.* Houndmill, Hampshire: Macmillan, 1989.

Mylne, Vivienne. *The Eighteenth-Century French Novel: Techniques of Illusion.* Manchester: Manchester Univ. Press, 1965.

Nerciat, Andrea de. *Le Diable au corps.* Paris: Borderie, 1980.

―――. *Le Doctorat impromptu.* 1788. Ed. Alain Chareyre-Méjan and Charles Floren. Aix-en-Provence: Actes Sud, 1993.

Nietzsche, Friedrich. *Human, All Too Human: A Book for Free Spirits.* Trans. Marion Faber with Stephan Lehmann. Lincoln: Univ. of Nebraska Press, 1984.

Panofsky, Erwin. *Studies in Iconology: Humanistic Themes in the Art of the Renaissance.* New York: Oxford Univ. Press, 1939.

Pontalis, J. B., and Jean Laplanche. *Fantasme originaire, fantasme des origines, origines des fantasmes.* Paris: Hachette, 1985.

Porter, Charles. *Restif's Novels; or, an Autobiography in Search of an Author.* New Haven: Yale Univ. Press, 1967.

Posner, Donald. *Antoine Watteau.* London: Weidenfeld & Nicolson, 1984.

―――. *Watteau: A Lady at Her Toilet.* New York: Viking, 1973.

―――. "Watteau mélancolique: La Formation d'un mythe." *Bulletin de la Société de l'histoire de l'art français,* 1973, 345–61.

Poulet, Georges. *Etudes sur le temps humain*. Paris: Gallimard, 1950.

Prévost, abbé. *Manon Lescaut*. Ed. Frédéric Deloffre and Raymond Picard. 2nd ed. Paris: Garnier, 1990. Trans. Leonard Tancock under the same title, intro. and notes by Jean Sgard (London: Penguin, 1991).

—————. *Mémoires d'un homme de qualité*. In *Oeuvres*, vol. 1. Grenoble: PUG, 1977.

Proust, Jacques. "Le Corps de Manon." *Littérature* 4 (1971): 5–21.

—————. *L'Objet et le texte*. Genève: Droz, 1980.

Rex, Walter. *The Attraction of the Contrary: Essays on the Literature of the French Enlightenment*. Cambridge: Cambridge Univ. Press, 1987.

Ripa, Cesare. *Iconologia*. Roma, 1603.

Roger, Philippe. "Au bonheur des dames sensées." Introduction to *Thérèse philosophe*. In *Oeuvres anonymes du XVIIIe siècle*, vol. 3, *L'Enfer de la Bibliothèque nationale*, vol. 5. Paris: Fayard, 1986.

Rosenberg, Pierre, ed. *Vies anciennes d'Antoine Watteau*. Paris: Hermann, 1984.

Ross, Kristin. "The Narrative of Fascination: Pathos and Repetition in *Manon Lescaut*." *The Eighteenth-Century: Theory and Interpretation* 24 (1983): 199–210.

Rousseau, Jean-Jacques. *Les Confessions*. Ed. Bernard Gagnebin and Marcel Raymond. In *Oeuvres complètes*, ed. Gagnebin and Raymond, vol. 1. Paris: Gallimard, Bibliothèque de la Pléiade, 1959.

—————. *Julie, ou la nouvelle Héloïse: Lettres de deux amants habitants d'une petite ville au pied des Alpes* (1761). Ed. Henri Coulet and Bernard Guyon. In *Oeuvres complètes*, ed. Bernard Gagnebin and Marcel Raymond, vol. 2. Paris: Gallimard, Bibliothèque de la Pléiade, 1964. Trans. William Kenrick under the title *Eloisa, or a Series of Original Letters*, 2 vols. (1803; reprint, Oxford: Woodstock, 1989). Trans. Philip Stewart and Jean Vaché under the title *Julie, or the New Heloïse* (Hanover, N.H.: Univ. Press of New England, 1997).

Russo, Elena. *First-Person Narratives: Prévost, Constant, Des Forêt*. Stanford: Stanford Univ. Press, 1996.

Sade, marquis de. *Histoire de Juliette*. Vols. 8 and 9 of *Oeuvres*, ed. Gilbert Lely. Paris: Au Cercle du Livre précieux, 1962–64.

—————. *Idée sur les romans, suivi de L'auteur des Crimes de l'amour à Villeterque, Folliculaire*. Ed. Jean Glastier. Paris: Ducros, 1970.

Saint-Amand, Pierre. *Séduire ou la passion des Lumières*. Paris: Méridien-Klincksieck, 1987. Trans. Jennifer Curtis Gage under the title *The Libertine's Progress: Seduction in the Eighteenth-Century French Novel* (Hanover, N.H.: Univ. Press of New England for Brown University, 1994).

Saul, John. *Voltaire's Bastards: The Dictatorship of Reason in the West*. New York: Free Press; Toronto: Maxwell Macmillan International, 1992.

Segal, Naomi. *The Unintended Reader: Feminism and Manon Lescaut*. Cambridge: Cambridge Univ. Press, 1986.

Semiek, Andrej. *La Recherche morale et esthétique dans le roman de Crébillon fils*. Studies on Voltaire 200. Oxford: Voltaire Foundation, 1980.

Sgard, Jean. *L'Abbé Prévost: Labyrinthes de la mémoire*. Paris: PUF, 1986.

———. "La notion d'égarement chez Crébillon." *Dix-huitième Siècle* 1 (1969): 240–49.

———. *Prévost romancier*. Paris: Corti, 1968–89.

———. *Vingt études sur Prévost d'Exiles*. Grenoble: Ellug, 1995.

Sheriff, Mary. *Fragonard: Art and Eroticism*. Chicago: Chicago Univ. Press, 1990.

Showalter, English. *The Evolution of the French Novel, 1641–1782*. Princeton: Princeton Univ. Press, 1972.

Singerman, Alan. *L'Abbé Prévost: L'Amour et la morale*. Genève: Droz, 1987.

Sollers, Philippe. *Le Cavalier du Louvre*. Paris: Plon, 1995.

———. *La Fête à Venise*. Paris: Gallimard, 1991.

———. *Les Surprises de Fragonard*. Paris: Gallimard, 1987.

Starobinski, Jean. *Jean-Jacques Rousseau: La Transparence et l'obstacle, suivi de Sept essais sur Rousseau*. 1971. Reprint, Paris: Gallimard, 1976.

———. *Le Remède dans le mal: Critique et légitimation de l'artifice à l'âge des Lumières*. Paris: Gallimard, 1989.

Stewart, Philip. *Engraven Desire: Eros, Image, and Text in the French Eighteenth Century*. Durham, N.C.: Duke Univ. Press, 1992.

———. *Half-Told Tales: Dilemmas of Meaning in Three French Novels*. North Carolina Studies in the Romance Languages and Literatures 228. Chapel Hill: University of North Carolina Department of Romance Languages, 1987.

———. *Imitation and Illusion in the French Memoir-Novel, 1700–1750*. New Haven: Yale Univ. Press, 1969.

Thérèse philosophe (1748). Oeuvres anonymes du XVIIIe siècle, vol. 3, *L'Enfer de la Bibliothèque nationale*, vol. 5. Paris: Fayard, 1986.

Tomlinson, Robert. *La Fête galante chez Watteau et Marivaux*. Genève: Droz, 1981.

Trousson, Raymond, ed. *Romans libertins du XVIIIe siècle*. Paris: Laffont, 1993.

———. *Les Romancières du grand siècle*. Paris: Laffont, 1996.

Versini, Laurent. *Laclos et la tradition: Essai sur les sources et la technique des Liaisons dangereuses*. Paris: Klincsieck, 1968.

Vidal, Mary. *Watteau's Painted Conversations: Art, Literature, and Talk in Seventeenth- and Eighteenth-Century France*. New Haven: Yale Univ. Press, 1992.

Voltaire. *Dictionnaire philosophique*. London, 1764.

———. *Romans et contes*. Paris: Gallimard, 1972.

Wagner, Peter, ed. *Erotica and the Enlightenment*. Frankfurt: Peter Lang, 1991.

Wald Lasowski, Patrick. *Libertines*. Paris: Gallimard, 1980.

INDEX

Winners of the Walker Cowen Memorial Prize

Elizabeth Wanning Harries

The Unfinished Manner: Essays on the Fragment in the Later Eighteenth Century

Catherine Cusset

No Tomorrow: The Ethics of Pleasure in the French Enlightenment